Reports of the death of direct mail have been greatly exaggerated, and Bob Bly proves it in this powerful new book, *The Direct Mail Revolution*. With email response rates dropping like rocks, postal mail is poised for a major comeback. Bly's book—which could be called "Direct Mail 2.0"—serves as both a superb primer for those who've never managed a direct-mail campaign before and an excellent refresher for those who have.

—RICHARD ARMSTRONG, DIRECT-MAIL COPYWRITER

Marketers are starting to realize that digital marketing is not the end-all solution for direct marketing. Bob's new book arrives just in time. It's a vital resource that helps organizations improve their ROI when implementing direct-mail promotions to clients and prospects.

—MICHAEL BORKAN, CEO OF TALON MAILING AND MARKETING

The Direct Mail Revolution is a treasure trove of easy-to-follow how-to advice on direct mail and digital marketing tricks of the trade. Both novices and professionals alike can boost their income from the proven direct-mail campaigns, valuable checklists, and sales funnels alone. Must read!

—ANDREW S. LINICK, PH.D., THE MARKETING COPYOLOGIST® AND FOUNDER OF THE COPYWRITER'S COUNCIL OF AMERICA™

Of all the books I've read in 50 years of being in the mail order business, Bob's new book is one of the best I've ever read!

—GEOFFREY FELDMAN, MDG MARKETING SERVICES, LLC

Bob is a first-rate copywriter and direct marketing strategist. I would recommend this book to anyone who either wants to brush up on their direct-mail marketing or get involved in this proven marketing channel to grow their business.

—BRUCE BROWNING, PRESIDENT OF OLLEYMAY MEDIA

THE DIRECT MAIL
REVOLUTION

SPECIAL OFFER INSIDE

HOW TO CREATE PROFITABLE
DIRECT MAIL CAMPAIGNS
IN A DIGITAL WORLD

ROBERT W. BLY

Entrepreneur Press®

Entrepreneur Press, Publisher
Cover Design: Andrew Welyczko
Production and Composition: Eliot House Productions

This publication is designed to provide accurate and authoritative information
in regard to the subject matter covered. It is sold with the understanding that the
publisher is not engaged in rendering legal, accounting, or other professional services.
If legal advice or other expert assistance is required, the services of a competent
professional person should be sought.

Entrepreneur Press® is a registered trademark of Entrepreneur Media, Inc.

Library of Congress Cataloging-in-Publication Data
Names: Bly, Robert W., author.
Title: The direct mail revolution: how to create profitable direct mail campaigns in
a digital world / by Robert W. Bly.
Description: Irvine, California : Entrepreneur Press, [2019] | Includes bibliograph-
ical references and index.
Identifiers: LCCN 2018046448| ISBN 978-1-59918-630-6 (alk. paper) | ISBN
1-59918-630-6 (alk. paper)
Subjects: LCSH: Direct marketing. | Sales letters. | Marketing—Graphic methods.
Classification: LCC HF5415.126 B5829 2019 | DDC 658.8/72—dc23
LC record available at https://lccn.loc.gov/2018046448

Printed in the United States of America

23 22 21 20 19   10 9 8 7 6 5 4 3 2 1

This book is for Dr. Krishna Maruri

CONTENTS

Chapter 2

PART II
CREATING AND PRODUCING DIRECT-MAIL CAMPAIGNS

Chapter 3

PART III
DIRECT-MAIL COMPONENTS AND FORMATS

PART IV
INTEGRATING DIRECT MAIL AND DIGITAL MARKETING

ACKNOWLEDGMENTS

Some sections of this book were published, in slightly different form, in several earlier and now out-of-print books of mine, *Power-Packed Direct Mail*, *The Complete Idiot's Guide to Direct Marketing*, and *The White Paper Marketing Handbook*. Others appeared, also in slightly different form, in direct-response industry trade publications including *DM News*, *Business Marketing*, and *Target Marketing*.

I would like to thank Bob Diforio, my agent, for finding a good home for this book at Entrepreneur Press. Thanks also to my editor, Jennifer Dorsey, for making the book much better than it was when the manuscript first crossed her desk. And to Vanessa Campos, thanks for bringing the book to the attention of businesspeople who can profit from it.

Lastly, I want to thank the many marketers who let me share their ideas, tactics, and samples of their work in this book. I can't name you all. But you know who you are, folks.

THE NEW DIRECT-MAIL REVOLUTION

When email marketing began around 1978, email's low cost (essentially free), ease of sending (just click a button), speed of transmission (almost instant), and superior response rates made many marketers think direct mail (DM) had become obsolete.

But the use of marketing tactics is usually cyclical. Today, email open and click-through rates have declined. Thanks to spam filters and firewalls, email deliverability has dropped dramatically. Worse, people are bombarded with so many emails that they have their finger poised over the delete key as they go through their inbox. And they fear viruses, malware, phishing schemes, and other online scams. As a result, direct mail has made a dramatic comeback.

POWERFUL EVIDENCE OF DIRECT MAIL'S COMEBACK

Did you know that direct-mail response rates took a tremendous leap in 2017? According to the Direct Marketing Association's (DMA) 2017

"Response Rate Report," direct mail offered a 5.1 percent response to *house lists* (the marketer's customers and prospects) and a 2.9 percent response to rented lists across all DM formats. (In comparison, the response rate for all digital channels combined in 2017 was 2 percent.)[1] In 2015, the response rates from house and outside lists were 3.7 percent and 1.0 percent respectively, and in 2010 were 3.4 percent and 1.4 percent.

Another reason for the rebirth of direct mail is that, despite the rising costs of paper, postage, and mailing lists, direct mail generates a tremendous return on investment (ROI). On average, U.S. advertisers spend $167 per customer on direct mail annually to sell $2,095 worth of goods per buyer.

Even more important, in the decade from 2006 to 2016, the total volume of mail handled by the U.S. Postal Service (USPS) fell 27.7 percent. With less mail competing for the consumer's attention, your direct-mail piece has a better chance of being noticed, read, and responded to. Need more convincing? Check out these facts:

- A 2017 DMA report says that direct mail continues to provide the best response rate of any marketing channel; for example, *a #10 DM package* mailed to a house file had an average response rate of 4.37 percent.
- The Winterberry Group, a marketing consulting firm, says that 29 percent of marketers' media budgets is still spent on direct mail.
- In 2013, U.S. companies sent out a staggering 80 billion pieces of direct mail, which stood out against the reduced volume of "regular" mail.
- More than 80 percent of local small businesses use direct mail to reach their customers.
- Branded products on average get a 1,300 percent ROI from direct mail.[2]
- Direct-mail packages generate 78 percent of all donations made to nonprofits.

---

[1] https://www.iwco.com/blog/2017/07/25/2017-dma-response-rate-report/

[2] http://www.ez24x7.com/blog/25-direct-marketing-statistics-prove-direct-mail-works/

- More than 40 percent of recipients scan or read the direct-mail pieces they get.
- Eighty-five percent of consumers will open a piece of mail if it catches their attention.
- Consumers are 22 percent more likely to purchase products promoted via direct mail than they are products advertised through email.[3]

These statistics demonstrate that direct mail is making a huge comeback in the multichannel marketing world.

WHY I WROTE THIS BOOK

Clearly, there are good reasons to add direct mail as an arrow in your marketing quiver. But in this digital era, a growing number of marketing professionals have no idea how to conduct a successful direct-mail campaign. That's the ever-widening knowledge gap that *The Direct Mail Revolution* aims to close so you too can profit from this revitalized marketing channel.

The Direct Mail Revolution is organized in four parts with a total of 17 chapters:

- Part I gives you a high-level overview of what direct mail is, how it works, and how to plan profitable DM programs.
- Part II gives you all the important elements needed to create successful direct mail including offers, lists, copy, graphics, production, and testing.
- Part III introduces you to the different types of direct-mail elements and formats including sales letters, brochures, reply elements, self-mailers, and postcards.
- Part IV shows you how to integrate direct mail with the web and covers landing pages, content marketing, email, and integrated multichannel marketing campaigns.
- The appendices also have useful resources for producing direct mailings, from mailing list brokers and printers to letter shops

---

[3] https://www.iwco.com/blog/2017/07/25/2017-dma-response-rate-report/

and graphic designers. Throughout the book, you'll find tables, charts, and checklists to help you plan and execute winning DM campaigns.

After reading this book, you'll have a newfound confidence in the power of direct-mail marketing—as well as the knowledge you need to generate unprecedented response rates, leads, sales, and profits with your own mailings.

WHO SHOULD READ THIS BOOK

Some marketers are already using direct mail but want to improve their response rates—or perhaps they're thinking about trying a direct-mail campaign but aren't sure how to go about it. If you have picked up this book, you probably fall into one of the following categories:

- *Fortune 1000 companies.* Chief marketing officers, marketing managers, product managers, and brand managers at billion-dollar corporations. These large corporations have big marketing budgets. In 2014, the top 200 advertisers in the U.S. collectively spent $137.8 billion on marketing.
- *Small-to-midsize businesses (SMBs).* A small business is usually defined as an organization with less than $50 million in annual revenue. A midsize enterprise is an organization that makes more than $50 million but less than $1 billion in annual revenue.[4] There are 28 million small businesses in the United States.[5]
- *Independent contractors.* Solopreneurs, service businesses, freelancers, consultants, independent contractors, and other self-employed professionals. These people often need advice on direct mail but may not be able to hire a professional. This book can help them do their own direct-mail campaign on a shoestring. According to the Small Business and Entrepreneurial Council, nearly nine out of ten U.S. companies have fewer than 20 workers.

---

[4] https://www.gartner.com/it-glossary/smbs-small-and-midsize-businesses

[5] https://townsquared.com/ts/resources/small-business-united-states-numbers/

✉ *Marketing services professionals.* Digital agencies, traditional ad agencies, PR firms, graphic design studios, printers, consultants, and other marketers have clients who may want direct-mail promotions as part of the mix.

ABOUT THE DM SAMPLES IN THIS BOOK

Throughout the book, you'll find numerous direct-mail examples. You may notice that a number of them are not new but are classic exemplars of tried-and-true direct-mail techniques. I'm deliberately including these for your reference for several reasons.

First, while the usage of direct mail today is making a comeback, the quality of many of today's mailers (certainly not all) is often subpar. That's because in the digital age, many marketers simply do not have the knowledge or experience to create winning DM packages—a problem this book was written to correct.

Also, without access to the response rates generated by these new DM pieces, we do not know how well they worked—or whether they worked at all. And who wants to emulate a direct-mail package that bombed?

Years ago, more marketing professionals had experience in creating direct mail. As a result, their mailings were, to be frank, much better on average than the average DM packages produced today. I have reprinted a lot of classic examples because they better illustrate what makes direct mail work.

Some I created myself, and for many others, I knew the marketers who produced them. Therefore I have been privy to the response data and know for a fact that they worked and were profitable. I can confidently hold them up as examples of winning DM promotions.

Also, while marketing methods evolve, the core of direct-mail marketing is human psychology. As Claude Hopkins noted in his classic book, *Scientific Advertising,* human psychology has not changed in ten centuries. Therefore, the direct-mail principles illustrated in the mailings I show and discuss in this book are as relevant and effective today as they were years or even decades ago. How do I know this? Because these same direct-mail techniques continue to get good results across demographic categories— even with Millennials.

PRINT IS FAR FROM DEAD, EVEN AMONG MILLENNIALS

Millennials are the largest group of business-to-business (B2B) customers: A 2014 Google report showed that of all potential buyers who researched B2B products, 46 percent were categorized as Millennials, a 19 percent uptick from 2012. Those numbers have continued to grow in the past few years. Today, Millennials make the majority of purchasing decisions at work (73 percent, to be exact), with 34 percent acting as the sole decision-makers for corporate purchases. They also make up the bulk of consumer purchase decision-makers, being a fourth of the total population with a combined $200 billion in annual buying power. In short, this group has massive purchasing influence—and they use it.

With so much marketing migrating from offline to online channels, some marketers believe Millennials are more receptive to digital content and marketing than to print. But there is plenty of evidence to the contrary. For instance, a 2015 article in *The Washington Post* reports that according to a 2014 survey, 87 percent of college textbooks purchased were print editions, vs. only 9 percent for ebooks and 4 percent for books from file-sharing sites. Despite the perception that we have migrated to a digital age, half the $197 billion U.S. ad market is still offline.

Millennials are still influenced by direct mail, in some cases favoring it over other communication or marketing channels:

- 75 percent of Millennials find value in the mail they get in their mailbox.
- 92 percent are persuaded to make a purchase decision based on direct mail as opposed to 78 percent who are persuaded to purchase thanks to an email.
- 90 percent would rather receive promotional items in the mail as opposed to their email inbox.
- 63 percent of responders to direct mail within the past three months actually made a purchase.
- An overwhelming 82 percent of Millennials read direct mail they get from retail brands. Those surveyed who also enjoy looking through catalogs they get in the mail total 54 percent.

✉ 49 percent of Millennials use print coupons at retail stores, with three out of four making use of grocery inserts found in direct mail or the newspaper.

So if you thought direct mail was only for the post-AARP crowd, think again.

WHY OUR BRAINS PREFER INK-ON-PAPER MARKETING

Why hasn't digital advertising killed off print? According to a study conducted by the Centre for Experimental Consumer Psychology at Bangor University, the physicality of print creates an emotional connection for those who handle it. Ink on paper makes a deeper impression in the brain than something nonphysical, like a digital message. The study used magnetic resonance imaging (MRI) to chart how respondents' brains reacted to print content vs. digital or virtual copy. The results showed a higher rate of brain stimulation for those reading content on paper; our brains perceive physical material to be more genuine.

Researchers at Temple University also used MRI measurements of brain activity to study consumers' responses to advertising. Their 2015 study found that people recalled the content of print ads better than digital ads and had more emotional responses to print content, which resulted in buying decisions. Cynthia Mascone, editor-in-chief of *Chemical Engineering Progress*, wrote in her editorial "Print Is Not Dead" that these emotional responses make for easier recall when making purchase decisions and "triggered activity in the area of the brain . . . associated with a higher perceived value and desirability of the advertised product or service, which can signal a greater intent to purchase."

YES, YOU CAN DO DIRECT MAIL

So in the digital age, an ink-on-paper sales letter or direct-mail package your customers can hold in their hands really distinguishes you from the digital-only marketers sending their messages solely via email.

Many marketers avoid direct mail because they are afraid it's too difficult, cumbersome, costly, time-consuming, or confusing. Others would like to try direct mail but don't know where to start.

With this book in hand, you won't be one of the clueless—or the fearful. Instead, with confidence, you'll create powerful direct-mail campaigns that trounce the competition, get noticed beyond the glut of emails clogging up the prospect's inbox, and generate more interest, readership, responses, leads, and sales.

Higher response rates. More leads and sales. Marketing results that knock your socks off. What more could any marketer ask for?

PART I

DIRECT-MAIL PLANNING AND STRATEGY

SPECIAL OFFER INSIDE

Pre-mailing planning is the key to maximizing direct-mail response and ROI. Yet too many marketers do little or no planning, invariably to their detriment. Proper planning is the foundation of creating high-response direct mail.

Chapter 1

GETTING STARTED IN DIRECT MAIL

I've been writing direct mail steadily since the beginning of my career as a freelance copywriter in the early 1980s—and I love it. Like many Americans, I look forward to getting the mail every day and seeing what surprises and even treasures await. The legendary speaker Dottie Walters called direct mail "the free marketing university in your mailbox."

As it happens, your self-education in direct mail should logically start with this "mailbox university" and should follow these three simple principles:

1. *Study.* Always study your "junk mail." Every day. Read it both as a consumer who is a potential buyer of the product and as a marketer looking to learn the techniques the mailers are using to generate leads and sales.

2. *Save.* Whenever you come across a mail piece that gets your attention, save it in a swipe file. A *swipe file* is a collection of sample direct-mail pieces you use for reference, information, inspiration, and ideas—and to keep tabs on what your competition is doing.

3. *Pay attention*. Pay particular attention to mailings you get multiple times, and the more times you get them, the closer you should look. Why? Because these mailings are actually making money for the marketers. Direct mail is expensive, so if the mailings weren't profitable, they would not be sent out repeatedly. Mark with a red X all swipe file samples you have received two or more times to identify them as winning mailings.

> ✉ **TIP**
>
> You should also become a direct-mail buyer. Start responding to more of the direct-mail packages you receive. Buy the product. Doing so will get your name on more mailing lists and multiply the volume of direct mail you get, study, and store in your swipe file, greatly accelerating your DM education.

THE DIRECT-MAIL RENAISSANCE

As I stated in the introduction, we are currently experiencing the rebirth of direct mail. Suddenly, marketing isn't just electrons anymore. It's also ink on paper again.

There are three major factors that have triggered the new bull market in direct mail:

1. *Digital overload*. Electronic marketing often works very well. But many market segments are so bombarded with digital communications that they are becoming increasingly numb to it. According to the International Association of Business Communicators (IABC) website, "We're living in a revolution . . . the internet has enabled anyone with a keyboard to speak up, and suddenly, everyone is, creating a maelstrom of spam, noise, and hype." This noise is amplified by social media. According to market research firm The Radicati Group, in 2015 there were more than 205 billion emails sent and received daily worldwide—that's about 7 million emails in the time it took you to read this sentence (about 30 seconds). The average office worker got 121 emails a day.

2. *Decline in post office deliveries*. Usage of the U.S. Postal Service (USPS) has declined. The USPS reports that from 1995 to 2013,

the volume of first-class mail in the United States dropped by 61 percent. That's good news for direct-mail marketers. As direct-mail writer Paul Bringe once observed, "When the feed is scarce, the chickens will scratch at anything." With less clutter in the consumer's mailbox, your mailing stands out more. And the lower volume has resulted in significantly higher response rates.

3. *It works.* Digital marketers have discovered that, rather than being outmoded, direct mail is yet another arrow in their quiver of traffic-generating marketing methods. In Part IV, we'll learn the best practices for integrating direct mail into a multichannel marketing program. The result: a synergy that makes both direct mail and digital marketing more effective.

SO WHAT EXACTLY IS "DIRECT MAIL"?

Direct mail is unsolicited paper advertising or promotional material (that is, material the recipient has not requested) sent to an individual or company through the mail. It is usually sent via the USPS, though some is sent via alternative methods, such as FedEx or United Parcel Service (UPS). Marketing consultant Shell Alpert once designed a direct-mail promotion that was delivered to prospects by carrier pigeons.

Direct mail seeking new customers is sent to rented mailing lists, containing the names and addresses of people your company has not done business with before. This is called "acquisition mail" because it is used to acquire new customers.

The purpose of an acquisition mailing is to turn strangers into first-time customers by getting them to order one of your products. For instance, if you get a mail order catalog from a company you have never bought from before, it is an acquisition mailing.

Alternatively, you can use the mailing to generate a lead rather than a direct sale and then follow up to convert the prospect into a customer.

Direct mail is one example of a type of marketing called either direct response or direct marketing: that is, any type of advertising that seeks some sort of reply from the recipient. The reply is usually sent to the marketer (you) by the consumer via mail, phone, fax, an online form, email, or text. Don't dismiss the fax machine as a reply option. Many businesses, especially doctors, still use them every day.

Other types of direct marketing include:

- Telemarketing, most commonly cold calls to rented prospect lists
- Half-hour infomercials as well as two-minute direct-response TV (DRTV) commercials giving a toll-free 800 number or URL for ordering; for example, those long, late-night TV commercials that sell steak knives, diet products, exercise machines, or get-rich-in-real-estate home-study programs are all examples of DRTV
- Radio commercials asking the listener to call a toll-free phone number, which is usually repeated three times or more
- Magazine and newspaper ads containing reply coupons, toll-free numbers, or URLs you can use to request information, order a product, or send for a sample
- Email marketing that drives you to a web page where you can download a free white paper or order a product with your credit card or PayPal
- Google ads, banner ads, and other online ads that hyperlink to a web page where you can make an inquiry or place an order
- Any other marketing that invites you to reply directly, either to request something free or order a product or service

"Everything I do is direct response," Howard Ruff, publisher of the financial advice newsletter *Ruff Times*, once said. "How can you measure how well you are doing if you don't use direct response?"

Along with acquiring new customers and leads by mailing to rented lists, organizations also send direct mail to existing customers to get additional orders, a list known as the "house file."

Although often seen as less glamorous than acquisition mailings, customer mailings can actually be more profitable. First, mailings to house files tend to be less elaborate and expensive than cold mailings to rented lists, because the customers already know you and your products, so less education is required. And because you are mailing to your own database, there is no list rental fee involved.

Second, existing customers are five to ten times more likely to respond and order than prospects from rented lists. Roughly 60 to 80 percent of your business is derived from your current customer base, while 20 to 40 percent comes from new customers.

WHO USES DIRECT-MAIL MARKETING?

Traditionally, direct marketers have sold products to consumers through the mail, eliminating the retailer, distributor, and middleman. But today, direct-marketing techniques are also used to support sales reps, agents, and distributors, and in some cases to get products onto the shelves in stores (or to get people to come into stores or showrooms to buy the products).

One early direct marketer was Richard Sears of Sears, Roebuck, and Company fame. He originally worked in a train station; and in 1886, Mr. Sears began writing letters to sell pocket watches to station masters at other train stations. In 1893, he founded Sears, which grew to become one of the nation's leading mail-order catalog houses.

Lester Wunderman, chairman of Wunderman, Ricotta & Kline, a New York City advertising agency, came up with the term *direct marketing* in 1967. Prior to that, it was called *mail order*.

Actually, mail order is a specialized form of direct marketing. In mail order, also called *one-step* direct marketing, the customer orders the product directly from the ad, letter, catalog, circular, commercial, or whatever. In *two-step* direct marketing, also known as *lead generation*, the initial ad or mailer generates an inquiry or request for more information; the sale is made after follow-up with additional promotional materials or sales calls from telemarketers or sales staff.

Direct mail is also sometimes referred to as junk mail, but many direct-marketing professionals consider the term an insult and take great offense when you call their work "junk mail."

According to direct-mail industry expert Gene Del Polito, the term *junk mail* was developed by the newspaper industry in the 1950s to belittle direct mail—which was competing with newspapers for valuable ad dollars.

In response to a negative *New York Times* article on advertising mail, Del Polito observed in a 1994 letter to the editor, "The *Times* does not explain why an ad for a fast-food chain or a supermarket supplement carried in a newspaper is OK but the very same ad sent through the mail is 'junk.'"

However, everyone uses the term "junk mail" all the time, and I suspect the average person doesn't really know what direct marketing or direct response is—nor do they care. But, as a marketer, you probably should.

The book you are reading will teach you what direct mail is and how to use it to boost your sales—whatever business you're in and whether you use it as a stand-alone promotion or integrate it into a multichannel marketing campaign. And, as you'll soon find, its advantages are numerous.

ADVANTAGES OF DIRECT MAIL

Despite rumors to the contrary, the internet has not killed direct mail. As you read in the introduction, even today, direct mail is a widely used and fast-growing area of marketing. Consider these facts:

- More than 80 percent of consumers at least give a quick read to the direct mail they get in their mailbox.
- Seven out of ten Americans say that physical mail is "more personal" than email.
- A 2017 study by Royal Mail MarketReach found 87 percent of people surveyed consider direct mail "believable."
- Direct-mail response rates have increased on average 14 percent since 2008, while email response rates have dropped 57 percent during that same period.
- Sixty-seven percent of online brand searches are made in response to a printed piece, such as a direct-mail package or other paper-and-ink promotion.

Obviously, direct mail is just one of the many weapons in your advertising arsenal, especially in the digital age. So you may ask, "Why spend money on direct mail? With that money, I could run Google pay-per-click (PPC) ads, create a YouTube channel, call prospects on the phone, hire a salesperson or search engine marketing specialist, write a blog post, or fund a social media campaign."

The answer is that direct mail has a number of unique characteristics that make it the ideal choice in many marketing situations. The rest of this section explores these characteristics in detail.

Direct Mail Can Reach Prospects That Online Marketing Sometimes Can't

There are more than 60,000 postal mailing lists commercially available for rental; even more important, direct-mail lists typically contain a lot of data about the prospects on the list and allow you to select names by various criteria—for instance, people who have credit cards, enter sweepstakes, live on a farm, earn six-figure incomes, or own luxury cars. Email lists typically don't offer the same degree of selectivity. Also, many mailing lists contain the names of proven mail order buyers, making them highly responsive to direct-marketing offers.

Direct Mail Is Response-Driven

Although it can do many things, direct mail is primarily a *response* medium. Few other offline advertising techniques can match direct mail when it comes to generating immediate replies in volume. If you want people to renew their insurance policies, visit your trade-show booth, request a demo of your new software, send for a free brochure, order some flowers for their anniversary, subscribe to your publication, or buy your multivitamin, direct mail is a good bet for you.

Direct Mail Can Pay For Itself—Quickly

No other form of offline advertising can give you such a rapid return on your investment. This is especially true with lead-generating B2B direct mail, where the size of individual orders is larger than in consumer mail order. A single sale can sometimes cover the cost of the entire mailing. For instance, a mailer I wrote to promote an MRI machine only sold one unit. But the product cost $700,000, and the entire cost of the mailing to 2,000 prospects was less than $5,000, giving the manufacturer an ROI of 140 to 1.

And in mail-order sales, a package that is profitable—that is, one that generates $1.50 to $2 or more in revenue for every $1 spent—is literally a money-generating machine. You simply keep mailing to more names on more lists and keep collecting the money until sales fall off and the piece stops being profitable.

The Response to Direct Mail Can Be Measured—Scientifically and Precisely

When you run an ad, do you know how successful it will be? If your goal is to build an image for your brand, how can you measure whether a particular ad or series of ads has changed the public's image of you, let alone *how* it has changed or how this may translate into higher sales? If your goal is to create brand awareness, how can you find out how many people are now familiar with your brand and what they think about it—and again, whether this change in perception has generated enough revenue to cover the cost of the advertising?

In direct mail, simply by counting the orders or inquiries that come in from a mailing, you know whether it was profitable. For example, let's say you send direct-mail pieces to 2,000 prospects. Your cost, including postage, rented mailing lists, and printing, is $0.70 per package for a total mailing cost of $1,400.

The mailing generates 40 leads. Therefore, your cost per lead is $35, and your response rate is 2 percent. With follow-up, you persuade eight of these prospects to buy your product. Your conversion rate is 8 out of 40 leads—or 20 percent—and your cost per sale is $175.

The product sells for $1,000 per unit. Eight units sold gives you revenue of $8,000 for the mailing. You would have had to generate $1,400 in sales for the mailing just to break even, but at $8,000 in sales, you have earned more than five and a half times break-even . . . a successful promotion by any standard.

Direct Mail Stands Out

In a world overloaded with digital marketing, direct mail can really stand out. Prospects often pay more attention to paper and even greater attention to envelopes, especially ones that contain objects such as books, coins, product samples, seeds, and other items.

Direct Mail Can Be Tested

When a major automobile manufacturer, airline, or fast-food chain begins a new advertising campaign, they are already committed, having spent hundreds of thousands or millions of dollars to create and run newspaper inserts, magazine ads, and TV and radio commercials—with no real clue as to whether the campaign will be effective and the money well-spent.

As you will see, you can effectively test a direct-mail piece by mailing only a few thousand or even a few hundred pieces at a cost ranging from hundreds of dollars to a few thousand. If the mailing is successful, you can do a larger run secure in the knowledge that your investment will pay off handsomely.

On the other hand, if the test mailing is a flop, at least you haven't spent much time, effort, or money. Your losses are minimal. You haven't blown your yearly ad budget, taken out a second mortgage on your home, or dipped into retirement or college funds.

And if the mailing is so-so—neither a clear success nor an obvious failure? You proceed cautiously, refining the piece and testing variations until you hit on a promotion that generates an acceptable profit in a small test. Once you prove the mailing is a winner, only then do you invest substantially in its production and distribution.

Direct Mail Can Be Rolled Out with Confidence

Once a direct-mail campaign has proved successful in a small test, it can be rolled out rapidly and easily, meaning you mail more pieces to more names and more lists—testing the performance of each list before renting names in volume.

The initial work is in the creation, testing, and refinement of the piece. This aspect of direct mail is as labor-intensive as any other form of marketing—and more so than some (for example, creating a direct-mail piece is more complex and time-consuming than creating a newspaper insert, email, or blog post). But once the piece is developed, rolling out is simply a matter of printing more mailers, ordering the lists, and tracking the results. It doesn't require the ongoing efforts that trade-show marketing, seminar marketing, telemarketing, in-person selling, and many other forms of promotion do.

If you create a mailing piece that is a big success, you can just sit back and collect the cash—sometimes for months or even years. However, experienced direct marketers continually refine and test different mailings to generate even more profitable results. Also, virtually all direct-mail pieces, even the most successful, eventually see a drop-off in responses, so new packages must be tested and a winner found to take the old mailer's place when it finally wears out.

Direct Mail Is Selective

"Effective advertising is that which reaches, at the lowest possible cost, the most people who can and will buy what you have to sell," said Herschell Gordon Lewis, a successful direct-mail writer, author, and teacher. With direct mail, you can send your message straight to your best prospects and customers without wasting money advertising to people who are not potential buyers.

For example, a printer in New Jersey who specializes in restaurant menus wants to target restaurant owners and managers in the New York–New Jersey area. What's the best way to reach them? If they run ads in one of New Jersey's business magazines, they are wasting their ad dollars on the 99.9 percent of subscribers who are not in the restaurant business. If they advertise in national restaurant trade journals, they are also wasting money because only a small percentage of the magazine's subscribers are located in their area.

But by using direct mail, the printer can selectively send their advertising message to people who own or manage restaurants in New York and New Jersey only. Thus, direct mail—not print advertising—is the printer's best bet for reaching the greatest number of qualified prospects at the lowest possible cost.

As a rule of thumb, if you are selling to a mass market with hundreds of thousands or millions of prospects, space advertising (magazine and newspaper ads) and broadcast advertising are the most cost-effective form of promotion, at least offline. The cost of contact is just pennies per person, and because so many of the readers and viewers are potential customers, there is little wasted circulation.

If you are selling to an extremely small and narrow market, with perhaps only a few hundred customers, why spend your money and creativity on advertising *or* mailing? Just call them on the phone, visit them in person, or both. The market is small enough that you can manage that.

But if you are selling to a midsize market, with thousands or tens of thousands of prospects, or one that is a subsegment of a larger market (for example, you are selling to radiologists as opposed to all medical doctors), direct mail is often the best way to reach them. The market is large enough to justify the time and effort spent developing and producing the mailing, which may be the marketing channel of choice if there is no trade magazine or newsletter in which to run ads.

Direct Mail Lets You Speak Directly to Your Prospect's Needs and Concerns

Because you can be highly selective about who receives your mailer, it can be quite specific about how your product or service relates to the prospect's needs. Instead of making broad statements about product features, as general advertising tends to do, you can focus on the specific problems, requirements, and desires of your target market and then show how your product addresses these issues.

For example, a company in Maryland sells filtration equipment used in various industries. Although the filters work essentially the same way wherever they are used, the benefits they deliver are different in each industry. In pharmaceutical manufacturing, the filters contribute to drug purity, ensuring patients don't get sick from contaminants. In semiconductor manufacturing, they remove contaminants from the manufacturing process to prevent defective chips, which increases yields and profits. Mailings aimed at each industry addressed these specific benefits, generating more interest and response than any generic filter advertising could.

Direct Mail Is Personal

TV is a mass medium, with every commercial reaching thousands or millions of viewers. Websites are online for all to see, not just for you. Newspapers and magazines are mass media, too, and your ad competes with all other ads in the issue for attention.

Direct mail is different. Your sales letter arrives in its own envelope, separated from other advertising messages. Even though the recipient knows it is advertising, its appearance resembles that of a personal letter, which receives a warmer reception. The letter can be written using personal pronouns (*I, me, we, you*), and it is signed by an individual, not a corporation. It speaks in conversational language, addressing the reader one-on-one. It can even be personalized with the recipient's name and address, and mailed in an envelope that looks like business or personal mail.

Make your direct mail warm, human, personal, and friendly, and people respond accordingly. Direct mail achieves a level of me-to-you communication not possible in an ad, commercial, or annual report. Write your sales letters in a natural, informal style, like one good friend telling another about something interesting they want to share.

Direct Mail Is a Flexible Format

Of all the print marketing options, direct mail gives you the most flexibility in format, graphics, design, and copy. Your sales letter, for instance, can be as long or as short as you like: from one page to eight, or even more.

You can include a small pamphlet, a flier, a jumbo-size brochure, or even a poster. You can have two or more letters, multiple brochures, two or more order forms. You can place a microchip in your mailing so that when the reader opens it, they hear a spoken message or music. You can use an aromatic patch so the mailer smells of steak or flowers or perfume, or insert a packet of seeds, which causes the envelope to make noise when handled. One of my recent mailings was a brochure that, when opened, played sound from a selection of educational and promotional videos.

You can use color to get attention (try sending your letter in a bright red or jet black envelope!). You can add a third dimension by enclosing a solid object, such as a gift or product sample. The possibilities are endless. Compared with a magazine ad in which you're confined to a 7-by-10-inch space (or less), or a banner ad, which limits you to a certain number of pixels, direct mail gives you much more freedom. This flexibility can boost your sales if you learn how to harness and use it creatively.

One extremely successful information marketer sent out a mailing asking their affiliates to help them promote their new product. Attached to the letter was a $50 bill. Did it get my attention? You bet. I felt beholden to read their letter and at least consider their offer—and in fact, I did promote the product to my email list. Fundraisers today are affixing nickels to their letters, and the coins show through a glassine window in the outer envelope.

Direct Mail Accommodates Shoestring Budgets

Direct mail can be expensive to write, design, and print, but a simple yet effective mailing can be produced on a small budget. Mailings can be complex packages with

- inserts and color brochures
- pop-ups
- other elaborate gimmicks.

Or you can send something much less expensive—a one-page letter in an envelope, or even a simple 3-by-5-inch postcard.

Another advantage is that you can mail as many or as few pieces as you want. When you run an ad in a magazine with a circulation of 40,000, you must pay for the privilege of reaching all 40,000 people. The magazine doesn't lower the cost of the space simply because only a few of its readers are potential customers for your business.

With direct mail, you can control your quantities precisely and therefore your budget. For instance, say you've developed a one-page sales letter that costs $0.70 apiece to mail (including postage and printing). If you can afford to spend only $200, send 285 letters. Only public relations and the web rival direct mail for cost-effectiveness and ability to generate results on a limited budget. And have you looked at the cost of renting email lists lately or the charges from email distribution services and software? The idea that email marketing is free is erroneous. It may cost less than direct mail, but email is hardly free.

DRAWBACKS OF DIRECT-MAIL MARKETING

Despite these advantages, direct mail, as with every other marketing method, has its drawbacks.

Overall, even with today's healthy response rates, rising paper, printing, postage, and list costs make it a challenge to profit from a single direct-mail package, especially when selling products directly from a one-step mailing. When you're trying to generate leads for more expensive products, the sales potential is usually large enough that just a few sales will pay back the cost of the mailing many times over.

But direct mail used to sell low-priced consumer products via direct order has always had a slim profit margin. A slight shift in response or cost per thousand pieces mailed can quickly transform a losing package into a winner—or vice versa.

The rest of this section delves into some hard facts you should be aware of as you venture into the direct-mail marketing world. You can make a lot of money with direct mail, but there are a few negatives to keep in mind.

Increasing Postage Rates

The United States Postal Service (USPS) raises rates whenever poor management, inefficient operation, or rising operating costs create a need for a bigger revenue stream. And even though third-class bulk-rate mail is the most profitable category for the post office, it is the third-class mailers who are often hit with the biggest rate increases.

When there is a rate change, it is virtually always up. The price of postage almost never declines, with rare exception—for example, the USPS' Every Door Direct Mail (EDDM) service, introduced in 2011, costs less in postage than standard direct mail. The EDDM service enables marketers to deliver direct mail to every household in a given zip code or town—hence the name "Every Door"—at significantly lower cost.

Thanks to a 2017 proposal from the Postal Regulatory Commission (PRC), postage rates could increase up to 40 percent during the next five years. Such a big jump could easily put smaller and marginally profitable catalogs and direct-mail marketers into the red. Higher postage rates raise direct mail's cost per thousand, making it increasingly difficult to break even, let alone make a profit.

Rising postage costs have driven mailers to look for alternatives to the standard #10 (business envelope–size), third-class, bulk-rate direct-mail package, including double and regular postcards, trifold self-mailers, and fliers.

Increased Production Costs

The cost of production—paper and printing in particular—has increased significantly over the past decade. Mailing lists are also more expensive, especially highly targeted, specialized lists. Add higher postage, and you get a substantial increase in the cost per thousand pieces mailed. A higher cost per thousand means the mailing must generate a higher percentage response to make money.

So how do you calculate whether the direct-mail promotion cost is low enough and the product profit margin high enough to allow you to make a good profit on the mailing? A little simple math can show you how much money your direct-mail sales can bring you.

Let's say we are sending out a direct-mail package offering an automotive toolkit that sells for $59.95. For this price, the customer gets a variety of hand tools and a free tool chest. The seller's cost of goods is $10.

The customer also pays $9.95 shipping and handling, which just about covers those costs, so we make no profit from that portion of the sale. For each sale, we collect a net total of $59.95 from the customer. So our profit per order is $59.95 minus $10 cost of goods, or $49.95 per sale.

Now, our direct-mail piece costs $700 per thousand. Divide that cost by the $49.95 we make per sale, and we have to make 14 sales per thousand DM packages mailed to break even. That requires a 1.4 percent response rate, which is realistically achievable. If the response rate is 2.8 percent, we'll double our money.

We call this a *break-even* analysis because we know in advance what response rate we need to break even as well as what response would make us money. To save you from having to do this calculation on your own, I have a free tool online that can do it for you: https://www.dmresponsecalculator.com.

No "Hipness" Factor

Many marketers see direct mail as old school, old hat, and out of date. So it is often difficult to persuade your managers, especially younger ones, to test it despite the many reasons given in this chapter to do so. People like

AVOID MAKING MARKETING DECISIONS BASED ON YOUR PERSONAL PREFERENCES

When deciding whether to use direct mail, crafting the copy, and designing the DM package, follow the advice of master copywriter Peter Betuel, who says, "Don't let personal preference get in the way."

It doesn't matter that you personally don't like "junk mail," long-copy sales letters, outer envelope teasers, or sweepstakes. What matters is what works. And in direct mail, you don't have to guess at what works. You can determine it by testing.

Graphic artist Ken Weissman warns: "Making marketing decisions based on your subjective judgment may lead to the slow death of your business over time." ✉

what's hot, and to many, direct mail is not; they are largely unaware of today's direct-mail resurgence.

"One Flop and Done" Mindset

The most common mistake that keeps businesses from enjoying the increased sales and profits direct mail can bring is the belief that if they tried direct mail once and it didn't work, that means it will never work for them.

When a direct-mail package succeeds, it can be a gold mine, but it can take many tests before you hit on a winner. When launching a new mail order product, the success rate is typically one or two winners out of every ten attempts. In writing direct-mail packages to test against existing *controls* (successful packages), the test beats the control maybe 25 percent of the time, ties it 50 percent of the time, and loses approximately 25 percent of the time.

The biggest mistake you can make is to do one mailing, have it flop, and conclude that direct mail doesn't work. Yes, I have had direct mailings that were winners the first time out of the gate. But many others were marginal or outright failures. Still, if I believed in the offer, I didn't give up. Eventually, many that flopped initially were made to work successfully.

Later in the book, I talk about testing, how to determine why a mailing didn't work, and ways to improve it to create a winner.

THE DIRECT-MAIL MINDSET

The more you embrace a "direct-mail mindset" in both offline and online marketing channels, the greater your response, ROI, sales, and profits will be. In multiple tests, promotions that were primarily focused on direct response out pulled promotions for the same product that featured branding messages, often by as much as tenfold. Having worked as a direct-response copywriter for close to four decades, the direct-response mindset is ingrained in me.

Direct marketers religiously follow the ten fundamental principles of direct-mail marketing in everything they do because their only concern is response. Those principles are:

1. *Write in a direct-mail style.* Direct-response copy is characterized by several factors. For one, it's usually significantly longer than branding copy. It relies on proven principles of persuasion rather than "creativity." Instead of emphasizing pretty design and clever copy, it depends on salient sales arguments backed by extensive proof and facts.

2. *Put response first.* The primary objective is not to enhance image, build a brand, increase awareness, or entertain. It is to get more inquiries, leads, orders, and sales.

3. *Don't allow branding guidelines to interfere with performance.* In large corporations, a primary focus is on maintaining branding guidelines in copy and graphic design with standards that must not be violated. But in direct response, using boilerplate copy or graphics from branding manuals that don't fit the promotion can actually depress response.

4. *The offer is prominent and emphasized.* The offer is never an after-thought. It is carefully thought out and worded, prominent in the promotion, and easy to find.

5. *Free, special discount offers, and guarantees are included.* Direct-mail copywriters strive to work free offers, discounts, and guarantees into

every promotion. Without these components, direct-mail response rates are usually lower than they are with them.

6. *Calls to action (CTAs) are repeated and prominent.* Make your *call to action*—which is where the consumer can accept the offer—prominent so it catches the eye and is easy to find. Put the CTA in two or three places in the promotion. The standard placement of the CTA is at the end of the sales letter, on the back page of the brochure, or on the reply form. If the offer is exceptionally strong, consider putting the CTA in the lead of the letter or even above the salutation as part of the headline.

7. *Target direct-response buyers.* Direct-mail campaigns work best when targeting direct-response buyers—people who have demonstrated that they will buy a product online or from a print ad, mailer, or catalog.

8. *Have a back end.* The real money in direct response is made on the *back end*—sales of additional products to customers who have bought a first product. Without a back end in place, you are leaving money on the table.

9. *Be a tightwad.* Direct marketers, unlike their Madison Avenue counterparts, are careful not to overspend. If a campaign is too costly, it becomes increasingly difficult to make money with it.

10. *Test everything.* Brand advertisers roll out huge campaigns without meaningful, real-world testing, relying instead on less effective methods such as surveys and focus groups. Therefore, they risk failing big and losing a lot of money. Direct-mail marketers start by testing small with live promotions where consumers vote with their credit cards, not their opinions. This is a truer indicator of whether the offer will work; if it doesn't, your losses are minimal because your test was modest and inexpensive.

60 WAYS TO USE DIRECT MAIL

To close this chapter, let's brainstorm. Here are five dozen ways smart marketers are using direct mail to build their businesses. Can you think of any others you might be able to profit from?

1. Generate inquiries
2. Follow up on sales leads
3. Qualify prospects
4. Sell a product or service directly
5. Generate appointments for salespeople
6. Get prospects to request your brochure or catalog
7. Fulfill inquiries generated by advertising, PR, or other promotions
8. Use as a cover letter when sending brochures and catalogs
9. Transmit information
10. Distribute product samples
11. Make an announcement
12. Introduce a new product or service
13. Introduce a product upgrade or enhancement
14. Educate consumers about your product, company, or industry
15. Alert customers about a change in company policy or pricing
16. Thank customers for their business
17. Ask customers for more business
18. Ask customers for referrals
19. Sell accessories and supplies
20. Sell directly to accounts too small for salespeople to call on or located outside your salespeople's territories
21. Invite people to attend a product demonstration, seminar, or sales presentation
22. Get people to visit your trade-show booth
23. Renew subscriptions, contracts, insurance policies, or service agreements
24. Upgrade subscriptions, contracts, policies, or agreements
25. Educate customers and prospects about new trends, methods, or technologies
26. Motivate the sales force
27. Recruit new dealers or distributors
28. Increase sales activity of existing dealers and distributors
29. Keep in touch with customers between sales calls
30. Remind prospects of your existence

31. Ask prospects to join a club or monthly service
32. Thank customers for recent orders
33. Create goodwill
34. Remind inactive customers of your existence
35. Build a mailing list of qualified prospects
36. Update mailing lists and customer files
37. Conduct surveys, market research, or opinion polls
38. Gather information about customer needs, problems, or buying habits
39. Announce discounts, price-off specials, and other deals
40. Introduce your company to new residents in a town (by mailing to "new mover" lists)
41. Test whether your product has appeal to a specific market
42. Determine which feature or benefit of your product is most important to buyers
43. Stimulate additional sales among current customers
44. Bring prospects into your store or showroom
45. Announce a change of address or new location
46. Distribute promotional newsletters and bulletins
47. Distribute ad reprints and article tear sheets to salespeople and customers
48. Correct and clarify rumors and word-of-mouth about your company
49. Bring important news to customers first, before it appears in advertisements or is released to the press
50. Revive inactive leads or accounts
51. Reach secondary or smaller markets that don't justify a large sales or ad budget
52. Distribute price lists, data sheets, and other ordering information to purchasing agents
53. Screen out people who are not genuine prospects
54. Conduct a sweepstakes or contest
55. Promote special events
56. Sell seasonal merchandise
57. Offer a free analysis, cost estimate, review, or consultation

58. Distribute business gifts and premiums
59. Sell new products and services to old customers
60. Raise funds for charitable events and nonprofit organizations

Chapter 2

PLANNING: THE PROFESSIONAL APPROACH

You wouldn't spend $100 million on a new national advertising campaign without carefully setting goals and objectives. Yet many advertisers will dash off a quick sales letter and mail it to hundreds or thousands of customers without a second thought. In direct marketing, planning is the professional approach.

Your plan need not be elaborate or complex, but by analyzing your audience, selecting your message, and establishing your sales goals, you increase your mailing's chances of success.

This chapter shows you how to plan a direct-mail project of any scope and size, from a one-page sales letter to a series of sophisticated mailings sent to thousands—or even hundreds of thousands—of prospects. We will cover the ten key steps of planning a direct-mail campaign, which are:

1. Selecting the medium
2. Selecting the product or service to promote
3. Establishing objectives
4. Targeting the right market

5. Finding mailing lists
6. Choosing a format, tone, and style
7. Determining your unique selling proposition
8. Identifying supporting features and benefits
9. Creating your offer
10. Scheduling your mailing

Let's explore each of these steps in greater detail.

STEP 1: SELECTING THE MEDIUM

The first question to ask when planning a direct-mail campaign, especially in today's multichannel marketing world, is: "Is direct mail the best medium for accomplishing our objectives? Or should we be using other media, either instead of direct mail or in conjunction with it?"

What other ways are there to promote your product? Some of the methods available to you include:

- Email marketing
- Sales representatives
- Space advertising
- Directory advertising
- Banner advertising
- Social media marketing
- Google AdWords
- Online video
- Public relations
- Exhibitions and trade shows
- Event marketing
- Catalogs
- Brochures
- Telemarketing
- Case histories
- Seminars
- Webinars
- Podcasts
- Newsletters

- ✉ Free-standing inserts
- ✉ Premiums, incentives, business gifts
- ✉ Teleseminars

And there are many others. A useful tool for choosing the right marketing channels is a comparative analysis of sales tools, or CAST. Figure 2.1 on page 28 shows a blank CAST worksheet you can copy and use.

How does CAST work? Create a separate CAST worksheet for each campaign promoting a specific product to a specific audience. Write in the product and the audience (or market) at the top of the sheet.

Next, in the far-left column, list all the marketing channels you would ever consider using; some possibilities are already filled in, and there are spaces so you can add others. Then rate each channel for its effectiveness in the ten categories listed across the top row of the table on a scale from 1 to 5; 1 means ineffective, 3 means average, and 5 means extremely effective.

Following are the ten categories in the CAST worksheet and an explanation of each.

Impact or Impression

How memorable is the medium? How much of an impact does it make on the consumer's awareness of the product? A TV commercial broadcast during the Super Bowl would have a high impact; a small newspaper ad would rate lower. Email can be great at generating responses, but much of it is forgotten almost instantly, so it would rate low in this category.

Size of Audience

Is the medium effective at reaching large numbers of people? Direct mail can reach only those people whose names are on a mailing list or who get the mailing when someone else passes it along to them. A newspaper ad reaches only those who read that newspaper. A billboard reaches only those who drive along that road. A website can potentially reach every internet user on earth, though it is unlikely to do so. You may write great blog posts, but is anyone reading them? Theoretically, SEO reaches everyone on the internet, but in reality, it touches just a small percentage of

Figure 2.1. **Comparative Analysis of Sales Tools (CAST)**

Product:									
Audience:									
	Impact or Impression	Size of Audience	Cost per Contact	Sales Lead	Message Control	Flexibility	Timing Control	Repetitive Contact	Credibility	Closing the Sale
Websites										
Email										
SEO										
Content Marketing										
Blogs										
Telemarketing										
Sales Rep										
Space Advertising										
TV Advertising										
Radio Spots										
Google Ads										

Figure 2.1. **Comparative Analysis of Sales Tools (CAST)**, continued

	Impact or Impression	Size of Audience	Cost per Contact	Sales Lead	Message Control	Flexibility	Timing Control	Repetitive Contact	Credibility	Closing the Sale
Banner Ads										
Billboards										
Directories										
PR										
Trade Shows										
Catalogs										
Brochures										
Direct Mail										
Case Studies										
Seminars										
Newsletters										
Premiums										
Others:										

the people who have searched your specific keywords. With telemarketing, you are limited by the speed at which you can make phone calls.

Cost Per Contact

What does it cost to reach a potential prospect with your message? If an ad in a magazine with a circulation of 50,000 costs $5,000, the cost per contact is $0.10. If a mailing costs $500 per thousand to mail out, the cost per contact is $0.50. If it costs $150 to send your salesperson out on the road to visit one prospect, the cost per contact is $150. If your telemarketer makes ten $5 phone calls to get through to one person, the cost per contact is $50. If your bid for a keyword on Google was accepted at $3 per click, the cost per contact is $3.

Sales Leads

Is the medium effective for generating sales leads? Billboards may get consumers to think about your product, but they usually don't generate inquiries. Direct mail, by comparison, is strong at bringing back responses. Email is, too.

Message Control

Do you have control of the message in your promotion? You do when you buy an ad in a newspaper or magazine because it appears exactly as you wrote and designed it. With radio advertising, DJs often take liberties with copy, and your commercial might not come across quite the way you envisioned. On Facebook, the site, not you, controls whether users will be allowed to see your ad or boosted post. And it dictates to a large degree what you can say in your ad, the copy of which is subject to their approval. When you send out a press release to the media, you don't know how much editors will rewrite it or even if it will run at all.

Flexibility

Can you make rapid changes if the promotion isn't working? A telemarketing script can be changed from one phone call to the next. A web page can be updated in minutes. But if you've created 5,000 DM pieces and sent them to the post office, it's too late to change anything until you print and mail another batch. And it can take weeks before you know the results of your initial test.

Timing Control

Do you have precise control over when your message will reach the consumer? When you run an ad in the Sunday paper, you know most of your audience will read it Sunday. Emails can be delivered at a precise date and time. Bulk rate direct-mail delivery cannot be controlled precisely, only roughly. And the USPS reports that in 2015, about 1.4 billion pieces of mail were classified as "return to sender"—and any mailings that get returned never reach their audience at all.

Repetitive Contact

Can you use the medium to expose your market to the message again and again? TV and radio commercials can be run many times. A speech you make to the local chapter of a trade association, on the other hand, can be given just once. PR is also more of a one-shot deal: If you send out a press release and your local newspaper runs it on the front page, sending the same release to them next week won't get you additional coverage.

Credibility

People are skeptical about advertising, and direct mail is a form of paid advertising. Promotion always has less credibility than "editorial." That means an article about your business in your local newspaper has greater credibility with subscribers than a paid ad or a sales flier inserted in the same paper.

Closing the Sale

When deciding which marketing channels to use, you should choose the ones most effective at achieving those objectives most important to you. Let's say you want to generate leads. If only direct mail, email, and directory advertising are rated 5 on a scale of 1 to 5 (1 = worst, 5 = best) in lead generation, then these would be the best vehicles for your lead-generation program.

STEP 2: SELECTING THE PRODUCT OR SERVICE TO PROMOTE

Once you have decided to use direct mail, what product should you choose to feature? The answer is not always as obvious as you might think.

Do you feature one product or the entire product line? Do you sell the deluxe version, the midline model, or the low-cost basic model? Pushing the deluxe version will bring in more money per order, but the higher price might hurt response.

Do you sell the product with supplies, accessories, and options as a complete package, or do you sell the basic product now and then upsell the buyer on the supplies and accessories after the initial purchase?

The question you must answer is this: What exactly are you selling?

Let's say you are a bank offering a special low rate on 15-year fixed-rate mortgages. How would you write a direct-mail pitch for this offer? You could talk about the benefits of this particular mortgage, the special interest rate, the advantages of fixed vs. adjustable-rate mortgages, and the fact that it will be paid off in only 15 years rather than the standard 30.

But, as good as it is, this mortgage is not for everybody. Some people want variable rates. Some want 30-year mortgages for the lower monthly payments. Some are willing to pay a slightly higher interest rate if the upfront costs are lower. Maybe, then, your letter should talk about how your bank offers a complete line of home mortgages—"the right mortgage to fit your financial needs"—rather than focus on this one specific type. Which approach works best?

Or let's say you sell a complete line of equipment used in chemical plants. You have many different products for sale, but your customers tend to purchase multiple items, each with different functions. Do you use each mailing to highlight an individual product? Or should each mailing sell your full product line?

Maybe your products are similar to those of your competitors. In that case, would you be better off stressing service, price, fast delivery, or the reliability and reputation of your firm rather than trying to convince your customers that the products themselves are superior?

What exactly are you selling?

Here are two hints to help you answer that question:

1. *One at a time.* Except for catalogs, most successful direct mail sells one thing at a time. Selling two or more items in the same mailer usually doesn't work.

2. *Keep it simple.* The simpler your offer is, and the easier it is to understand, the better the response. Don't clutter your mailer with too many options, models, colors, and accessories. As a rule, the fewer choices you offer customers, the better.

When you give the recipient too many options to consider, they may put the mail piece aside to think about it, which depresses response. A decision deferred is often a decision never made.

STEP 3: ESTABLISHING OBJECTIVES

Why are you sending out a direct-mail package? Most people answer, "To increase profits and sales," or, "To get leads for new business."

But how many leads? Of what quality? How much profit? How many sales?

Once you have chosen the medium and the product, you can set concrete, measurable goals—the more specific, the better. Why is this important? Because if you don't have a goal—a specific result you want from the mailing— you can't know whether it has achieved its objective. Only by defining your sales objective can you determine whether the mailing succeeds.

Some people say a 1 percent response is good, but that's highly dependent on circumstances. For a mail campaign of 5,000 self-mailers asking people to pay $895 to attend a seminar, a 0.5 to 1 percent response is excellent . . . and highly profitable. But if you're going for leads, not sales, and you offer a free gift with no strings attached (such as a book, coffee mug, or calendar) to everyone who requests your brochure, a 2 to 5 percent response or even higher is possible with a highly targeted list, a great product, and an irresistible offer.

Comparing a sales-generating mailing with a lead-generating mailing, or a free gift offer with a straight offer, or the orders generated for a $10 product with those for a $1,000 product, is meaningless. You have to set objectives that make sense in terms of your audience, your product, your offer, your price point, and your sales methods. One manufacturer may want leads for its salespeople, while another sells its product directly through a catalog. The type of response you want, and how *much* response you want, is a decision you must make.

Also, do you base your revenue forecasts on just the immediate sale the direct-mail package generates or on the *customer lifetime value* (CLV) of the responses? CLV is how much money a new customer is worth to you over the length of their relationship with your company. If the average sale is $100, and the average customer places ten orders a year, they are spending $1,000 annually. If that person remains an active customer for five years, their CLV is $5,000.

That's important because if you calculate marketing budgets and returns based only on initial sales, it will sharply limit what you can afford to spend. If the initial order generated by the mailing is worth $100, and you spend $100 in marketing to acquire that new customer, then you will only break even on the sale.

But if you calculate the ROI of a $100 marketing acquisition cost based on a CLV of $5,000, it's a handsome 50 to 1. If you approach your marketing from that perspective, you will be willing to spend more than your competitors, who base their budgets on initial sales only, and you can ultimately outperform them.

Here are some objectives taken from actual direct-mail marketing plans. The names, numbers, and products have been changed to ensure privacy, but the excerpts are real.

Example 1: Direct-Mail Marketing Plan Objectives Overview

There will be a major direct-mail campaign to promote the capabilities of the GENEX graphics software package. Staggered mailings for this direct-mail campaign will begin in late April or early May, and the campaign will total approximately 12,000 pieces when finished. Approximately 2,000 letters will be mailed each month for a total of six months. Depending upon the level of response, we can expect approximately 60 inquiries from each mailing of 2,000. Prospects will be invited to see a free demonstration of the GENEX system. The secondary response option is to receive a free white paper on desktop graphic design.

Example 2: Direct-Mail Marketing Plan Objectives List

- ✉ *Program offering*: 15 percent discount on purchase of SM-15 system. Customer to trade in old model SM-10 in exchange.

- ✉ *Audience*: Approximately 350,000 office managers. Ninety percent own ten or more SM-10s.

- ✉ *Goal*: Convert 2 to 3 percent of target audience.

- ✉ *Benefits to customer*: Increased capabilities of new system. Opportunity to acquire state-of-the-art equipment at significant cost savings.

- ✉ *Problems to overcome*: Alienation due to customer dissatisfaction with SM-10 technical support. Reluctance to spend money. Many customers satisfied with current product, and do not realize the benefits of new smart technology and new phone app.

Example 3: Direct-Mail Marketing Plan Goals List

GOALS FOR *SMOOTHFLOW* DIRECT-MAIL CAMPAIGN

1. Inform current customers and sales reps that Racom Membranes and SmoothFlow Filters have joined to offer a complete line of micron filters under the banner name SmoothFlow-RM Filtration Systems.

2. Explain to customers the benefits of having a single source for all filter requirements.

3. Ease fears among customers and assure them that the SmoothFlow is not as effective as other membrane filtration because adding the Racom Membrane improves performance.

4. Generate sales leads. Offer customers new SmoothFlow-RM filtration catalog available in print or as a PDF download.

5. Distribute new sales sheet (to be enclosed with sales letter).

Having seen these companies' plans for direct-mail marketing, how would you craft your own goals? Sum up your objectives in a short paragraph or two. Think about the response you want as well as the results you can realistically hope to achieve. The act of writing down objectives will help focus the rest of your efforts.

"Every company must write their own marketing plan," Ray W. Jutkins of Rockingham Jutkins Marketing wrote in one of his agency's pamphlets. "No one from the outside can tell you what your objectives will be. Consulting on how to do it and using professionals experienced in marketing to aid you with your thinking, planning, and ideas may be good investments. However, when push comes to shove, you and your company must decide your objectives and direction."

The break-even formula and calculator provided earlier can help you determine the percentage response rate you need to cover the costs of the mailing. Your goal might be to double that—in other words, get a response rate that generates $2 in net sales for every $1 you spend on the mailing.

Though it may surprise you, many direct marketers are content to break even on their acquisition mailings, and some are even willing to lose some money. Why? Because they are gaining valuable new customers, and they know they will make their money on the back-end selling additional products to those customers.

STEP 4: TARGETING THE RIGHT MARKET

The fourth critical step is to determine whom you are selling to. In other words: Who is the audience? Who is the prospective buyer? Who will receive, read, and hopefully respond to your letter?

The beauty of direct mail is that you can use it to reach *only* those people who are potential buyers for your product or service. This is called *target marketing*. It means that with direct mail, you can target your market using multiple selection criteria, including age, income, gender, geography, home value, marital status, vehicle driven, occupation, hobbies, and interests, to name just a few. Selection criteria for B2B mailing lists include the company's industry, type of product, annual sales, number of employees, and number of locations.

For example, one management consulting firm has found they can successfully sell their consulting programs only when they can reach the CEO of the client company. If they were to advertise in general business magazines, they would waste a lot of money because most of the readers are *not* CEOs. But they can easily rent a mailing list of CEOs and send their message to those executives only.

Who are your ideal customers? Are they male or female? Young or old? Rich or poor? New wave or grass-roots? Corporate or entrepreneurial? City slickers or country folk? Married or single? What do they do for a living? Where do they live? What are their hobbies and interests? If you can accurately describe them, chances are there's a mailing list of people just like them available for rent.

Sometimes you may be selling one product to many different types of customers, each with different interests and concerns. In that case, you can use a standard brochure to describe the product and then tailor your cover letter to your different markets. For example, a financial advisor selling investments might stress income in a letter to retired couples but highlight lower taxes in a letter to doctors, lawyers, and other high-income professionals.

In B2B marketing, you often have to reach multiple purchasing influencers within each client company. Let's say you're selling enterprise software to midsize firms. Mail aimed at CEOs would talk about service, commitment, and your company's reputation and track record. A sales letter to the CFO would stress the cost savings and quick ROI. Another letter, aimed at IT professionals, would cover the technical details and explain how the software integrates easily with existing legacy systems. And a fourth letter, sent to the users, would stress the software's capabilities, features, and improved productivity.

STEP 5: FINDING MAILING LISTS

It is not enough to know your customers. You must also be able to find a mailing list of such people. Without a mailing list, you can't do a mailing.

Mailing list selection is not as simple as novices think. Old pros know it is one of the most difficult and time-consuming aspects of direct mail.

There are two basic categories of mailing lists: compiled lists and response lists. *Compiled lists*, as the name implies, are lists compiled from various sources, such as directories, membership lists, and trade-show attendees. Compiled lists are more complete than response lists when it comes to reaching the greatest number of prospects in a given market (e.g., chiropractors in New York City). They can work well for direct mail designed to drive people to a URL with a landing page (a page on your website designated specifically for the DM campaign).

Response lists consist of prospects who have responded to other marketers' offers; for example, by purchasing a product through a catalog or replying to a direct-mail package. They are less comprehensive than compiled lists because not everyone in a given market is a responder. But they tend to generate more orders, because you are mailing only to people you know respond to direct mail. When you want to sell a product directly from your DM package, response lists work best 90 percent of the time. Mailing list selection is covered in greater detail in Chapter 4.

STEP 6: CHOOSING A FORMAT, TONE, AND STYLE

Next, think about what type of mailing piece you want to send out. Will it be big or small? Expensive or low-budget? Flat or bulky? Will it be a full-blown direct-mail package with a letter, color brochure, inserts, order forms, and reply cards, or just a simple postcard? Will you use a hard sell in the copy or a low-key, professional approach? Will it be splashy and bright or quiet and dignified? Will it be a one-shot mailing or a series? Will you follow up with an email? Will you include the URL of an online form as a response option?

There are many possible formats to choose from. Selecting the right one for you is based largely on your subjective judgment, knowledge of your audience, the type of offer, and your budget. Part III describes in detail the many different mailing formats available. You'll learn how to put together sales letters, direct-mail packages, self-mailers, postcards, and other types of direct mail.

One piece of advice: When in doubt, try a good old-fashioned sales letter in an envelope with a reply card. It's relatively inexpensive and works more often than not. However, if your primary goal is to get a phone call to your 800 number or drive traffic to a landing page, a postcard might be your best bet. The way to settle the issue is to test. It is axiomatic in direct marketing that you can never know in advance which promotion will be a winner. The only way to find out is to test.

STEP 7: DETERMINING YOUR UNIQUE SELLING PROPOSITION

Next, decide which sales appeal to stress in your letter. Your product may have many features that appeal to buyers, and depending on whether you're after leads or sales, you may decide to mention all or just some of them. But successful copy focuses on *one* central sales appeal.

First, pick the *key sales appeal.* This is the benefit that is most important to your customers. If they are primarily concerned with cost, the sales appeal would be *saves money.* If they are more concerned with performance, it might be *performance guaranteed, fastest data delivery,* or *highest reliability.* Then write a mailing piece based on this theme. You'll talk about other features and benefits, too. But these will be presented so that they support and reinforce the main message.

Why does successful advertising copy highlight one key benefit rather than many? Herschell Gordon Lewis had a saying: "When you emphasize everything, you emphasize nothing." Pioneering ad executive Rosser Reeves coined the term *unique selling proposition* (USP) for the number-one factor that makes your product, service, or offer different and better than all others. When you highlight one key point—your USP—and drive it home again and again, you get your message across, and it sticks in the reader's mind. One famous USP is M&M's "Melts in your mouth, not in your hand." Another is, "Red Bull gives you wings," a reference to the energy boost the drink delivers.

How do you know which product benefit is most important to your customers? Again, through testing. For example, you could run two Google or Facebook ads or test two sales letters or postcards. One says, "Easy to install," while the theme of the other is, "Maintenance-free." By seeing which draws the best response, you will know whether your customers are more concerned with ease of installation or minimal maintenance.

Your own experience, or that of your sales force, is also a helpful guide, but you should still test it to see if you are right. If one theme doesn't work well, you can easily switch to another. That's a major advantage of direct mail: It's easy to test and reasonably inexpensive to change.

Another way to find out what customers want is through market research. This can be as informal as talking to a few customers at a trade show or as elaborate as a marketing survey or focus group. Usually, simply getting out there and talking to customers is the best and least expensive way. Formal market research, though helpful, is sometimes overrated and often not necessary.

Remember, you can always learn which sales appeal works best through a simple direct-mail test. Companies that use direct mail in volume may do a series of mailings, with each piece highlighting a different sales appeal, e.g., "saves energy" vs. "costs less than other brands."

STEP 8: IDENTIFYING SUPPORTING FEATURES AND BENEFITS

Now make a list of all the secondary sales arguments you might include in your copy. Remember to talk about benefits, not just features. A *feature* is a descriptive fact about a product or service, such as size, weight, material, form, or function. A *benefit* is what the user of the product or service gains as a result of the feature.

For example, a feature of a wristwatch is that it is luminescent: The hands and numbers glow in the dark. The benefit is that the wearer can easily read the time, even at night or in a dark room.

To uncover your product's benefits, divide a sheet of paper into two columns—Features on the left and Benefits on the right. Look at your product or study its sales literature. In the Features column, list every fact you can find about your product. Now, in the Benefits column, try to think of how each feature can help your customer. In other words, how does the feature save the buyer time or money, make their life easier, or satisfy their needs in some other way?

For instance, a feature of a car might be that it has all-weather tires. The benefit is that you can use these tires all year round. You don't have to switch to snow tires in the winter, so you save money (the cost of buying snow tires) and time (driving to the shop to have the tires switched twice a year).

Figure 2.2 on page 41 shows a features and benefits list for a common object: a No. 2 pencil.

Figure 2.2. **Features and Benefits of a No. 2 Pencil**

Features	Benefits
Pencil is a wooden cylinder surrounding a graphite core.	Can be sharpened as often as you like to ensure clean, crisp writing; writes smoothly and easily
One end is capped by a rubber eraser.	Convenient eraser lets you correct writing errors cleanly and quickly.
Eraser is attached with a metal band.	Tight-fitting band holds eraser snugly in place—won't fall off.
Pencil is 7½ inches long.	Lasts a long time
¼ inch in diameter	Slender shape makes it easy to hold, comfortable grip.
No. 2 hardness	Writes smoothly yet crisply
Yellow exterior	Bright, attractive; stands out in a pen holder or desk drawer
Sold by the dozen	Convenient 12-pack saves trips to the store.
Also available by the gross at a discount	Accommodates the needs of schools and businesses; saves money
Made in the USA	A quality product that supports our economy
Hexagonal shape	Won't roll off your desk

This example may seem trivial because of the product's simplicity. But creating a features and benefits list is immensely helpful when preparing to write copy about unfamiliar or more complex products and services.

STEP 9: CREATING YOUR OFFER

Now that you've decided on your main and supporting sales arguments, the next step is to determine what offer you want to make. The offer is simply what you send to people who respond to the mailing, combined with what they have to do to get it.

Successful direct mail usually has a free or discount offer, or it gives people a bonus gift, called a *premium*, when they respond. One of the main reasons people respond to mailings is to save money. Another is to get something for free. In direct-response TV and online ads, the buy-one-get-one-free approach (aka BOGO) works well.

People are often afraid of being tripped up by unethical direct-marketing schemes or high-pressure salespeople, so your offer should have no strings attached. Stress that your offer is free, there is no obligation to buy, and you have a money-back guarantee. Shoppers don't want to commit themselves to a purchase, and buyers want to be reassured that they won't be ripped off. Your offer should address these needs.

The action you want your prospect to take is part of the offer. Use phrases that will move the reader to action, like "Send no money now," "Try it FREE for 15 days," "Mail the no-obligation Trial Request Form today," "Call us toll-free," "Complete and mail the enclosed reply card." Here are some examples of successful offers:

"If this book does not give you all the help you think it will, just return it anytime within 60 days and you will get your money back in full."	Boardroom Reports ($29.95 book sold by mail)
"If you return the enclosed card to us, I will send you the next issue of *Inc.* free. Without cost or obligation to you."	*Inc.* (magazine subscription)
"To get your free Preview Booklet, just complete and return the postage-free reply card. Or visit [URL] now."	Time-shares

In your copy, you should sell the offer, not the product. If you're selling a handbook for $59 and the customer can return it within 15 days, then you're not really selling a $59 book; you're selling the opportunity to examine the book risk-free for two weeks without cost or obligation.

A FEW WORDS ABOUT RETURNS AND REFUNDS

Traditionally, direct-mail marketers using hard offers have aimed for a refund rate below 10 percent. Anything higher usually means one of two things. One, your direct-mail copy makes the product sound so much better than it is that buyers are disappointed when they receive it. Or two, the product delivered for less value than they expected for the price you charged, and your customers feel ripped off and return it.

But there is a third reason for returns that applies mainly to high-priced offers and luxury items: *buyer's remorse.* The product is worth the money, but the purchase is so extravagant, so much of an unnecessary indulgence, that the buyer feels guilty, changes their mind, and returns the item even if they really like it.

For soft offers, the problem is the *pay-up rate.* For instance, magazine publishers who use soft offers for subscription marketing send an invoice along with the first issue. The pay-up rate is the percentage of buyers who actually pay the invoice.

Many consumers will keep the first issue they got for free but never pay. The invoice amount is too small for the publisher to chase the subscriber for payment, and the copy of the magazine is worthless to them. Instead, if the invoice is not paid after several billing reminders, the publisher just cuts off the subscription. ✉

With a *soft offer,* the customer can read the book for 15 days for free. Then, if they like the book and want to keep it, you send an invoice for payment; this is also called a *bill-me* offer.

With a *hard offer,* the buyer pays for the book upfront, but if they are not satisfied, they can return it for a full refund.

See the difference? Asking someone to plunk down $59 for an unknown product sold by an unfamiliar company through the mail is scary. You probably wouldn't get many orders. But offering to let people look at your book for 15 days and *then* decide whether they want to buy, is a more attractive deal. Even bookstores don't let you do that!

The same approach works in industrial direct mail. No direct-mail letter, no matter how clever, will persuade an engineer to order your $50,000 reverse-osmosis water purification system sight unseen. But a good letter *can* get an engineer to ask for a free demonstration of the system, which gets the salesperson in the door and paves the way for the sale.

Many different offers are possible. Should you offer a 30-day trial, a free pamphlet, a free pocket calculator, a one-year guarantee, or a 20-percent discount? Choose the offer you feel your prospects would respond best to and test it. See which offer works best. Figure 3.1 in Chapter 3 gives you a checklist of offers proven to work in both direct mail and multichannel marketing campaigns.

STEP 10: SCHEDULING YOUR MAILING

Budget and objectives determine the scope of a mailing. For example, if you want to generate 100 orders, and you anticipate a 1-percent response rate, you must mail 10,000 pieces. At $600 per thousand pieces mailed, your cost is $6,000.

Timing is critical to some mailings and less important in others. Some offers can be mailed year-round with continued strong response, while others are seasonal. For example, for catalogs selling gift items, the Christmas season is the most important, and they mail heavily in September, October, and November. Offers for self-help and self-improvement programs do best in January, after the indulgences of the holiday season and the resolutions to do better in the new year.

The other big decision is whether to do a single mailing or a series of mailings. If your market is large and your budget limited, you can probably mail one piece for many months or even many years before exhausting the available names.

On the other hand, if you have a small market, you need a variety of promotions. If you mail just one piece again and again, you will soon experience a decline in response rate.

THE DIRECT MAIL REVOLUTION

How many pieces should you have in your series, and at what intervals should they be mailed? Marketing consultant Jeffrey Lant says you should make contact with your market seven times in an 18-month period. Others advise you should mail more frequently, as often as once a month.

Once, to mail that frequently was costly, and as a result, almost no one did. But now, if you can get direct-mail respondents to give you their email address, it's easy and inexpensive to contact them that often (or even more) via follow-up emails as well as letters and postcards.

Direct mail is as much art as science and more trial and error than anything else. You come up with an idea, test it, and refine your work based on the results. The advantage is that you *can* measure results, which isn't possible with many other types of marketing.

CREATING AND PRODUCING DIRECT-MAIL CAMPAIGNS

SPECIAL OFFER INSIDE

In Part II, I'll show you how to create all the important elements of a successful direct-mail package. These include coming up with strong offers, finding the right mailing lists, writing the copy, designing and printing package elements, and testing.

Chapter 3

CREATING IRRESISTIBLE DIRECT-MAIL OFFERS

First, recall from Chapter 2 that an offer is simply what your prospects get when they respond to your mailing, combined with what they have to do to get it. For example: "Call this toll-free 800 number or mail the enclosed reply card to order a free home security audit today."

THREE OFFER ELEMENTS

The offer has three key elements. The first is the *substance* of the offer itself: Is it a discount? A BOGO (buy one, get one free)? An extended warranty or guarantee? Free shipping? A free bonus gift with your purchase? Buy on installment and make no payments for a full year?

Let's look at some examples of how that substance is conveyed. Here are just a few of the offers in the many direct mailers I received while writing this chapter:

- The American Association of Retired Persons (AARP) offered me a year of membership for $16, three years for $43, or five years for $63, plus a free insulated travel bag as a bonus gift for joining now. They also enclosed a faux membership card and said I could use it until I received my real one in the mail once I joined.

- The AARP Auto Insurance Program lists a toll-free number you can call for a free, no-obligation quote on car insurance, and it gives you a free calculator when you request the quote. In a separate promotion for life insurance, people who call for a rate quote get a free personalized pen and pencil set.

- *The New York Review of Books* offers a one-year subscription for $79.95, a savings of $99.05 off the cover price, and as a bonus gift, you get a free *New York Review* canvas tote bag. You can cancel your subscription at any time for a full refund on all unmailed issues.

- MDHearingAid sent a mailer inviting me to purchase a hearing aid for less than $200 with a 45-day, risk-free, money-back guarantee; free batteries are included.

- Hawthorne Village sent a mailer selling a miniature Christmas village nestled within a large, handcrafted Christmas tree replica. It costs $149.99, payable in four installments of $37.50. It's a soft offer, in that you don't pay upfront but are billed later. It comes with a one-year, money-back guarantee and a certificate of authenticity.

- U.S. Career Institute is selling a home-study course in how to work at home as a medical-billing specialist. The offer is a free information package.

- Renewal by Andersen has multiple offers in their flier: 1) a 20 percent discount on windows and patio doors, 2) free installation, 3) free "window and patio door diagnosis," 4) a discount card good for an additional $250 off your window and patio door offer when you respond by June 12, and 5) financing with no payment required until one year after purchase.

- The Garden Patch sells, direct by mail, a plant box with potting mix and seedlings for growing tomato plants. The cost is three for $105, plus shipping and handling. They guarantee you will grow tomatoes or they will refund your money.

- *Consumer Reports* offers a one-year subscription to their magazine (eight monthly issues) for $20. You also get the annual auto issue, the 2018 and 2019 *Buyers Guide*, and a special bonus report on nutrition—items with a total list price of $96.84. You send no money. And when you receive your first issue and bonus report, if you change your mind about subscribing, you don't have to pay—and you can keep all materials received for free.

The second key element is the *wording* you use to describe the offer. The substance of the offer and the way it is phrased must be accurate, clear, and appealing.

Wording matters. Even a small change can make a huge difference. For instance, a software company was offering a "30-day trial" of its product. When they changed the wording to a "30-day free use," response increased by 10 percent. A "trial" means hard work. But everyone wants to use a product for free.

The third element is the *design and placement* of the offer copy. Do you mention the offer only at the close of your sales letter? Or also upfront? What about on the outer envelope? Is it in plain type, or is it larger than the rest of the lettering? Underlined? Boldface? In a box? Does the box have a plain border or is it designed to look like an important certificate?

Coming up with the right offer should not be an afterthought. Just changing the offer alone, with everything else in the mailing left the same, can boost response rates between 10 percent and 900 percent, as incredible as that sounds.

Many different offers have been tried and tested over the decades. Figure 3.1 provides a checklist of some offers known to work well in direct mail as well as multichannel marketing campaigns.

Figure 3.1. **Checklist of Basic Offers**

[ ] Free white paper	[ ] Free information kit
[ ] Free brochure	[ ] Free mobile app download
[ ] Free booklet	[ ] Invitation to attend a free webinar
[ ] Free catalog	[ ] Free information
[ ] Free newsletter	[ ] More information

Figure 3.1. **Checklist of Basic Offers,** continued

[ ] Free trial

[ ] Free use of product

[ ] Free product sample

[ ] Discount certificate

[ ] Free coupon

[ ] Use of toll-free hotline

[ ] Free advice

[ ] Free consultation

[ ] Free survey

[ ] Free analysis

[ ] Free estimate

[ ] Free problem evaluation

[ ] Free product demonstration

[ ] Have a sales representative call

[ ] Add me to your mailing list

[ ] Not interested right now—try me again in the future

[ ] Not interested—here's why:

[ ] Free audio CD

[ ] Free DVD

[ ] Free gift for providing names of friends who might be interested in the offer

[ ] Free special report

[ ] Money-back guarantee

[ ] Double-your-money-back guarantee

[ ] Free sample issue

[ ] Send no money now—we will bill you

[ ] Cash with order

[ ] Order by credit card

[ ] Enter our contest and win prizes

[ ] Enter our sweepstakes and win prizes

[ ] Enter our drawing and win prizes

[ ] Discount for new customers

[ ] Discount or other special offer for past customers

[ ] Your name removed from our mailing list—unless you order now

[ ] Introductory offer on small trial orders

[ ] Free price-off coupon when you request catalog

[ ] Extra discounts for large volume purchases

[ ] Free gift with volume orders

[ ] Extra discount for payment with order

[ ] Seasonal sale

[ ] Warehouse inventory reduction sale

[ ] Special clearance sale

[ ] Remnant sale

[ ] Buy at low prices now before prices go up

[ ] Free gift item in return for your inquiry

[ ] Free gift item with your order

Figure 3.1. **Checklist of Basic Offers,** continued

[ ] Free gift item with paid in advance order	[ ] Complete and mail description of what you need for a prompt price quotation
[ ] Surprise bonus gift with your order	
[ ] Extra quantity with paid order	[ ] Send no money now—pay in easy monthly installments
[ ] Order now—we won't bill you until [specify date]	[ ] Reply today—while the reply form is still handy
[ ] Order X amount of product/service now, get Y amount free	[ ] Order today—supplies are limited
[ ] Order product X—get product Y free	[ ] Offer good until [date]
[ ] Call toll-free number	[ ] This offer is for a limited time only
[ ] Go to URL	[ ] Subscribe today
[ ] Mail reply card	[ ] Become a member
[ ] Complete and mail order form	[ ] Discount with trade-in of your old equipment
[ ] Complete and mail questionnaire	

There are many more. Start a swipe file and have a separate section for interesting offers you might be able to use for your product or market.

DIRECT-MAIL SUCCESS DEPENDS ON THE OFFER

Direct marketers rely heavily on finding just the right offer to wake up bored consumers, get them to take notice, and persuade them to respond to their ads and mailings.

To get maximum response from your direct mail, you must understand the following:

- The offer is without question among the most important factor in the success of any direct-marketing piece or campaign.
- The strategic planning, selection, and testing of offers—can determine the mailing's success, regardless of how well-designed or well-written the piece is. As a rule, the more valuable and risk-free

the offer seems to the reader, the better your response will be.

☒ How you present the offer—the copy used to describe it, the graphics, and the emphasis placed on it—is also vitally important. The more attention you can draw to the offer, the higher your response rate will be. One study, reported in *Target Marketing* magazine (4/07), showed that direct mail focused primarily on the offer gets an average of ten times more orders than direct mail that targeted the recipient's attention to brand messages.

☒ The clearer and more understandable your offer, the better your response. The lack of a clear, distinct offer can significantly depress response.

☒ Response rates increase when you add a deadline, time limit, or other "act now" sense of urgency to your offer.

It has been estimated that 30 percent of the effectiveness of a direct-mail package depends on the offer, 40 percent on the mailing list, 15 percent on the copy, and 15 percent on the design (see Figure 3.2).

Figure 3.2. **Elements of a Winning Direct-Mail Package**

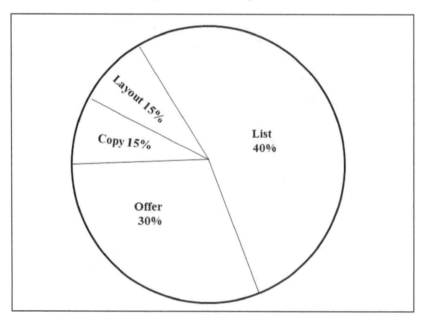

THE SIX CHARACTERISTICS OF AN IRRESISTIBLE OFFER

The best offers share these six common characteristics. To boost your response rates, your offers should incorporate as many of them as they can.

1. Winning Offers Are Different or Even Unique

The best offers are fresh and new. When copywriter Bill Jayme wrote the direct-mail package that launched *New York* magazine, he proposed a sweepstakes. Sweepstakes have long been used to sell magazine subscriptions, but none has ever offered the prize Jayme dreamed up: dinner at Gracie Mansion with New York City's mayor.

Most investment newsletters offer free special reports as premiums. *The Sovereign Society*, a newsletter on offshore investing, offered something different: a free Swiss bank account, a gift not given by any other investment newsletter.

Most business magazines offer either discounted subscription rates or standard premiums like special reports, tote bags, or calculators. *Advertising Age* had a successful control where the premium was a ceramic coffee mug. Mugs are nothing special. But this one was imprinted with a mockup of an *Ad Age* cover. If the subscriber was Jan Smith, the headline was personalized to read: "Jan Smith Chosen as Marketing Genius of the Year."

2. Winning Offers Are Something Prospects Desire

An unusual offer only works if it's something people really want. For instance, a publisher was selling a reference manual on how to manage local area networks (LANs). Response rates doubled when a new direct-mail promotion offered a disk with free software—a collection of utilities for LANs.

The 100-percent increase in orders confirmed that network administrators obviously wanted to get their hands on this software. The outer envelope teaser read: "Yours FREE!—5 Powerful Programs to Help You Manage Your LAN More Efficiently and Easily—See Inside for Details on This Special Time-Limited Offer."

On the other hand, a financial newsletter mailed a renewal promotion that offered as a premium a pack of playing cards with

PUT AN EXPIRATION DATE OR TIME FRAME ON YOUR OFFERS

State that the offer expires on a specific date or within a certain time frame. If you don't, people will continue to demand you fulfill the offer long after your promotion has run its course. And without a time limit, you are legally required to do so. One colleague offered an expensive Mont Blanc pen without including an expiration date, and the company had to give away $100 pens long after the promotion was over. It cost them a lot of money, and the marketing manager who made the error incurred the displeasure of their boss. ✉

the editor's picture on them. Not surprisingly, it flopped. Who would subscribe to an expensive investment newsletter in exchange for a measly deck of cards?

Subscriber surveys for that newsletter indicated the readers liked the stock recommendations but wanted more mutual fund suggestions. The next mailer offered a free DVD of the editor giving mutual fund advice and was a big success.

3. The Offer Should Have a High Perceived Value, Especially in Relation to Fulfillment Costs

Free software has traditionally worked well as a premium. Software has a high perceived value in relation to the cost of goods. Software packages can easily sell for $49 to $300 or more, yet a CD with code on it can be duplicated for about a dollar. But how much do you pay for a deck of playing cards? About a dollar, right? Therefore, the perceived value of the playing cards offered by the financial publisher above is only a dollar—not much of a motivation to renew a newsletter subscription that cost around $79 a year.

In a promotion tied in with its sponsorship of the Olympics, IBM offered a special IBM Olympic pin as a premium. In reality, the pin probably only cost and was worth a buck or so. But the mailer copy hinted that it could become a collectible, creating an impression of potentially high value (people do in fact collect Olympic memorabilia). A mailing selling a series of audio dramas based on stories from the Bible offered as a bonus gift a set of privately minted coins, each featuring a different Biblical figure.

4. Dramatize the Brand or Product's Unique Selling Proposition (USP) with Your Offer

The Sovereign Society is a newsletter about offshore investing. The symbol for offshore investing has long been Swiss bank accounts. Therefore, the offer of a free Swiss bank account with a subscription to *The Sovereign Society* supports and dramatizes the newsletter's USP: making money and increasing privacy by investing offshore in things like Swiss bank accounts.

Even when the offer does not at first glance seem closely related to the product, a clever copywriter can find a connection. Many years ago, *Newsweek* magazine offered a free radio as a premium for new subscribers. On the surface, a radio seems like a poor choice: In the news arena, radio and magazines compete with each other. But take a look:

Dear Reader:

What's the fastest way to get the news?

It's on the radio. That's why *Newsweek* wants you to have—as an introductory gift for new subscribers—this superb AM/FM radio.

But what's the best way to get the news?

You won't get just headlines and a rough outline of the news; with *Newsweek,* you'll get the news in depth . . .

The copy used the differences between these media to make a logical connection between the premium and the product.

5. Make It Easy for the Prospect to Accept the Offer

You should make it as easy and convenient for the prospect to accept your offer as possible. To begin with, offer multiple response mechanisms: a toll-free phone number, a fax number, a URL or a hyperlink to a landing page, even a paper reply element and business reply envelope. Different prospects respond in different ways.

In a direct-mail package, enclose a fax-back form or *business reply card* (BRC) with your letter. If you want customers to enclose payment with their order, or if privacy is a concern, also include a *business reply envelope* (BRE). Yes, even in the digital age, where we have online order forms and QR codes, enclosing a reply card or form still boosts direct-mail response.

One reason for this is because when the prospect opens the envelope, the elements of the package separate. So the order form,

> ✉ **TIP**
>
> If the envelope and letter in the direct-mail package are printed on white paper, consider printing the reply element on canary yellow or robin's egg stock (a light blue) to make it stand out from the other elements.

which features the offer, stands out. In addition, the reply element is a visual indicator to the reader. It says, "This is one of those letters where you get something when you respond." So more recipients reply.

In a print ad, consider including a coupon or a bind-in BRC opposite the ad. On the web, your landing page should ask for the minimum information from the prospect when collecting leads. If you are building your opt-in email list, ask for name and email address only. When you have multiple fields for the user to complete, use an asterisk (*) to indicate which are mandatory, and make as many fields as possible optional. Conversion rates decline incrementally for each additional field you force the prospect to fill out.

6. Minimize the Buyer's Risk and Obligation

Do whatever you can to minimize sales pressure on the prospect. If you follow up leads by phone instead of with the field sales force, say in your copy, "No salesperson will visit." If you don't follow up leads by phone, say, "No salesperson will call."

When offering anything free—a white paper, a webinar, even a brochure—say that it is free. Don't substitute the weaker "complimentary" when writing to a high-level business audience because you think "free" is unprofessional or will offend them. It won't.

"Free" is perhaps the most powerful word in direct-mail copy. Everybody wants free stuff, and businesspeople and professionals are no exception.

A health-care agency sent a direct-mail piece inviting doctors to attend a symposium. They did an A/B split test of two versions; the only difference was that B offered a free pocket diary as a gift for attendance. Version B, with the free gift, out pulled version A sixfold. Busy doctors were persuaded to give up an afternoon by a free pocket diary that cost the health agency about a dollar.

Does the buyer have to agree to sit through a presentation or demonstration or complete a survey? If they are not required to take further action once they accept the offer, note this in your copy by saying, "There's no obligation, nothing to buy, and no commitment of any kind."

OFFERS FOR LEAD-GENERATION DIRECT MAIL

In a two-step direct-mail campaign, where you are generating leads rather than direct sales, there are four basic offers: soft, hard, negative, and deferred.

Soft Offer for Lead Generation

In lead-generating direct mail, the simplest and most common offer has traditionally been a free brochure and other information describing the product or service. In direct mail, this typically reads, "For a free brochure on the Widget 3000, complete and mail the enclosed reply card today." What the prospect gets is a brochure describing your product. What they have to do to get it is fill in and mail a reply card.

The key to the soft offer is that the odds of your prospect being ready to buy the minute they open your mailer are low. It's the ideal response option for prospects who might be interested in your product in the future but not today. They can get sales literature that tells them more about the product without speaking to a salesperson, which they are probably reluctant to do at this early stage in the buying cycle.

Hard Offer for Lead Generation

The soft offer is for prospects not yet ready to buy; the hard offer attracts those who are readier to purchase. In the hard offer, the marketer encourages the prospect to call or request that a salesperson contact them. The offer is made more attractive by calling it a briefing, demonstration, initial consultation, evaluation, free estimate, needs assessment, or initial appointment.

These hard offers all involve direct person-to-person contact between buyer and seller: over the phone, in a face-to-face meeting, or via Skype. During these conversations, the salesperson attempts to persuade the prospect to buy the product or service.

The Negative Offer

The negative-offer option on the reply card reads as follows:

[ ] Not interested right now because: _____

Typically, the sales letter refers to the negative offer using the following language:

P.S. Even if you are not interested in [name of product or service], please complete and return the enclosed reply card. Thank you.

The negative offer provides a response option for people who are prospects (that is, they have a need or problem your product addresses), but for some reason don't want to buy from you right now.

Normally, people who are uninterested in your offer will not respond to your mailings. But by adding a negative-offer option, you will get responses from a small portion of them. And often, by following up, you can answer their objections, overcome their hesitancy, and convert some of them to actual leads, increasing the total number of leads generated by the mailing.

The Deferred Offer

The deferred offer encourages responses from prospects who don't have an immediate need but may have a future requirement for your product or service. The deferred-offer option on the reply card reads as follows:

[ ] Not interested right <u>now</u>. Try me again in: _____

_____ (month/year) _____

The deferred-offer option box tells the prospect, "If you don't need us now but may in the future, you can use this box to let us know, without getting calls and annoying follow-up from salespeople now." Use the deferred offer if you think a significant number of prospects are more likely to need your services in the future. Note: If they say to try them again in June, call them in May. That way, you are more likely to reach them before they have made a purchase decision.

USING MULTIPLE OFFERS IN ONE MAILER

In most lead-generating mailings, you should have two or three offers. The best results usually come from having three: a hard offer, a soft offer, and either a negative or a deferred offer. At minimum, you should have both a hard and soft offer.

The primary offer is the one you hope your prospects will respond to, and the one you emphasize in your copy and graphics. For example, if you want a face-to-face meeting with your prospects, a hard offer asking for an appointment would be the primary.

The secondary offer gives those prospects who will not take you up on your primary offer a second chance to respond. Introduce the secondary soft offer at the end of your ad or letter copy; for example, "P.S. For a free special report on underpublicized tax-saving strategies offered by our firm, just complete and mail the enclosed reply card."

OFFERS FOR ONE-STEP DIRECT MAIL

One-step direct-mail packages allow the customer to order the product directly from the mailing—which is still called mail order marketing. In mail order, the definitions of hard and soft offers are different than for lead-generation offers.

Hard Offers for One-Step Direct Mail

In mail order, a hard offer requires the customer to pay for the product in advance. The seller ships the product only after payment is received via check, money order, or credit card. Use of a hard offer eliminates credit and collection problems because buyers are not billed—everyone pays upfront.

There are several methods to make hard offers more palatable when selling products directly through mail order. One is to allow the prospect to pay in installments; for example, instead of one large upfront payment, the prospect can make three smaller payments, often spaced two weeks or a month apart. Another is to offer a small discount as an incentive to pay all at once, as opposed to paying full price over the installment payments.

Soft Offers for One-Step Direct Mail

The soft offer in mail order selling is the classic "bill-me" offer. Here, the prospect can order and receive the product with no money upfront. The seller sends a bill and is paid later. The advantage of the bill-me offer is to overcome price resistance. The disadvantage is that many customers often don't pay the invoice.

Mailings and ads for collectibles often use soft offers, sending you the necklace, porcelain figure, or collectible plate without getting paid first. The standard copy for these offers reads, "Send no money now. We will bill you later." Most of these collectible mail order offers also allow you to pay in installments once you receive the item.

Magazine subscriptions have been sold via direct mail with soft offers for many decades. The offer here is, "May I send you an issue of *XYZ* magazine absolutely FREE? There's no risk or commitment of any kind." If the subscriber decides they don't want to continue, they write "Cancel" on the invoice and send it back in a postage-paid envelope provided by the publisher. And the magazine issue is theirs to keep.

LEAD MAGNETS

The key to boosting response from free offers is to give away free content, also known as a *lead magnet*. Unlike a brochure, which is a sales document, the lead magnet is more desirable because it contains useful how-to information. But the marketing objective of lead-magnet offers is to get more recipients to respond. Lead magnet offers can often double response rates. Offering a free white paper or special report (see Figure 3.3) can dramatically increase responses to your mailings.

Figure 3.3. **Special Report Used as a Lead Magnet**
Even though the report is free, the price of $15 is shown on the front cover to create higher perceived value.

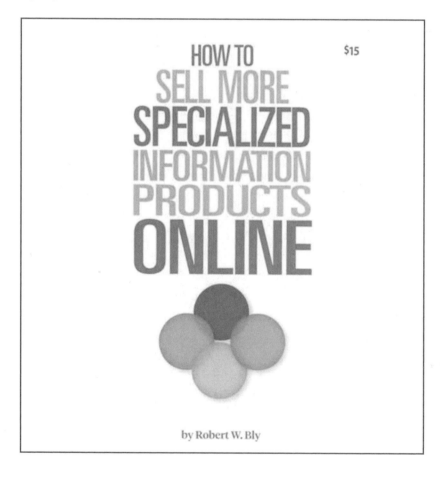

Lead magnets are effective for several reasons. First, today's business prospects, despite being overloaded with reading material, are information seekers, always on the lookout for advice, ideas, and information to help them do their jobs better. Many publishers charge handsomely for such information sold as seminars, books, newsletters, and manuals. So when people see they can get similar information from you in the form of a free booklet or special report, they respond. After all, if it's free, they have nothing to lose.

Second, most people are so busy they flip through mail and ads at a frantic rate. The free-booklet offer, with perhaps a cut-out coupon in the ad and a picture of the report, has attention-grabbing power. It forces the reader to stop and peruse your copy. The reader thinks, "Oh, this is one of those ads offering something free. Let me look for a second and see what I can get." So they call or clip the coupon and request the booklet.

Third, people like getting things for free. In the direct-marketing seminars I give nationwide, there is always someone in the audience who says, "Aren't free offers much less effective in business-to-business than consumer marketing? Come on, really, how excited can an executive get about a free booklet or report?"

The fact is, they do get interested, and the specific offer of free information dramatically increases ad and direct-mail response rates in both B2B and consumer advertising.

The free lead magnet is so effective and so important that for most marketers using direct mail to generate leads, I think it's a mistake not to include a free content offer in your mailing.

The reason is simple: Unless the prospect has an immediate, urgent need to pick up the phone and call you, they're largely indifferent to your mailing. It's just another sales pitch—one of many they will receive by mail or phone that day. The prospect feels no need to respond, and doesn't. The free content offer solves that problem. It says, "Even if you have no immediate need, don't have time to read our mailing, and don't want to think about our product right now, at least mail back the reply card. You'll receive something of value in return"—and thus converts inaction to a response.

Here are some typical titles from successful lead magnets offered in actual direct mail and print ads:

- ✉ "15 ways to improve your collection efforts"
- ✉ "14 winning methods to sell any product or service in a down economy"
- ✉ "Should I Personalize? A direct personalized guide to direct mail"
- ✉ "Choosing business software"
- ✉ "A guide to desktop design"
- ✉ "Family-owned businesses: the 3 most common pitfalls . . . and how to avoid them"
- ✉ "A special report: Productivity Breakthrough Projects"
- ✉ "33 ways to make better displays: What every marketing executive should know about point-of-purchase display marketing"
- ✉ "Steel Log: glossary of metal terms"
- ✉ "7 questions to ask before you invest in IT training . . . and one good answer to each"

AUDIO AND VIDEO LEAD MAGNETS

One way to create additional interest and make your lead magnet stand out even more is to produce your information in the form of an audio CD, online mp3 file, DVD, or streaming video.

While audio and video can be delivered digitally, we find that a physical CD or DVD used as a lead magnet often gets better results: When

STRATEGIC OFFERS

Offers of useful information can be effective at increasing response rates. But even better is to craft the content of your lead magnet so it *also* solves a marketing problem. For instance, companies selling rings by mail order lose sales because potential customers do not know their ring size, and therefore cannot be sure that the ring, bought sight unseen, will fit. The solution is to provide a piece of cardboard with labeled holes in various ring sizes, enabling the customer to determine their ring size before they order. The inexpensive measuring device cuts down on refunds and increases response rates. ✉

the envelope with the lead magnet arrives, the disk's bulk makes the recipient more curious to open it.

Other advantages? Disks usually get past secretaries who screen mail. Because a disk has a higher perceived value and is a tangible object, it won't get thrown away with the rest of the paper mail.

Experience has shown that prospects will take the time to either listen to or view the disk, or at least pass it on to the right prospect within the organization. Printed pieces are not treated with the same degree of importance. Finally, even if the prospect doesn't immediately listen to or view the disk, they will probably keep it in a desk drawer, rather than throw it away. So every time they open the drawer, they will see the item—and its label imprinted with your company name and phone number.

> ✉ **TIP**
>
> When you mail an envelope with a CD or DVD inside, add this teaser to the outer envelope in large, bold type: "Magnetic Media Enclosed" to boost open rates.

ENHANCING THE HARD OFFER IN LEAD GENERATION

"Have a salesperson call" is probably the most widely used hard offer in B2B lead generation. It paves the way for the in-person sales visit that, for many marketers, is a crucial step in getting the prospect to buy. In practice, however, very few prospects will ask a salesperson to call or visit. The reason for this is twofold.

First, prospects don't view salespeople as helpful or beneficial. In fact, the word *salesperson* signals to the prospect that sales pressure will be exerted—something most people want to avoid. Second, most prospects don't want to hear your "sales pitch" or "presentation." Again, the word *sales* implies that the prospect will be subjected to high-pressure selling tactics aimed at benefiting the seller, not the buyer.

The solution is to repackage the offer with skillful copywriting and a change in tactics, to convert a perceived "sell job" into a meeting that is beneficial for the prospect. In a nutshell, this is done by replacing the words *sell* and *sales* with more benefit-oriented words.

To start with, don't use the term *salesperson* when referring to the person who will follow up with the prospect. Replace it with any of the following (or create your own title, as appropriate):

- account representative
- senior consultant
- technical specialist
- account manager
- account supervisor
- application specialist
- program manager
- program planner
- senior specialist

For example, if you are selling financial services, don't say, "Have a sales representative call." Say, "Have a financial consultant call" or "Have a financial planner call" (if your salespeople are truly financial planners). If you are selling a relational database, say, "Have a database specialist call."

Next, don't use the words *sales call*, *sales pitch*, or *sales presentation* when referring to the initial appointment you are seeking with the prospect. Instead, suggest that they contact you to arrange one of the following:

- initial appointment
- free, no-obligation consultation
- free estimate
- free analysis
- needs assessment
- audit
- exploratory meeting
- evaluation of their requirements
- initial planning session
- free demonstration
- executive briefing
- free seminar

Therefore, your hard offer might now read:

Have a technical consultant call to arrange a free analysis of my network requirements. I understand there is no cost for this initial analysis—and no obligation.

If you phrase your offer this way or in a similar fashion, you will get more responses than if you simply say, "Have a salesperson call."

GUARANTEES

If you are selling directly from your mailing, be sure to back your hard offer with a powerful guarantee, either of service, support, or return of money.

For a product, the best offer is a strong, long, unconditional money-back guarantee. For example: "If for any reason . . . or for no reason . . . the X-100 Widget is not for you, return it within 60 days and we will refund your money in full—no questions asked."

A longer guarantee period will generally out pull a shorter one. A 10-day or 15-day guarantee period is not long enough for the prospects to evaluate your product and decide whether it is for them. They will feel rushed and may just return your product without trying it to avoid being stuck with it once the deadline expires.

A 30-day guarantee is sufficient for most products, and I think 60 or 90 days is even better. Many books on direct marketing say to offer a one-year guarantee, but this can be a problem with products that are frequently updated, such as software or annual directories—the prospect could just return the old product and ask for the new one after a year.

Make your guarantee as unconditional as possible. The more conditions you put on the guarantee, the less the prospects are likely to trust you—and buy from you.

The best offers contain an unconditional money-back guarantee. Prospects are wary of offers that seem conditional or that might obligate them in any way. The offer should be easy to take advantage of, easy to understand, risk-free, and require no commitment or obligation on the prospect's part.

For instance, one seller of mail order books offered a refund, but only if the book was returned "in salable condition." If there is a nick on the front cover and you refuse to give a refund, you create ill will and most likely a complaint with the Better Business Bureau. Even if the book is scratched or pages are ripped, give the customer the benefit of the doubt (it could have been damaged in transit) and issue their refund in full, promptly and cheerfully.

DEADLINES AND OTHER ACT-NOW INCENTIVES

Putting in some incentive or reason for the reader to respond now instead of later usually increases responses. People are bombarded by direct mail, sales messages, and offers daily. Your best chance of getting a response is to give them sufficient motivation to respond right now, while the piece is still in their hands.

How do you get the prospect to act now instead of later? The simplest way is to put a time limit in your copy. This can either be a specific date ("Offer expires March 15") or a generic time limit ("You must reply within 15 days to take advantage of this special free offer").

Which is better? A specific date is good if you have enough control over the timing of your mailing to ensure that delays in printing and mailing don't make the deadline obsolete—for instance, you don't want prospects to get a "reply by April 15" mailing on May 2. If you can't control the timing, or if you print your letters in large quantities and mail them regularly, a generic "respond within the next 15 days" offer may be better from a logistics perspective: no matter when the mailing arrives, it's always accurate.

A variation is the limited-number offer: "This offer is limited to the first 200 people who respond to this letter." This tactic gets prospects' attention because they have no idea how many pieces you mailed and therefore want to reply right away to ensure that they are one of the first 200 to respond.

Also, giving a reason for the time-limited offer adds credibility. For the first 200 to respond on a mailing selling art prints, that reason could be a limited supply of signed first editions.

If you don't want to be specific about deadlines, use this language in your sales letter:

> But I urge you to hurry. This offer is for a limited time only. And once it expires, it may never be repeated again.

MAIL-ORDER OFFERS

For direct mail that seeks to generate an order directly from the DM package, rather than a sales lead, here are aspects of mail order that make consumers regularly buy products promoted through direct mail and other media, such as print ads, radio, TV, and telemarketing. To be fair, many of these advantages also apply to merchandise ordered online that is delivered to you via USPS, UPS, or FedEx:

- *Price*. Many mail-order buyers cite lower prices as the reason they buy through the mail. A common theme in mail-order copy is, "Because we eliminate the middleman, we can offer our products direct to you from the factory, at prices significantly below retail." In the retail supply chain, the manufacturer, wholesaler, distributor, and/or store puts their own mark-up on the product to make a profit, which often makes the product more expensive than if you bought it directly.

- *Convenience*. Whenever I need paper for my photocopier, I pick up the phone, call Nancy at Minolta, and place an order. It takes less than a minute. The supplies I need come to my doorstep a few days later. And they send me a bill I have 30 days to pay. Why on earth would I want to get in my car, drive to a store, pay cash out of my pocket, and lug a heavy box all the way home? When I order from a catalog, I find it quicker and easier to call the toll-free number than to go online and search for the product I want. However, if I am totally out of paper, which I am careful to not let happen too often, I will buy a ream or two of copier paper from an office supplies store until my shipment arrives by mail.

- *Time*. Every time I go to the mall, it takes 10 minutes just to find a parking space. Then I have to fight the crowds, deal with rude salespeople, and waste time selecting merchandise only to learn that it's out of stock. Many people don't have the time to go shopping and prefer to order through the mail.

- *Fun*. Mail order buying is a lot of fun. It's exciting to get colorful mailings and catalogs, read through all the interesting offers, and look at the beautiful pictures. My wife and I especially enjoy the food catalogs from Harry & David in Oregon; reading a Harry & David catalog is like walking through the finest gourmet store— browsing the seller's website does not quite match it. And when your merchandise does arrive, it's like getting an unexpected gift from a friend. There's a pleasure in opening the box not unlike unwrapping your presents at holiday time. Blue Apron sends "meals in a box," which consist of the ingredients packaged with the recipe. The delight of opening the box and finding the goodies inside also adds an element of fun and surprise.

* *Availability.* A big appeal of mail order is that it offers people an opportunity to buy many interesting, unusual, or odd products they cannot get locally. Each year, for example, we order bulbs of beautiful, exotic flowers that local greenhouses don't carry. Take a look at mail order advertising—print, TV, and web. They frequently use the phrase "not available in stores." This tells the customers that if they don't order from you, they won't be able to get the product at all.

* *Free trial.* If I buy a book from a bookstore, I'm stuck with it even if I discover after the first ten pages that it's boring. But when I order books by mail, I can keep them for 15 or 30 days, read them, and then decide whether to keep the book and pay for it—or return it without cost or obligation of any kind. Although we have had our share of problems with getting the wrong merchandise and dealing with incompetent telephone representatives from some mail order houses, returning mail order merchandise is generally easier—and less costly—than going back to the store.

* *Service.* To get your business, mail order companies often offer a lot of extras that retailers don't provide; free delivery, free gift-wrapping, free gifts, discounts for being a good customer, discounts for prompt payment, buy-now-pay-later privileges, help with ordering and merchandise selection, toll-free telephone numbers to call, direct-mail and email notifications of when it's time to buy again, and reminders of what you bought last time. Is your local department store as generous or helpful?

* *No sales pressure.* If you've ever set foot in a car dealership or time-share resort, you know what sales pressure is. In direct-mail selling,

you can study the catalog or mail piece, and ponder the offer in your home without being pressured by a salesperson. Yes, some direct-marketing companies exert undue pressure with telephone follow-ups. But it's a lot easier to hang up the phone than it is to get out from under the thumb of a live salesperson.

SETTING YOUR GOALS

Everyone has a different goal in mail order. Some people expect to make money with every mailing and every product. For them, a direct-mail piece that breaks even is a disappointment. A piece that loses money is a disaster.

In his book *Mail Order* (Boardroom Books, 2004), mail order guru Eugene Schwartz says he considers any mail piece a success that generates revenue that is 1.3 times break-even or greater. So if a mailing costs $500 per thousand, he would want revenue of at least $650 per thousand.

In addition, success has varied meanings depending on your industry and your product. Howard Shenson, author of *Shenson on Consulting* (John Wiley & Sons, 1994), says that when promoting seminars, for example, your mailing must generate at least double the cost of the mailing for the seminar to be profitable.

But others are more willing to break even or take a small loss on the first mailing because they know most mail order enterprises make their money on repeat business. They view the initial mailing as an expense they will recover in future mailings. The purpose of that first mailing is not just to sell a product but also to gain a customer.

Someone who buys in response to your direct-mail package is of great value to you. Once people buy your product, they have proved themselves to be mail order buyers. That's important because many people aren't willing to buy through the mail. Even better, they have shown they will buy your type of product by mail and will spend at least the amount of money you charged them.

By building your customer list, you are building your mail order business. That list is a gold mine; typically, the response you get to your "house list" of customers will be anywhere from two to ten times greater than you can get from a rented or compiled list. The real profits in mail order lie in later mailings to your customers, offering more products like the one they already bought.

What's more, if your list gets large enough, you may be able to generate additional profits by renting it to other firms. A professional list management company can act as your agent, marketing the list in exchange for a percentage of the profits. You generally need a minimum of 25,000 names (and preferably 50,000) before list managers will be interested. However, if your list is highly specialized and you know your market, you may be able to rent it directly to other firms.

SEVEN GUIDELINES FOR DM TESTING

Here are some final guidelines to make your direct-mail offers as strong as possible:

1. Don't underestimate the importance of offers.

2. The product or service is key, but a good offer can often mean the difference between a so-so and a super response.

3. Invest time in creating and testing your offers. Most marketers don't spend nearly enough time on this crucial step.

4. You can never tell which offer will pull best. Constantly try and test different offers.

5. When in doubt, the surest way to increase response is to make the offer free and without risk or obligation of any kind.

6. In selling to businesses, include both a hard and a soft offer.

7. In lead-generation mailings, always include a free booklet or other free information offer as the soft offer in addition to your "meet-with-me-now" hard offer. ✉

Chapter 4

MAILING LISTS

A *mailing list* is a list of people who are potential customers for your product or service. It contains their names and postal addresses so you can send out mailings to the people on the list. Some postal lists also include the prospect's email address and phone number.

A mailing list can be a list of customer and prospect names you've collected over the years. It can be a list of people or companies compiled from a variety of sources, including warranty registration cards, club membership rosters, trade-show attendees, or industry or professional directories—for example, members of the American Medical Association or your local chamber of commerce. Or it can be a list of people who have previously responded to a direct-marketing offer either by buying a product or by requesting more information by mail, phone, or online.

You can rent mailing lists from many different sources, or you can put together your own list. Depending on how you count, there are thousands of different lists available for rental on the market today.

You can select only those portions of a list that are right for your offer, sorting it by state, city, zip code, industry, income, job classification, gender, and many other categories.

THE IMPORTANCE OF THE LIST

A mailing list is more than a means of reaching your market. The list *is* the market. About 40 percent of your mailing's success depends on using the right lists. So finding and testing lists is critical to your direct-mail success.

To judge whether your product should be promoted by direct mail, ask yourself, "Is there a mailing list of my customers available?" If there is, you can use direct mail. If not, it will be very difficult to reach your prospects by mail—unless you can create your own list.

Most experts agree that selecting the right mailing list is the most important factor in your mailing's success.

Whom you mail to is more important than what you mail. The best-performing lists in a given mailing can out pull the losers in the same list test by as much as 10 to 1. I have firsthand experience in a list test where that is exactly what happened. In other words, proper list selection can increase response tenfold. Instead of 100 replies, you can get 1,000 if you choose the right list of prospects to mail to.

For example, let's say the New York City Ballet sends out a mailing offering season tickets at a 20 percent discount. If you dislike ballet, no direct-mail copywriter will persuade you to buy those tickets no matter how skilled they are.

On the other hand, if you're a ballet lover and have been thinking of going more often, this mailing will be very appealing to you. You might very well buy the tickets even if the mailing is not particularly persuasive. Merely informing you that the discount tickets are available might be all you need to open your wallet.

You can see that an offer for season tickets to the ballet would do much better when mailed to a list of ballet lovers than to the general public. Lists of people who attend other cultural events, such as the symphony and the theater, might also work well.

In other words, if you're selling gourmet steaks by mail, don't rent the subscriber list of the *Vegetarian Times*. You may think you write persuasively enough to get vegetarians to start eating steak. But advertising doesn't work that way. As mail order master Eugene Schwartz pointed out in his book *Breakthrough Advertising* (Bottom Line Books, 2004), "The purpose of advertising is not to create desire; it is to focus the consumer's existing desires onto your product as a way to fulfill them."

Although the information in this chapter applies to every type of mailing, from small to large, I pay extra attention to an often-ignored area: getting lists for small mailings (50 to 5,000 pieces). This is a special problem area, since most mailing-list firms have a minimum order of 5,000.

IDENTIFYING LIST REQUIREMENTS

In Chapter 2, you read that one of the ten key steps in planning a mailing is targeting the right market. This determines which list to use and thus what kind of requirements your list should have.

When selling to consumers, look for a list of prospects who have responded to similar offers in the past. If you're selling a diet plan, the best list would be of people who have paid for other weight-loss programs in the past, such as Weight Watchers members. For selling those fine steaks I mentioned above, test a list of buyers from a barbecue sauce catalog.

If such targeted lists are unavailable, you could mail to more general lists of people you think are likely to respond to your offer. If you're selling a luxury round-the-world vacation, you might mail to lists of millionaires, corporate executives, and other people who can afford to indulge themselves.

In B2B direct mail, choose lists by industry and job title. You could, for example, get a list of process engineers and plant managers at chemical plants in Florida and California that employ 100 people or more. (Size and location are also popular selection factors for industrial mailings.)

Don't neglect secondary markets when selecting lists. A manufacturer of telecommunications equipment started out mailing exclusively to telecommunications managers at small and midsize companies. But it soon discovered that independent telecommunications consultants have a big say in determining what systems their clients purchase. So the manufacturer added these consultants to its mailing list, and sales finally began to rise.

HOW MANY NAMES ON THE LIST SHOULD YOU MAIL?

Sometimes the size of your mailing may be limited by the actual number of names available. Often, for highly specialized offers, there may be only a few thousand or even a few hundred names on the list. But for other products, such as laptops or tablets, the potential market is in the hundreds of thousands or even millions.

In that case, your budget determines how many names to rent and how many pieces to mail. If you've budgeted $5,000 for the mailing, and your mailing costs $1 apiece (including postage and list rental), then you can afford to mail 5,000 pieces.

If there are more names on the list than you can afford to mail to, select only the best prospects—the people who most closely fit your profile of the "ideal customer." For example, if location is important, you might select only those prospects in your state. If the list is still too large, start breaking it down by zip code until you get the 5,000 prospects closest to you.

MINIMUM LIST RENTAL REQUIREMENTS

When you rent mailing lists from list brokers, managers, compilers, owners, and other resources, the standard minimum order is 5,000 names, although some may allow a smaller order, such as 1,000 to 2,000.

So what do you do if your mailing plans are less ambitious? There are several options. First, you can always rent the 5,000 names, use only as many as you need, and keep the remainder for future mailings. Of course, lists get outdated quickly, so if you don't do additional mailings within six months or so, some of the names and addresses will be obsolete.

Second, if you're mailing to your "house list"—prospect and customer names you've collected through the years—rather than a rented list, quantity poses no problem. You simply address as many envelopes and sales letters as you need. Don't overlook salespeople's personal files as a source of names. Ask your salespeople to send you copies of their prospect lists. People with whom your sales force has had personal contact with are usually highly responsive to mail describing new products and services.

A third alternative for B2B marketers is to compile your own list from directories, magazine articles, industry directories, or other published sources. This is an excellent way to get good lists for smaller, industry-specific mailings. In some cases, it is the best way. Most mailing-list firms are unaware of these specialized lists.

To self-compile a small, targeted list, get the major magazines serving your market or industry, go through them, and record the name and contact information of every company running a full-page ad. These are the companies that have money to spend. Then go online or get on the phone and get the name and title of the executive at each company who is your best prospect.

A fourth option is to rent mailing lists from organizations that don't require a minimum order of 5,000. These include publishers, trade associations, professional societies, seminar sponsors, and other organizations that have their own lists but are not in the list business full time. Often, you can rent the membership rosters of local chapters of national associations rather than the larger national list.

RENTING MAILING LISTS

Lists can be rented from many different resources. You pay a fee, which is typically $50 to $350 or more per thousand names, for the right to use the mailing list one time.

The person renting you the list gives you the names either on pressure-sensitive labels, "Cheshire" (ungummed) labels, a disk, a thumb drive, or in some other electronic form. If the list comes as a computer file, you can use it to print the recipient's name and address on the outer envelope or any other package component.

Standard list-rental agreements allow you to use the list once. If you want to use it again, you have to pay another fee. Some people think they can just copy the labels or the data files and mail to the list as many times as they like without paying.

But they can't. Beyond the fact that it's dishonest and illegal, list owners and managers have taken precautions to identify cheaters. For one thing, the list contains several fake names. Anything you mail to those names will actually go to the person renting you the list. If they receive two of your mailings addressed to a fake name, and you've only paid to use the list once, you're caught. Penalties are stiff, and list managers don't tolerate cheaters. So if you want to use a list more than once, you'll have to pay for it. However, a small but growing minority of list owners and managers are now offering the option of unlimited use of a list for a fixed fee—it is, of course, much higher than the single-use fee.

If someone from a rented list responds to your mailing, their name goes into your prospect or customer file, and you can now mail to them as often as you wish, without paying any additional fee to the list company. You own the name.

There are basically two types of lists available for rental: response lists and compiled lists.

Response Lists

For most consumer offers, *response lists* are best. These are lists of people who have responded in some way to an offer made through the mail, in a print ad, or in a TV commercial.

Experience shows that people who have responded to direct-marketing offers in the past are likely to do so again. Some folks just love to buy through the mail, while others hate it. This is why you usually get better results with response lists than with a list of names someone has collected.

But beware. Experience also shows that people who respond to one type of offer will not necessarily respond to a different type. So your best bet is a list of people who have responded to or expressed interest in a similar offer.

For example, let's say you are selling a home-study course on computer programming. Your first choice might be students who have taken introductory computer courses at local community colleges. But when you mail to this list, you get poor results. Why? Because even though these people have demonstrated an interest in learning about computers, they are not proven direct-response buyers. Many people who enjoy taking courses with live instructors would never consider doing it by mail.

A better choice might be people who have already responded to offers on home-study courses in electronics or other similar subjects. These people have demonstrated willingness to study by mail and have an interest in technology. You mail to this list and get good results. The response list has worked for you.

You might then do a small test mailing to a third list: people who have responded to home-study courses in unrelated subjects. You might find that this type of person just loves to take courses by mail and will respond to offerings in a wide variety of subjects. This list is worth testing (see Chapter 8 for advice on how to do a direct-mail test).

Here are some other factors to consider when selecting response lists:

- ✉ *How frequently do the people on the list order products by mail?* The more often, the better.
- ✉ *What was the date of their last purchase?* The more recent, the better.
- ✉ *What is the average size of their purchase?* People who have responded to $29 offers in the past may not respond to $149 offers; the latter may be too rich for their blood.
- ✉ *What type of offer did they respond to?* A person who received a free calendar for subscribing to a magazine may not respond to your subscription mailing unless you also offer a free gift. Someone who buys through direct-response TV commercials may turn a cold shoulder to direct mail. Look for people who have responded to similar offers and media.

Compiled Lists

As the name implies, a *compiled list* is a list of names that someone has put together from other sources. The most common sources include car registrations, association memberships, club directories, guest book signatures, public records, and warranty card registrations. As we've discussed, compiled lists are usually not as good as response lists for mail order offers.

But there are a limited number of response lists, and sometimes compiled lists can work unexpectedly well with certain direct-response offers. There are many more compiled lists available than there are response lists, so by using compiled lists, you can reach out to more potential customers. You get the best results when the people on your list match the profile of your "ideal customer."

In B2B direct mail, you can specify a list by industry, job function, and title. For a recent mailing, I went to my list broker with the following specifications: "IT managers, systems analysts, and programmers in banks, insurance companies, and financial-services firms with 100 employees or more." The broker produced a list matching my requirements exactly.

Take the time to build a profile of your ideal customer, and then describe them to your list broker. The more closely the people on the list fit your description, the better your response will be.

Think about sales opportunities that exist in your industry. If you own a restaurant or gas station, one good market might be lists of people who have just moved to your town, called "new mover" lists. Experience proves that new residents will spend eight to ten times more than established residents. One reason is that someone who is new to the area does not have a regular auto mechanic, pizza delivery service, or dry cleaner. So if you reach them first and they are satisfied with your service, you can become their regular go-to source; their lifetime customer value can be enormous.

SELF-COMPILED VS. RENTED COMPILED LISTS

If you market to a small niche market with only a few well-known players, you may simply compile your mailing list yourself. However, if your target market has thousands of prospects, you are better off renting a compiled list from a list broker. One advantage of compiled lists is the ability to select segments of the list and mail to those names only. For instance, an investment advisor may want to mail only to investors who are close to retirement age and have an IRA worth $1 million or more. ✉

Conversely, mailing to people who don't match your specifications can be disastrous. One company selling software did a mailing to midsize businesses that generated zero response. Following up by phone, they discovered their error: The software ran only on Apple computers, and none of the companies on the list owned them. They then did a second mailing to a list of Apple owners and this time got some inquiries in response.

Other Mailing List Categories

In addition to response lists and compiled lists, there are several other types of lists direct mailers use including the following:

- *Subscription lists.* Lists of magazine and newsletter subscribers are excellent for direct mail because they are all "response lists," in that a subscriber typically responds to a mailing to order a subscription. So we know that they are direct-mail buyers. Ask the list broker to confirm that the list was direct mail generated; online subscribers are not necessarily direct-mail responsive.

- *Paid circulation.* There are two types of magazine subscription lists: paid and controlled. Paid circulation subscription lists are lists of subscribers who pay for the magazine. Most consumer publications have paid subscriptions. Those marketers who favor paid circulation lists argue the subscriber has paid for the magazine and therefore is willing to spend money on mail order items.

- *Controlled circulation.* These are lists of subscribers who get the magazine for free. Many business, trade, and technical publications have controlled subscriptions. The reader fills out a "qualification card" that has been mailed to them, certifying that they hold a certain position within the industry that qualifies them to receive the publication free of charge. Those who favor controlled circulation lists are looking for more complete coverage of an industry, job title, or demographic. Because they are free, controlled circulation lists are generally bigger and contain a larger percentage of the market than paid circulation lists.

- *Donor lists.* Fundraisers rent lists of people who have donated to charitable and worthy causes by mail. But because donors are mail-responsive, direct-mail marketers use these lists for a variety of commercial offers as well.

- ✉ *Attendee lists.* Many mailers look for lists of people who have attended trade shows and seminars. Seminar attendees are especially attractive to marketers selling via mail order because many of them registered by mail and paid a substantial amount of money to attend.

- ✉ *Membership lists.* One way to target business and professional prospects is by renting membership lists of associations and professional societies. If your business is regional, contact local chapters of these groups and see if you can rent their lists of members and prospective members.

- ✉ *Credit card lists.* Direct-mail sales increase when you take credit cards, so many mailers seek lists of prospects who hold major credit cards.

- ✉ *Sweepstakes.* Some marketers use sweepstakes lists to increase sales. Sweepstakes can increase response up to 50 percent for some offers. However, some people like sweepstakes and some (like me) don't. Therefore, mailers planning to do sweepstakes should look to rent lists of sweepstakes participants if they are available in their market niche.

- ✉ *Databases.* A database is a collection of consumer names and addresses from which lists can be selected based on demographics, psychographics, and other lifestyle indicators. For instance, if you were doing a mailing to get people to subscribe to a newsletter on infertility, you could select women aged 30 to 45 who are married, don't have children, have a household income of $50,000 or more, and subscribe to other newsletters or magazines. Much of this information is added to the files in the database from third-party sources. As a result, the records in a database typically have more "selects" than ordinary mailing lists where extra demographic data has not been appended to the records. A "select" is simply a data point you can use to segment the list and choose names that are an optimal fit with your DM campaign; e.g., people who are grandparents.

- ✉ *Master B2B databases.* Some brokers, such as MeritDirect and Reach Marketing, offer big databases made by combining many different business mailing lists, removing duplicate names, and allowing you to select by firmographics and demographics; for example, size of company, annual sales, industry, and so forth.
- ✉ *Hotline names.* A hotline list is a selection from a response list of buyers who have bought something within the past 6 to 12 months. Since a prospect is more likely to buy again if he's bought something recently, hotline lists can be extremely effective and rent for a premium price.

RECENCY, FREQUENCY, MONETARY (RFM)

When I first got into direct marketing, I took a course in direct-mail copywriting at New York University with legendary copywriter Milt Pierce. One day I said, "Professor Pierce, why is it that as soon as I give a donation to a charity, they immediately send me another letter asking for more money? Don't they realize I just gave and therefore have no more money to give again so soon?"

Milt replied, "Because they know from experience that the person who just made a donation is the one most likely to give again."

Huh? This threw me. It seemed counterintuitive. "But if I just gave money to a charity, then I would feel I'd fulfilled my obligation for at least a while," I said. "And I might even be annoyed that they were coming back to me asking for more."

"Nonetheless," Milt replied, "experience proves that the person who just gave is the most likely to give again." And as Milt taught us, above all else, you can't argue with results. What matters is what works—not what you think should work. He explained that this practice of mailing to donors or customers as soon as you get their money is called *recency*, and it is part of a formula called RFM: recency, frequency, and monetary.

Recency refers to how recently the person made a purchase through direct response. According to RFM, those who bought most recently are most likely to buy. This is why it's usually worth paying a premium to rent the hotline names on a mailing list: the hotline names invariably outperform the other names on the list because of recency.

Frequency refers to how often the customer buys. The more often someone buys, the more responsive they are to additional mail order offers. This is why some mailing lists offer a selection called *multibuyers*, or customers who have bought more than once. Typically, multibuyers outperform the one-time buyers on the list.

Finally, *monetary* looks at how much money the customer spends, or the size of their average order. Look for mailing lists where the average order falls in the same range of your product's price.

Let's say you are selling a video program called "Overcoming Infertility: How to Have a Child When You've Been Trying Without Success." The price is $99. You rent a list of people who have subscribed to an infertility magazine for $12. You send out a mailing to the list, but it doesn't pull. Why not?

The problem is that while the people on the list have an interest in infertility and buy information by mail, they have not demonstrated that they will spend $99 in the mail. Twelve dollars, yes; $99, no.

The solution is to find a list of people who have, say, attended a workshop on infertility or bought a fertility test kit via mail order for $100. That way, you not only know the people on the list are mail order buyers and interested in infertility but also that they will shell out a large amount of money for the right offer.

WHERE TO RENT MAILING LISTS

To rent mailing lists, you can go to one of three sources: the list owner, the list manager, or a list broker.

List Owners

The list owner is the person or organization that originally collected, generated, or compiled the list. This could be a magazine publisher (for subscriber lists), trade association or professional society (for membership lists), trade-show producer or seminar sponsor (for attendee lists), mail-order company (for buyer lists), or any organization that has a list of customers or prospects.

List Managers

Some list owners rent out their lists directly. Most, however, prefer to hand it over to professional list managers. These firms actively promote the list and take care of the administrative details, such as shipping, billing, and so on.

The advantage of going to a list manager is that these people are experts in using mailing lists. They can look at your mailing piece, product, marketing plan, or even just a rough draft of your letter and recommend lists that would work well for your offer. List managers don't normally charge for their advice and recommendations; instead, they make their money from commissions paid to them by the list owners.

So one way to get started is to contact a reputable list manager. Many list brokers (see below) also offer list-management services. Call them, explain the nature of the mailing you are planning, and get their advice on which lists you should use. Also ask for a copy of their print or onlin list catalog; most list-management firms provide them at no cost.

List Brokers

A third source of mailing lists is the list broker, a company that gives you more personalized service than a list manager or owner. Again, there is no charge for using the list broker's service, since they get their commissions from list owners and managers. Unlike list owners and managers, who make money only if you rent their list, brokers have no financial incentive to recommend a particular list; the broker makes money regardless of

> ✉ **TIP**
>
> When a list broker recommends a mailing list to you, ask them to provide data on "tests and continuations." This will give you a list of direct-mail marketers who have tested the list recently as well as a record of which firms "rolled out" to more names on the list after the initial test. These reports are valuable for two reasons. First, you can see whether the list has worked for similar offers. Second, a high percentage of continuations—ideally 70 percent or higher—means the list is responsive; a low percentage means it doesn't get good results.

which lists you rent. Their incentive is to get you the best lists possible so you have a successful mail campaign and come back to them again. See Appendix I for a listing of select list brokers.

16 TIPS FOR PROFITABLE LIST SELECTION AND USAGE

Here are a few guidelines that will help you communicate your mailing-list needs to list brokers.

1. Your main responsibility is coming up with an accurate, detailed definition of your target market. If you can clearly describe your ideal customer, a list broker or manager can probably find the right list for you.

2. Be sure this definition is correct and complete. If you're selling custom hubcaps for Cadillacs by mail, make sure you insist that people on the list own Cadillacs.

3. Don't overlook your own resources. You may have access to directories, attendee lists, subscriber lists, and other sources that list managers don't know about. Compiling and collecting your own list can make sense, especially if your product is highly specialized and your market is small.

4. Most postal lists rented for one-time use range from $50 to $350 or more per thousand names. Business lists generally cost more than consumer lists.

5. In B2B direct mail, I have gotten excellent results from trade journal subscriber lists, trade-show attendee lists, and membership lists of professional societies and trade associations.

6. The first step in creating an ongoing, successful direct-mail program is to get your own in-house list in order—or start building one if you don't already have one.

7. Many lists offer *selects*. For a small additional cost, you can just select segments of the list, such as people in a specific state or zip code working for companies of a certain size, etc. If you know your market's demographics well, targeting those people on the list can produce an ROI far in excess of the modest extra cost of using selects.

8. Don't be intimidated by list people or their jargon. Mailing-list selection is a highly involved, complex subject. But you really don't need to know much about it—that's the job of the list broker or manager.

9. You can find list brokers and managers online or through referrals. They also advertise their services in such magazines as *Target Marketing* and *DM News*. Some are in Appendix I of this book.

10. Never rent the whole list at once. Always start with a few thousand names and test. Then, if successful, you can rent more names and mail more pieces.

11. Rand McNally and other companies sell maps of the United States by zip code, if you're inclined to go old school with a big paper map on your office wall. If you do regional or local mailings, such a map will help you select which zip codes to mail to. Maps are also available online, of course.

12. In consumer mail order, the best list contains people who have bought a product similar to yours, at a similar price, recently. If you sell rosebushes by mail, rent lists of people who have bought seeds and plants by mail.

13. In business mailings, look for lists of prospects who have demonstrated interest in your topic. For example, if you are promoting a seminar on total quality management, don't just rent compiled lists of engineers and managers in manufacturing. Rent lists of people who have attended quality seminars, subscribe to quality journals, or belong to a quality society or association.

14. Test lists, even those that on the surface seem to reach the same audience. Often one such list will surprise you and significantly outperform another list you thought was almost identical. You don't know which lists will be winners until you test.

15. For a small fee, the mailing-list provider can add a key code to the mailing labels. You can use this code to track which responses came from which lists. Of course, if the key code is not on the reply card or order form, you can't tell which list produced that response. That's why so many mailers affix or imprint the label on

the reply element, which shows through a glassine window on the outer envelope.

16. Add a few "seed" names to the list that are addressed to you and others in your company. Getting the mail piece with your seed label gives you an idea for how long it takes the mailing to get to others on the list.

You can also use these guidelines to review recommendations submitted by list brokers so you can better judge whether the list they are recommending is a good fit for your product and reaches the right prospects.

Chapter 5

WRITING DIRECT-MAIL COPY THAT SELLS

It has been said many times that in direct mail, copy is king." The great direct-mail marketer Malcolm Decker said, "Copy is the architect of the sale. If your copy can firmly engage your prospect—and keep them engaged—through reading, you're on your way to a sale."

COPY IS KING

Yes, other factors besides copy, notably the list and the offer, have greater influence on the direct-mail package's performance. But after initial testing, you gradually identify the best lists and offers. From that point on, *the major leverage you have for boosting response is through the copy.*

As for graphics, there is a long-running debate in direct mail about the importance of copy vs. graphic design. Rather than argue about it, let's just say that both are important and then do our best job of writing and designing every piece we produce.

However, unlike general advertising, where some ads are almost totally visual, direct mail needs words to sell.

Ad agency creative directors often treat copy as just another design element. In direct response, it is the copy that sells. So DM designers take great pains to make the copy readable and prominent; the main purpose of graphic design in direct mail is to make the copy easy to read.

KNOW YOUR PRODUCT

Once you have gone through the planning process outlined in Chapter 2 and have a clear definition of your audience and marketing objectives, the next step in writing copy that sells is to immerse yourself in your product.

Dig into the source material. Underline or highlight key information, facts, figures, or phrases that strike your fancy. Physician and nutritional supplement maker Dr. Al Sears once said to me, "Big ideas come from thorough research." Copywriter Don Hauptman, when writing direct mail to sell newsletter subscriptions, read through all the issues the client gave him; he said the big idea for the promotion was often buried in one of the articles.

Don't be afraid to "steal" sentences, paragraphs, or even entire headlines and concepts from previous ads or mailings. As copywriter John Francis Tighe once said, "We are not in the business of being creative. Rather, we are in the business of knowing what works and reusing it."

I cannot overemphasize this point. Many copywriters are afraid to study past materials because they fear their creative thinking will be tainted and they will be accused of being copycats. But remember, we are after sales, not prizes for originality.

After you complete your study on the background materials, you should be able to answer the following questions on pages 93–95. If not, get the answers by talking to subject matter experts (SMEs): product managers, salespeople, distributors, engineers, and marketing managers. Interviews with users of your product or potential customers can also be revealing.

Is all this research really worthwhile? "Digging pays off," says my friend and fellow DM copywriter Don Hauptman. "Superficial preparation usually generates anemic copy. Your research should be thorough. Learn everything you can about your product and your market."

Here are 50 questions you should ask before you start to write the copy according to my friend and professor Milt Pierce:

1. What are all the product benefits?
2. What are all the features of the product?
3. How is my product different from—and better than—the competition?
4. What does the buyer expect when they plunk down money for my product? And do we deliver?
5. What methods, approaches, and sales techniques is the competition using?
6. How is the audience for my product different from the general public?
7. How much can my buyer reasonably expect to pay?
8. Does my average buyer have a credit card or a checking account?
9. Will my product be purchased for business or personal use?
10. Can I expect to get multiple sales from my buyer?
11. What is the logical "back end" product to sell someone after they have purchased my product?
12. Will I need to show my product in color?
13. What's the "universe"—the total number of potential customers?
14. Who will buy my product? Teenagers or octogenarians? Men or women? Executives or blue-collar workers?
15. Is there a market for overseas sales?
16. Should I offer time payments?
17. Will my product be a good gift item?
18. Should my copy be long or short?
19. Should my copy be breezy or down-to-earth?
20. Should I test the price?
21. Should I test lists?
22. Should I test copy approaches?
23. Should I mail third class[1] or first class?

---

[1] https://bizfluent.com/info-8727173-third-class-mail.html

24. Is there a seasonal market for my product—and am I taking advantage of it?

25. Are there testimonials available from satisfied customers?

26. Can my direct mail be integrated with digital marketing?

27. Can I use a member-get-a-member approach? (In other words, can I ask buyers to give me the names of other people I can mail to?)

28. Do I need photographs or illustrations?

29. Which appeals have worked in the past for this promotion?

30. What objections might arise from a prospective customer? How can I overcome these objections?

31. Should I use a premium?

32. Should I offer a money-back guarantee?

33. Is this item also sold retail? Are there price advantages I can stress for buying direct?

34. Should I consider a celebrity testimonial?

35. Can I tie in my copy to some news event?

36. Can I tie in my copy to some holiday or other seasonal event?

37. Does my product sell better in a particular region or climate?

38. Would personalizing the mailing improve the effectiveness of my DM piece?

39. Should I consider using a sweepstakes?

40. Can my product be sold through billing inserts?

41. Can my product be sold through a two-step advertising campaign?

42. Should I consider using audio or video?

43. What must I do to give the reader a sense of urgency—so they will buy my product now?

44. Can I use scientific evidence in my sales approach?

45. Have I allowed enough time to create a direct-mail package?

46. Can I get my customer to order by phone? Online? Or by scanning a QR code with their smartphone?

47. What information will I want to get from my customer to make future sales possible?

48. What unsuccessful approaches have been used to sell this product in the past?

49. Can I get powerful "before" and "after" pictures?

50. Assuming I get a 10-percent return, am I prepared to fill all the orders?

While asking yourself all 50 questions may seem a cumbersome process, taking the time now will make sure you set your copy up for success.

THE "4S" FORMULA FOR CLEAR WRITING

There is an old saying that easy reading is hard writing. But it need not be. Although the art of copywriting—persuasion in print or on the screen—is based on testing and psychology, writing clear, concise copy that is easy to read is a simple skill to learn. Simple writing is the precursor to great copy: It doesn't matter how brilliant your promotion is if it's difficult to read.

The 4S formula is the quickest and simplest way to make your writing easy to read:

- *Small words.* Never use a big word when a smaller one will do. For instance, don't write "utilize" when you mean *use*. Mark Twain said, "I never write 'metropolis,' because I can get the same money for 'city.'"
- *Short sentences.* Read your sentences aloud. If you run out of breath before you get to the end, the sentence is too long. Break it into two sentences at the point where a new thought or idea begins.
- *Short paragraphs.* Especially in the lead of a sales letter, a long paragraph is a turnoff and a barrier to reading, which may make the recipient give up. For my direct-mail letters, the first two or three paragraphs are usually just one or two sentences long, which gently draws the reader into the rest of the copy.
- *Short sections.* For a sales letter that is two pages or longer, use subheads, centered and boldface, to break the copy up into bite-sized sections. Write the subheads so that if the recipient reads only those, he will still get the gist of the sales message.

THE BDF FORMULA FOR REACHING YOUR PROSPECTS ON A DEEPER LEVEL

How well do you really know your prospects?

Reading the list descriptions is a good way to learn about the people you are mailing to, but it's not enough. Knowing that you are writing to farmers, IT professionals, or plumbers is just the start. You have to dig deeper.

To write powerful copy, you must go beyond the demographics to understand what really motivates these people—who they are, what they want, how they feel, and what problems and concerns your product can help solve.

One direct marketer told me, "We want to reach prospects on three levels: intellectual, emotional, and personal."

The *intellectual* level, though effective, is not as strong as the other two. An intellectual appeal is based on logic—for example: "Buy the stocks we recommend in our investment newsletter, and you will beat the market by 50 to 100 percent."

More powerful is to reach the prospect on an *emotional* level. Emotions you can tap include fear, greed, love, vanity, and—for fundraising—benevolence. Going back to our stock newsletter, the emotional appeal might be, "Our advice can help you cut your losses and make more money, so you become much wealthier than your friends and neighbors. You'll be able to pay cash for your next car—a Lexus, BMW, or any luxury automobile you care to own—and you'll sleep better at night."

But the most powerful way to reach people is on a *personal* level. Again, from our stock market newsletter: "Did you lose a small fortune in the 2008 crash? So much that it put your dreams of retirement or financial independence on hold? Now you can gain back everything you lost, rebuild your net worth, and make your dream of early retirement or financial independence come true—a lot sooner than you think."

To reach your prospects on all three levels, you must understand what copywriter Mark Ford calls the buyer's *core complex*. These are the emotions, attitudes, and aspirations that drive them, as represented by the formula BDF, which stands for "beliefs, desires, and feelings."

> ✉ *Beliefs.* What does your audience believe? What is their attitude toward your product and the problems or issues it addresses?

- ✉ *Desires.* What do they want? What are their goals? What change do they want in their lives that your product can help them achieve?
- ✉ *Feelings.* How do they feel? Are they confident and brash? Nervous and fearful? Angry and resentful? What are their feelings about the major issues in their lives, businesses, or industries?

For instance, we did this exercise with IT people for a company that gives seminars in communication and interpersonal skills for IT professionals. Here's what we came up with in a group meeting:

- ✉ *Beliefs.* IT people think they are smarter than other people; technology is the most important thing in the world; users are stupid, and management doesn't appreciate them enough.
- ✉ *Desires.* IT people want to be appreciated and recognized. They also prefer to deal with computers and avoid people whenever possible. And they want bigger budgets.
- ✉ *Feelings.* IT people often have an adversarial relationship with management and users, both of whom they service. They feel others dislike them, look down on them, and don't understand what they do.

Based on this analysis, particularly the feelings, the company created its most successful direct-mail letter ever to promote the seminar, "Interpersonal Skills for IT Professionals" with a rather unusual headline: "Important news for any IT professional who has ever felt like telling an end user, 'Go to hell.'"

Before writing your copy, write out in narrative form the BDF of your target market. Share these with your team and make sure you agree on them. Then write copy based on the BDF.

Occasionally, insights into the prospects' desires and concerns can be gleaned through formal market research. For instance, a copywriter working on a cooking oil account came across this comment from a user in a focus group transcript: "I fried chicken in the oil and then poured the oil back into a measuring cup. All the oil was there except one teaspoon." This comment, buried in the appendix of a focus group report, became the basis of a classic TV ad campaign, The selling point was that the food did not absorb the oil when cooked in it and therefore did not come out greasy.

Veteran ad man Joe Sacco once had an assignment to write a campaign for a new needle used by diabetics to inject insulin. The users Sacco talked to all praised the needle because it was sharp. People who don't use syringes generally view sharp, pointy objects with alarm. But if you have ever given yourself or anyone else an injection, you know that sharper needles go in more smoothly, with no pain. So Sacco wrote a successful ad campaign

MUST YOU SAMPLE THE PRODUCT?

Ideally, you should get a free sample of the product and use it to gain familiarity and understanding with the thing you're writing about. However, it's not necessary, and sometimes it's not possible.

On one assignment, I had to write about a $32 million corporate jet. The company was nearby, so I drove there for a closer look at the exterior and interior. A short flight would have been better, but the company didn't want to spend the time or money on it, and it ultimately didn't hinder me.

Similarly, no industrial client is going to give you an expensive piece of equipment, such as a large valve, pump, or control panel. And a seller of luxury cars is unlikely to give you a loaner.

When I am writing about nutritional supplements, I get a sample bottle so I can see the packaging and the size of the pill. And if it might benefit me, I may take it while I am working on the assignment. But if I don't suffer from the condition the product targets, such as arthritis or back pain, there is no point to trying it.

When I worked for a division of a company that made radar systems for airports, I was lucky: An airport right down the road from our plant used our radar and invited me to see it being used by air traffic controllers and operating mechanically inside its dome. If it had been in the next state, I wouldn't have gotten the tour, but I'm confident the quality of my copy would not have suffered. ✉

based on the claim that the needles were sharp, therefore enabling easier, pain-free insulin injection.

Copywriter Don Hauptman advises, "Start with the prospect, not the product." With BDF, you can quickly gain a deeper understanding of your prospects before you attempt to sell them something. Your marketing campaign will be stronger as a result.

TEN TIPS FOR WRITING WINNING, PERSUASIVE DIRECT-MAIL COPY

Copywriting, more so than other types of writing, has a lot of rules and forms that have been developed and refined over time. Following these rules increases the odds that your direct-mail copy will work, though there is never a guarantee of results, nor can anyone accurately predict the response rate it will produce until the DM package is mailed and the replies are tallied.

1. Test Your Copy

Big consumer mailers test copy all the time. Small businesses, on the other hand, seldom track response or test one mailing piece or list against another. As a result, they repeat their failures and have no idea of what works in direct mail—and what doesn't. Big mistake. In direct mail, you should not assume you know what will work. You should test to find out.

Many years ago, copywriter Milt Pierce wrote a subscription package for *Good Housekeeping* magazine. His mailing became the "control" package for 25 years. That is, no package tested against it brought back as many subscriptions. The envelope teaser and theme of that successful mailing was "33 Ways to Save Time and Money." Yet Pierce said that when he applied the same theme to subscription mailings for other magazines— *Science Digest, Popular Mechanics, House Beautiful*—it did not do nearly as well.

2. Use a Letter in Your Mailing Package

The sales letter—not the outer envelope, the brochure, or even the reply form—is the most important part of your direct-mail package. A package with a letter will usually out pull a postcard, a self-mailer, or a brochure or ad reprint mailed without a letter.

A company tested two packages offering a copy of its mail-order tool catalog for $1. Package "A" consisted of a sales letter and reply form. Package "B" was a double postcard. The result? "A" out pulled "B" by a 3-to-1 ratio.

Why do letters pull so well? Because a letter creates the illusion of personal communication. We are trained to view letters as "real" mail and glossy fliers and brochures as "advertising." Which is more important to you?

One recommendation I often give clients is to try an old-fashioned sales letter first. Go to a fancier package once you start making some money.

3. Features vs. Benefits

Perhaps the oldest and most widely embraced rule for writing direct-mail copy is "Stress benefits, not features." But that doesn't always hold true. In certain situations, features must be given equal (if not top) billing over benefits.

"I've tested many mailings selling engineering components and products to OEMs (original equipment manufacturers)," said Don Jay Smith, president of the ad agency The Wordsmith. "I've found that features and specs out pull benefits almost every time."

Vivian Sudhalter, Director of Marketing for Macmillan Software Co., agrees. "Despite what tradition tells you," said Sudhalter, "the engineering and scientific marketplace does not respond to promise- or benefit-oriented copy. They respond to features. Your copy must tell them exactly what they are getting and what your product can do. Scientists and engineers are put off by copy that sounds like advertising jargon."

4. Have and Highlight a Great Offer

One way to boost response in your direct mail is to feature a free offer, such as a free home trial or bonus gift. For example, if I mail a letter describing a new midrange computer, my letter is not going to do the whole job of convincing people to buy the computer. But the letter can sway some people to at least show interest by requesting a free demo.

Write lead magnet titles in styles known to work well as offers in direct mail. When one of my clients decided to publish a catalog listing US software programs available for export overseas, I persuaded her to call the book *The International Directory of U.S. Software* because I thought people would think such a directory was more valuable than a mere product catalog. It worked.

Let's say you are selling an audio business course on 8 CDs, each covering an important business topic. Instead of inviting people to buy an 8-CD package for $240, say, "Order our 7-CD course today for $240, and you get an extra FREE CD (a $29 value) on improving customer service." It's the exact same product at the same price. But by positioning one of the CDs as a free bonus, you can likely increase orders because people love free stuff.

5. Make Your Copy Detailed and Specific

One of the quickest ways to kill response is to be superficial, to talk in vague generalities rather than specifics, to ramble without authority on a subject rather than show customers that you understand their problems, their industries, and their needs. What causes superficial copy? The fault lies with lazy copywriters who don't bother to do their homework (or ignorant copywriters who don't know any better).

To write strong copy—specific, factual copy—you must dig for facts. You must study the product, the prospect, and the marketing problem. There is no way around this. Without facts, you cannot write good copy. But with the facts at their fingertips, even mediocre copywriters can do a decent job.

Specifics get more attention and are more credible. For instance, instead of saying you made thousands of dollars last month, say you made $5,478.45. As ad man James Webb Young notes, specifics come from product research.

6. Lead with Your Strongest Copy

Some copywriters save their strongest sales pitch for last, starting slow in their sales letters and hoping to build to a climactic conclusion. But Leo Bott, Jr., a Chicago-based copywriter, once said that the typical prospect reads for five seconds before they decide whether to continue reading or throw your mailing in the trash. The letter must grab their attention immediately. So start your letter with your strongest sales point. Some examples of powerful openings:

- ✉ *"14 things that can go wrong in your company—and one sure way to prevent them"*: Envelope teaser for a mailing that sold a manual on internal auditing procedures
- ✉ *"A special invitation to the hero of American business"*: From a subscription letter for *Inc.* magazine
- ✉ *"Can 193,750 millionaires be wrong?"*: Envelope teaser for a subscription mailing for a financial magazine
- ✉ *"Dear Friend: I'm fed up with the legal system. I want to change it, and I think you do, too."*: Lead paragraph of a fundraising letter

Some time-tested opening gambits for sales letters include the following:

- ✉ Ask a provocative question.
- ✉ Go straight to the heart of the reader's most pressing problem or concern.
- ✉ Arouse curiosity.
- ✉ Lead off with a fascinating fact or incredible statistic.
- ✉ State the offer right up-front, especially if it involves money: saving it, getting something for an incredibly low price, or making a free offer.
- ✉ Tell readers something they already know.
- ✉ Tell readers something they don't know.
- ✉ Announce something new.
- ✉ Lead with a short quiz above the salutation.

Know the "hot spots" of your direct-mail package—the places that get the most readership. These include the letter headline, first paragraph, subheads, last paragraph, and postscript (it is often said that 80 percent of readers look at the P.S.); the brochure cover, subheads, and the headline of its inside spread; picture captions; and the headline and copy on the order form or reply card. Put your strongest selling copy in those spots.

7. Use the "Magic Words" of Direct-Response Copy

Not using the magic words that can dramatically decrease the response to your mailing because you fear they are overused or they don't tickle your creative fancy. Branding advertisers, operating under the mistaken notion that the mission of the copywriter is to be creative, avoid the magic words of direct mail because they think those magic phrases are clichés.

But just because a word or phrase is used frequently doesn't mean that it has lost its power to achieve your communications objective. In conversation, for example, "please" and "thank you" never go out of style.

So, what are the magic words of direct mail? Here they are:

- *Free.* Say free reference guide—not guide. Say free consultation—not initial consultation. Say free gift—not gift. Note: If the English teacher in you objects that "free gift" is redundant, let me tell you a story. A mail-order firm tested two packages. The only difference was that package "A" offered a gift, while package "B" offered a free gift. The result? You guessed it. The free gift order in package "B" significantly out pulled package "A." What's more, many people who received package "A" wrote in and asked whether the gift was free!

- *No obligation.* Important when you are offering anything free. If prospects aren't obligated to use your firm's wastewater treatment services after you analyze their water sample for free, say so. People want to be reassured that there are no strings attached.

- *No salesperson will call.* If true, this is a fantastic phrase that can increase response by 10 percent or more. Most people, including genuine prospects, hate being called by salespeople over the phone. Warning: Don't say "No salesperson will call" if you do plan to follow up by phone. People won't buy from liars. If you do plan to call, the fallback is "No salesperson will visit."

- *Details inside/See inside.* One of those should follow any teaser copy on the outer envelope. You need a phrase that directs the reader to the inside.

- *Limited time only.* People who file or set your mailing aside for later reading will probably never respond. The trick is to generate a response now. One way to do it is with a time-limited offer, either generic "This offer is for a limited time only," or specific "This offer expires 9/20." Try it!

- ⊠ *Announcing/at last/just released.* People like to think they are getting in on the ground floor of a new thing. Making your mailing an announcement increases its attention-getting powers.
- ⊠ *New.* "New" is sheer magic in consumer mailings. But it's a double-edged sword in industrial mailings. On the one hand, business and technical buyers want something new. On the other hand, they demand products with proven performance.

The solution? Explain that your product is new or available to them for the first time, but proven elsewhere—either in another country, another application, or another industry. For example, when we introduced a diagnostic display system, we advertised it as "new" to U.S. hospitals but explained that it had been used successfully for five years in leading hospitals throughout Europe.

8. Start with the Prospect—Not the Product

In my copywriting workshops, I teach students to avoid "manufacturer's copy"—copy that is vendor-oriented, that stresses who we are, what we do, our corporate philosophy and history, and the objectives of our firm.

You and your products are not all that important to the prospect. The reader opening your sales letter only wants to know, "What's in it for me? How will I come out ahead by doing business with you vs. someone else?"

Successful direct mail focuses on the prospect, not the product. The most useful background research you can do is to ask your typical prospect, "What's the biggest problem you have right now?" The sales letter should talk about that problem then promise a solution.

Don't guess what is going on in industries about which you have limited knowledge. Instead, talk to customers and prospects to find out their needs. Read the same publications and attend the same seminars they do. Try to learn their problems and concerns.

Too many companies and ad agencies don't do that. Too many copywriters operate in a black box and doom themselves merely to recycling data already found in existing brochures.

For example, let's say you have the assignment of writing a direct-mail package selling weed control chemicals to farmers. Do you know what farmers look for in weed control or why they choose one supplier over another? Unless you are a farmer, you probably don't. Wouldn't it help to speak to some farmers and learn more about their situation?

Read, talk, and listen to find out what's going on with your customers. In his book *Or Your Money Back*, Alvin Eicoff, one of the deans of DR TV and DR radio, tells the story of a radio commercial he wrote selling rat poison. It worked well in the consumer market. But when it was aimed at the farm market, sales turned up near zero.

Eicoff drove out to the country to talk with farmers. His finding? Farmers didn't order because they were embarrassed about having a rat problem and feared their neighbors would learn about it when the poison was delivered by mail.

He added a single sentence to the radio script: "The product is shipped to you in a plain brown wrapper." After that, sales soared.

Talk to your customers. Good direct mail—or any ad copy—should tell them what they want to hear. Not what you think is important.

9. Appeal to Multiple Senses

Unlike an ad, which is two-dimensional, direct mail is three-dimensional and can appeal to all five senses: sight, hearing, touch, smell, and taste. Yet most users of direct mail fail to take advantage of the medium's added dimension.

Don't plan a mailing without at least thinking about whether you can make it more powerful by adding a fragrance, or even a sound. You ultimately may reject such enhancements because of time and budget constraints, but they are worth considering.

For example, Chris Crowell, president of Structural Graphics Inc., says pop-ups can increase response up to 40 percent when compared with a conventional flat mailing. In a pop-up, when you open the mailer inside the envelope, a 3-D construct pops up, just as in a children's pop-up book.

Market research firms have discovered that enclosing a dollar bill with a market research survey can increase response by a factor of five or more even though $1 is surely of no consequence to business executives or most consumers. A common P.S. reads, "I know you don't need the dollar, but it may brighten the day of a child you know." Fundraisers often affix coins to the letter, and if this were not effective, they wouldn't keep using it.

Don't neglect this old standard. Enclose a product or material sample in your next mailing. We once did a mailing in which we enclosed a small sample of knitted wire mesh used in pollution control and product recovery. Engineers who received the mailing kept the mesh on their desks for months, as it was visually interesting and its malleability made it fun to play with.

An inexpensive gift such as a slide guide, measuring tape, ruler, or thermometer can still work well. A premium enclosed with the mailing, rather than offered to those who reply, is known as a *freemium*.

10. Write in the First and Second Person

The letter writer refers to themself as "I" and addresses the reader directly as "you." Don't use the more formal third person, writing in a corporate voice; for example, referring to yourself as "ABC Company" or "we" or to the reader as "the customer."

Because direct mail, unlike advertising, originated as a purely personal medium, you retain the warmth and feel of that personal communication by using the first and second person. Also, write in a natural, conversational style, like one friend talking to another. Avoid overly formal language. Use contractions, short words, short sentences, and short paragraphs.

SIX COMMON COPYWRITING MISTAKES

Top copywriter Mike Pavlish provides a concise list of six copywriting mistakes to avoid when drafting your direct-mail copy:

1. You don't differentiate your product and make it unique and superior to similar products.
2. You don't use enough sales copy to promote all your product benefits in a compelling way; the more you tell, the more you sell.
3. You don't use enough proof, credibility, and believability elements.

4. You don't tell what will happen if the prospect does not respond.

5. You don't have a great offer.

6. You don't make it urgent and close hard for an immediate response.

As you create your copy, keep these caveats in mind. Remember: you want to approach your potential customer as a trusted friend. How would you treat a friend? You would offer them something real and unique, tell them about the features of it, and prove to them that it's worth their time.

THE MOTIVATING SEQUENCE

"Amateurs may talk about creativity, but professionals insist on structure," copywriter Martin Chorich once told me. In direct marketing, structure is key: If your copy does not follow the formula for persuasion, it won't work, no matter how creative you get.

There have been numerous formulas for writing persuasive copy throughout the years. The most famous is probably AIDA, which stands for *attention, interest, desire,* and *action.* In copywriting seminars, I've taught a variation on AIDA known as the *motivating sequence.*

The rest of this section explores the five steps of the motivating sequence.

Step 1: Get Attention

Before your promotion can do anything else, it has to get your prospect's attention. It must get the prospect to stop, open the envelope, and start reading the materials inside instead of tossing it in the trash. You already know many methods of getting attention and see dozens of them in action every day. In TV and magazine advertising, sex is often used to gain attention for products ranging from soft drinks and cars to diet and exercise programs.

Other options: make a bold statement, cite a startling statistic, ask a curiosity-arousing question, put a bulky object in the envelope, apply a glossy coating to the envelope and letter, use a pop-up graphic—you get the idea.

Step 2: Identify the Problem or Need

Most products fill a need or solve a problem. But what are the chances that your prospect is thinking about this problem when they get your promotion? Probably not great.

So the first thing you have to do is focus their attention on the need or problem your product addresses. Only then can you talk to them about the solution.

Step 3: Position Your Product as the Solution to the Problem

Once you get the prospect to focus on the problem, the next step is to position your product or service as the solution to that problem.

This can be a quick transition; here's an example from a fundraising letter from the Red Cross:

> Dear Mr. Bly:
>
> Someday, you may need the Red Cross.
>
> But right now, the Red Cross needs you.

It pretty much lays out where the letter will go next, doesn't it?

Step 4: Offer the Reader Proof

As marketer Mark Joyner points out in his book *The Irresistible Offer* (John Wiley & Sons, 2005) one of the prospect's first questions when they receive your promotion is "Why should I believe you?"

You answer that question by offering proof. That proof comes in two flavors.

The first type speaks to your credibility. It convinces the prospect that you are a reputable firm or individual and can therefore be trusted. A diploma from a prestigious medical school displayed prominently on a doctor's office wall is an example of credibility. In a direct-mail piece for health offers, response improves if the letter is signed by an MD.

The second type of proof has to do with the product and convinces the buyer that your product can do what you say it can do. Testimonials, case histories, reviews, performance graphs, and test results are examples of proof in this category.

Step 5: Ask for Action

The final step is to ask for action. Your goal is usually to generate either an inquiry or an order. To ask for action in direct marketing, we make an offer, defined earlier in the book as what the reader gets when they respond to your promotion and what they have to do to get it.

In a lead-generating direct-mail package, the offer might be as simple as "Mail back the enclosed reply card for our free catalog." In a mail order online promotion, the offer might be "Click here and enter your credit card information to purchase our product on a 30-day money-back trial basis for $49.95 plus $4.95 shipping and handling."

I am willing to wager that every successful piece of copy you have ever mailed or emailed follows to some extent the steps in the motivating sequence—even if you've never heard of it before. That's because you have an instinct for how to sell.

So if you can sell instinctively, then what good are the motivating sequence and other persuasion formulas?

They're useful because when you have the steps written out in front of you, you can make sure no step is shortchanged or left out—increasing your odds of writing a winner.

BE CREDIBLE ABOUT WHAT YOU OFFER

A particular problem when writing direct-mail copy is the temptation to say your company is the best at everything: the best quality, the fastest delivery, and the lowest prices.

The problem with these claims is credibility. For instance, if you charge a rock-bottom price, how can you also afford to have the best quality and the fastest delivery?

It takes time to make the finest product in the industry—and you're going to have to charge more for the quality and labor.

Years ago, many companies had Figure 5.1 on page 110 posted on the wall. The three points of the triangle said "Top Quality," "Fast Delivery," and "Low Price." But under the triangle, in large type, were the words "PICK ANY TWO." The point was that you can't have everything; decide which of these qualities is most important to you and which you can let go.

Figure 5.1. **The Benefit Triad**

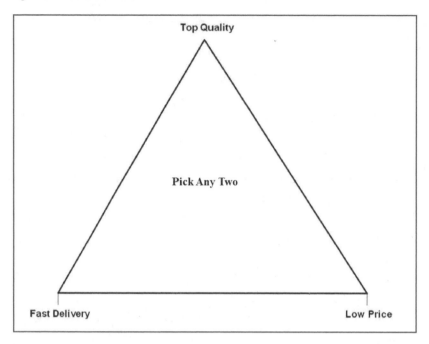

Use this principle to guide you. If you excel at two of the qualities, you can't believably promise the third as well. If you happen to be great at one of them—the best in the business, or close to it—you can stress that in your copy and let go of the other two.

You can even prove your main quality by noting how being superior in it means you can't possibly deliver on the other two. For instance, if you make fine crystal, doing it in an hour and charging just a few bucks makes no sense; if you are really as good as you say, the speed and cheap price make your claim of being the best crystal-maker seem unlikely.

THE NINE FUNDAMENTALS OF PERSUASION IN PRINT

What are the characteristics of effective direct-mail copy? Why does one mailing make a lasting impression and sell merchandise, while another falls flat and doesn't generate enough revenue to pay for itself?

Virtually all persuasive direct-mail copy contains the nine elements in the list below:

1. Gains attention
2. Focuses on the customer
3. Stresses benefits
4. Differentiates from the competition
5. Proves its case
6. Establishes credibility
7. Builds value
8. Is specific
9. Closes with a call to action

Not all sales letters will have all nine characteristics in equal proportions. Depending on the product, some of these elements will dominate your mailing while others will be subordinate.

Let's take telephone service as an example. If you are AT&T, Verizon, or Sprint, you have a long track record of success and a well-established reputation. Therefore, you will be naturally strong in elements five and six (proving your case and establishing your credibility).

However, a new telephone-service provider does not have a track record or reputation, so these two elements will not be the dominant themes in the copy. Instead, the strongest element might be number three (benefits the service offers customers) or perhaps number four (differentiation resulting from innovation and superior technology).

Each product or service has natural strengths and weaknesses. The copy should emphasize the strengths and play down the weaknesses. But all nine elements must be present to some degree, or the ad won't work.

The rest of this section discusses the nine elements of persuasion in a bit more detail with examples of how to achieve each in your copy.

1. Gain Attention

If an ad fails to gain attention, it fails totally. Unless you gain the prospect's attention, they won't read any of your copy and will miss the persuasive message you've so carefully crafted.

There are numerous ways to gain attention. Sex is certainly one of them. Look at the number of products—health clubs, cars, clothes, beer, soft drinks, chewing gum, perfume—that feature attractive bodies, both male and female, in their ads. It may be sexist or base, but it works.

Similarly, you can use cute visuals to get prospects to pay attention. Parents (and almost everyone else) are attracted to pictures of babies and young children. Puppies and kittens also strike a chord in our hearts.

Since so much advertising is vague and general, being specific in your copy sets it apart from other ads and creates interest. A letter promoting collection services to dental practices began as follows:

"How we collected over $20 million in unpaid bills over the past 2 years for thousands of dentists nationwide"

Dear Dentist:

It's true.

In the past 2 years alone, ABC Systems has collected more than $20 million in outstanding debt for dental practices nationwide.

That's $20 million these dentists might not otherwise have seen if they had not hired ABC to collect their past-due bills for them.

What gains your attention is the specific figure of $20 million. Every collection agency promises to collect money, but saying that you have gotten $20 million in results is specific, credible, and memorable.

Featuring an offer that is free, low-priced, or unusually attractive is also an effective attention-getter. A full-page newspaper ad from Guaranteed Term Life Insurance announced, "NOW . . . $1 a week buys Guaranteed Term Life Insurance for New Yorkers over 50." Not only does the $1 offer draw you in, but the headline also gains attention by targeting a specific group of buyers (New Yorkers over 50).

In public speaking you can gain attention by shouting or talking loudly. This approach can also work in copy, especially in retail advertising. An ad for the Lord & Taylor department store proclaimed in large, bold type:

"STARTS TODAY . . . ADDITIONAL 40% OFF WINTER FASHIONS."

Not clever or fancy but attention-grabbing—and interesting to shoppers looking to save money.

Another method of engaging the prospect's attention is to ask a provocative question. *Bits & Pieces,* a management magazine, began a subscription mailing with this headline: "What do Japanese managers have that American managers sometimes lack?" Don't you want to at least read the next sentence to learn the answer?

A mailing for a book club had this headline on the outer envelope:

Why is the McGraw-Hill Chemical Engineers' Book Club giving away— practically for FREE—this special Anniversary Edition of PERRY'S CHEMICAL ENGINEERS' HANDBOOK?

To chemical engineers, who know that *Perry's* costs about $125 per copy, the fact that someone would give it away is indeed a curiosity—and they would want to know the answer.

Injecting news into copy, or announcing something that is new or improved, is also a proven technique for getting attention. A mailing offering subscriptions to a health newsletter had this headline on the cover:

"Here Are Astonishing Nutritional Therapies and Alternative Treatments You'll Never Hear About From the Medical Establishment, the FDA, Drug Companies or Even Your Doctor . . ."

3 decades of medical research breakthroughs . . . revealed at last!

The traditional Madison Avenue approach to copy—subtle wordplay and cleverness—often fails to get attention because many people reading the ad either don't get it or, if they do get it, they don't think it's funny (or they do think it's funny but that still doesn't compel them to read the ad or buy the product). How often have you been entertained by a clever TV commercial and forgotten which product was being advertised as soon as it was over?

A newspaper ad for a New Jersey hospital promoting its facilities for treating kidney stones without surgery (it used ultrasonic sound waves to painlessly break up and dissolve the stones), carried this headline:

The End of the Stone Age.

Clever? Yes. But as a former kidney stone patient, I can tell you they are not a fun, playful subject, and this headline misses the mark. The kidney stone sufferer wants to know they can go to their local hospital, get fast, painless treatment without an operation and a hospital stay, and get rid of the stones that are causing them current discomfort. Here's a headline that would get their attention:

Get Rid of Painful Kidney Stones—Without Surgery!

The headline, while less clever, is more direct and works better with this topic and this audience.

2. Focus on the Customer

When writing copy, start with the prospect, not the product. Your prospects are interested primarily in themselves—their goals, their problems, their needs, hopes, fears, dreams, and aspirations. Your product or service is of secondary importance; all they really care about is whether it can address one of their wants or needs or solve one of their problems.

Effective copy speaks directly to a specific audience and identifies their preferences, quirks, behaviors, attitudes, needs, or requirements. A recruitment brochure for a computer consulting firm, for example, had this headline on the cover:

> Introducing a unique career opportunity only a few dozen computer professionals in the country will be able to take advantage of this year....

The headline is effective because it focuses on the prospects (IT professionals) and one of their main concerns in life (their career), rather than on the consulting firm and its history as most such brochures do.

Write from the customer's point of view—for example, not "Introducing our Guarda-Health Employee Benefit Program," but "At last you can combat the huge health insurance premiums threatening to put your small business out of business."

Weka Publishing, in a direct-mail package promoting the *Electronics Repair Manual,* a do-it-yourself guide for hobbyists and others who want to repair their own home and office electronics, as well as build cool electronic devices, uses copy that speaks directly to the personality type of the potential buyers:

If you're handy . . . fascinated by electronics and the world of high-tech . . . are happiest with a tool in your hand . . . and respond to household problems and broken appliances with a defiant, "I'll do it myself" . . .

. . . then fun, excitement, the thrill of discovery, time and money saved, and the satisfaction of a job well done await you when you preview our newly updated *Electronics Repair Manual* at no risk for a full 30 days.

A good way to ensure that you are focusing on the prospects, and not yourself, your product, or your company, is to address them directly in the copy as "you." For example:

Dear Health-Care Administrator:

You know how tough it is to make a decent profit margin in today's world of managed care . . . and how the HMOs and other plans are putting even more of a squeeze on your margins to fill their own already-swelling coffers.

But what you may not be aware of is the techniques health-care providers nationwide are using to fight back . . . and get paid every dollar they deserve for the important work they do.

This direct-mail copy, which successfully launched a new publication, works because it focuses on the prospect's problems (making money from their health-care business) and not on the publication, its editors, or its articles.

Copy that fails to focus on the prospect often does so because the copywriter does not understand the prospect. If you are writing to metal shop managers, attend a metalworking trade show, read a few issues of the trade publications they subscribe to, and interview some of your prospects in person or over the phone. Study focus group transcripts, attend live focus group sessions, or even accompany salespeople on sales calls to customers. The better you understand your target audience, the more you will have a feel for the way they think and what they think about. Then you can more effectively target copy that speaks to those concerns.

3. Stress Benefits

Although, depending on your audience, your prospects may be interested in both the features and the benefits of your product or service, it is almost never sufficient to discuss its features only.

Virtually all successful copy discusses benefits. Copy aimed at a lay audience would primarily stress benefits, mentioning features mainly to convince the prospects that the product can in fact deliver the benefits promised in the ad.

Copy aimed at specialists often gives equal play to features and benefits; it may even primarily stress features. But whenever a feature is described, it must be linked to a benefit it provides the customer. Buyers don't just want to know what the product is and what it does; they also want to know how it can help them achieve the results they want, such as saving money, saving time, making money, being happier, looking better, or feeling fitter.

In copy for technical products, clearly explaining the feature makes the benefit more believable. Don't just say a product has greater capacity; explain what feature of the product allows it to deliver this increased capacity. A brochure for a telecom manufacturer explains:

> CDMA gives you up to 10 times the capacity of analog cellular with more efficient use of spectrum. Use of a wideband block of radio frequency (RF) spectrum for transmission (1.25 MHz) enables CDMA to support up to 60 or more simultaneous conversations on a given frequency allocation.

A brochure for a computer consulting firm tells corporate IT managers how working with outside consultants can be more cost-effective than hiring staff, thus saving money:

> When you augment your IT department with our staff consultants, you pay our staff consultants only when they work for you. If the need ends tomorrow, so does the billing. In addition, various studies estimate the cost of hiring a new staff member at 30 to 60 percent or more of the annual salary (an executive search firm's fee alone can be 30 percent of the base pay). These expenditures are 100% eliminated when you staff through X-5 Staffing.

4. Differentiate Yourself from the Competition

Today your customer has more products and services to choose from than ever before. Someone walking into a supermarket can choose from a dizzying range of brands for everything from soda and cereal to baked beans and frozen pizza.

Therefore, to make your product stand out and convince the buyer that it is better and different than the competition, you must differentiate it from those other products in your copy. For example, Post Raisin Bran was advertised as the only raisin bran having "two scoops of raisins" in each box of cereal.

Companies that make a commodity product often differentiate themselves on the basis of service, expertise, or some other intangible. The industrial gas company BOC, for example, promotes itself as a superior vendor not because their product is better (one oxygen molecule is identical to another) but because of their ability to use oxygen and technology to benefit the customer's business. Here is copy from one of their brochures aimed at steel-makers:

> An oxygen supplier who knows oxygen and EAF steel-making can be the strategic partner who gives you a sustainable competitive advantage in today's metals markets. And that's where BOC can help.

A telecom manufacturer that competes with many other companies that manufacture telecommunications network equipment differentiates themselves by stressing the tested reliability of their switch, which has been documented as superior to other switches in the industry. One brochure explains, with specifics:

> The XPL-2000 Switch is one of the most reliable digital switches available for wireless systems today. According to the U.S. Federal Communication Commission's (FCC) ARMIS report, the XPL-2000 switch has the least downtime of any switch used in U.S. networks, exceeding Bellcore's reliability standards by 200%. With an installed base of more than 2,300 switches, the XPL-2000 Switch currently serves over 72 million lines in 49 countries.

5. Prove Your Case

Element 4, which we just discussed, claims product differentiation. Element 3 claims substantial benefits to buyers. The reason these elements cannot stand alone is that they are *claims*—ones made in a paid advertisement by the advertiser. Therefore, skeptical consumers don't usually accept them at face value. If you say you are better, faster, or cheaper and you don't back up your claims with proof, people won't believe you. For example, ABC Systems convinces dentists it is qualified to handle their collections by presenting facts and statistics in its direct-mail letter as follows:

> The nationwide leader in dental-practice collections, ABC Systems has collected past-due accounts receivables for 45,717 dental practices since 1963. Over 20 state dental associations recommend our services to their members.
>
> *ABC Systems can collect more of the money your patients owe you.* Our overall recovery rate for dental collections is 12.4% higher than the national average of 33.63%. (For many dental practices, we have achieved recovery rates even higher!)

BOC claims that the gas mixtures they sell in cylinders are accurately blended and that the composition listed on the label is what the buyer will find inside the container. They make this argument believable by explaining their blending and weighing methodology, again with specifics that make the copy credible:

> Each mixture component is weighed into the cylinder on a high-capacity, high-sensitivity equal-arm balance having a typical precision of ± 10 mg at 95 percent confidence. Balance accuracy is confirmed prior to weighing by calibration with NIST-traceable Class S weights. Electronic integration of the precision balance with an automated filling system provides extremely accurate mixtures with tight blend tolerances.

The most powerful tool for proving your case is to demonstrate a good track record in your field, showing that your product or service can deliver the benefits and other results you promise. One way to do this is to include case histories and success stories—testimonials from satisfied customers are another technique for convincing prospects that you can do what you say you can do. You can also impress prospects by showing them a full or partial list of your customers.

Share with readers any results your firm has achieved for an individual customer or group of customers. ABC Systems, for example, impressed dentists by telling them it has collected $20 million in past-due bills over the past two years alone—creating the perception of a service that works.

6. Establish Credibility

In addition to the benefits you offer, the products and services that offer these benefits, and the results you have achieved, prospective buyers will ask, "Who are you?"

In terms of persuasion, of the three major topics you discuss in your ad—the prospect, the product, and the product vendor—the last one is usually the least important. The prospect is primarily interested in themselves and their problems or needs. They care about your product or service only as a means of solving those problems or filling those needs, and they are interested in your company only as it relates to your ability to reliably provide that product or service.

However, the company can still influence purchase decisions. In the early days of personal computing, IBM was the preferred brand. This was not because IBM necessarily made a superior computer at a better price, but because if something went wrong, it could be counted on for fast, reliable, effective service and support.

As PCs became more common and local computer resellers and stores offered better service, IBM's reputation became less of an advantage, and their PC lost its dominance over the market.

Here are some examples of copy in which the company gives credentials designed to make the consumer feel more comfortable choosing them over other suppliers advertising similar products and services:

- We guarantee the best technical service and support. I was a compressor service technician at Ingersoll Rand, and in the last 20 years have personally serviced more than 250 compressors at over 80 companies.

- For well over a century, BOC has provided innovative gas technology solutions to meet process and production needs. We have supplied more than 20,000 different gases and gas mixtures—in purities up to 99.99999 percent—to 2 million customers worldwide.

- For nearly three decades, we have dedicated ourselves 100% to training managers, engineers, and others in environmental compliance-related subjects. Since 1989, our firm has conducted more than 1,400 workshops nationwide on these topics.

Credentials you can list in your copy include year founded, number of years in business, number of employees, annual revenue, number of locations, number of units sold, patents and product innovations, awards, commendations, publications, membership and participation in professional societies, seals of approval, agency ratings, independent survey results, media coverage, number of customers, and in-house resources (financial, technological, and human).

7. Build Value

It's not enough to convince prospects you have a great product or a superior service. You must also show them that the value of your offer far exceeds the price you are asking for it. You may have the best widget in the $100 to $200 price range of medium-size widgets, but why should the prospect pay $200 for your widget when they can get another brand for half the price? One argument might be a lower total cost of ownership. Although your widget costs more to buy, its greater reliability and performance can save their firm money that, over the long run, far exceeds the difference in price between you and brand X.

Stress cost of ownership vs. cost of purchase. The purchase price is not the only cost of owning something. There is the cost of maintenance, support, repair, refurbishment, operation, and, when it finally wears out, replacement. Therefore, the product that costs the least to buy may not cost the least to own; often, it is the most expensive to own!

Say you need to buy a photocopier. Copier A costs $900. Copier B costs $1,200. The features are essentially the same, and the reputations of the brands are comparable. Both have an expected lifetime of 120,000 copies. Most people would say, "Everything's the same except price, so buy copier A and save $300." Copier A compares itself feature for feature with Copier B and runs an ad with the headline, "Copier A vs. Our Competition . . . We Can Do Everything They Can Do . . . at 25 Percent Off the Price."

But you are the copywriter for the makers of copier B, and ask them what it costs to make a copy. Their cost per copy is $0.02. You investigate copier A, and find out that the toner cartridges are more expensive, so that their cost per copy is $0.04. You can now advertise copies at "half the cost of our competitor."

What's more, a simple calculation shows that if copier B is $0.02 cheaper per copy, and you use the machine to make 120,000 copies, your savings over the life of the machine is $2,400. Therefore, buying copier B pays you back eight times the extra $300 it cost to buy. This is additional ammunition you can use in your copy to establish that purchase price should not be the ultimate deciding factor and that copier B offers a greater overall value to the buyer.

If your product costs slightly more upfront but actually saves money in the long run, stress this in your copy. The term for this comparison is *total cost of ownership* (TCO). Everyone knows that the cheapest product is not automatically the best buy; corporate buyers are becoming especially concerned with TCO. Only government business, which is awarded based on sealed bids, seems to still focus solely on the lowest price. And even that is slowly changing.

The key to establishing value is to convince your prospects that the selling price is a drop in the bucket compared with the money your product will make or save them or with the other benefits it delivers. For example:

What would you do if the EPA assessed a $685,000 fine against your company for noncompliance with environmental regulations you *weren't even aware existed*?

Now get the special Anniversary Edition of PERRY'S CHEMICAL ENGINEERS' HANDBOOK . . . for only $4.97 (list price: $129.50) *with your No-Risk Trial Membership in McGraw-Hill's Chemical Engineers' Book Club.*

Another way to establish value is to compare the cost of your product with more expensive products or services that address the same basic need:

> The cost of *The LAN Manager's Companion*, including the 800+ page reference binder and NetWare utilities on diskette, is normally $189 plus $9.50 for shipping and handling. This is less than a LAN consultant would charge to advise you for just one hour of their time . . . yet *The LAN Manager's Companion* is there to help you administer and manage your network, year after year.

If your product or service is used over time, as most are, you can reduce the sticker shock that comes with a high upfront price by showing the cost over the extended usage period. For instance, a life insurance policy with an annual premium of $200 "gives your loved ones protection for just 55 cents a day." The latter seems more affordable, although the two prices are the same.

8. Be Specific

Nothing kills the selling power of a mailing faster than lack of content.

The equivalent in sales literature is what I call the "art director's brochure." You've seen them: showcase pieces destined to win awards for graphic excellence. Brochures so gorgeous that everybody falls in love with them—until they wake up and realize that people want *information* not pretty pictures. That's why white papers can often pull *double* the response of expensive, four-color sales brochures.

In the same way, direct mail is not meant to be pretty. Its goal is not to be remembered or create an image or make an impact but to generate a response *now*.

Make sure you can guarantee a good response by writing with specific language. Show customers that you get them—and their needs or problems—by offering pointed and concise copy that really speaks to them. Avoid talking in vague generalities.

Instead, do your homework. As a copywriter, it is your duty to do your due diligence and get to know your customer and what they need (or think they need).

Search for facts, study the product, get to know the prospect and their problem, then create customized copy that answers their needs and/

or wants. With the facts at your fingertips, you can go from being a so-so copywriter to a skilled marketer.

Don Hauptman, author of the famous mail-order ad, "Speak Spanish Like a Diplomat!" says that when he writes a direct-mail package, more than 50 percent of the work is in the reading, research, and preparation. Less than half his time is spent writing, editing, and revising.

Recently a client hired me to write an ad for a software package. After reading the background material and typing it into my computer, I had 19 single-spaced pages of notes.

How much research is enough? I recommend you collect *at least* twice as much information as you need—preferably three times as much. Then you will have the luxury of selecting only the best facts instead of trying desperately to fill up the page.

9. Close with a Call to Action

Copy is written to bring about change—that is to get your prospects to change their opinion, attitude, beliefs, purchasing plans, brand preferences, or immediate buying actions.

To achieve this, your copy must be specific about the action the prospect should take if they want to take advantage of your offer or at least find out more.

Tell them to complete and return the order form, call the toll-free phone number, visit your website, come to your store, request a free estimate, or whatever you want them to do. Specify the next step explicitly in your copy, or few people will take it. Here are some examples:

> When you call, be sure to ask how you can get a FREE copy of our new audio CD, *"How to Get Better Results From Your Collection Efforts."* In just 7 minutes listening time, you'll discover at least half a dozen of the techniques ABC Systems uses—and you can use, too—to get more people to pay what they owe you.

> For a complimentary copy of the SECRETS OF BUILDING A WORLD-CLASS WEBSITE DVD, complete and mail the survey enclosed or fax it today to 1-888-FAX-2IBM (1-888-329-2426).

Think it's time to talk with a gas supplier that really knows your business and has real solutions to your problems? Call your BOC representative today. Or visit our website at https://www.boc.com.au/shop/en/au/gases.

Chapter 6

DIRECT-MAIL GRAPHIC DESIGN

For decades, the old mail order masters believed direct mail should have low production values, crude graphics, and cheap paper stock. Their maxim was that ugly always outperforms beautiful and slick. The logic was that plain-looking mailings look like real personal mail, while mailings with slick graphics look like advertising.

Even today, there is some truth to that. In many tests, though not all of them, I see the "downscale" package designs out pull the fancy ones. So it makes sense to test one against the other.

There is one guiding principle: If you are selling a product or service that is a real bargain to a lower demographic market, cheaper mailings usually work better because they are congruent with the audience, product, and offer and they create the perception that your offer is a bargain.

Conversely, elegant, elaborate mailings work better for upscale audiences and expensive products and services, such as private banking invitations or million-dollar condos on the shore sent to wealthy people. If these mailers looked cheap, rich people would not read them or believe that the offer was good enough for them.

Avoid overuse of branding guidelines and especially graphics, which will also clue recipients in that your mailing is advertising. A direct-mail piece that looks like personal mail doesn't necessarily fool the recipient, but it creates a feel of a one-to-one communication that is key to getting people to open, read, and respond.

"Often I will create a package that has elements that do not look as if they have an organic unity," said copywriter Milt Pierce. "However, this is deliberate. The disunity will engender a sense of tension that would not have otherwise existed. This makes the overall package more exciting."

COLOR IN DIRECT-MAIL DESIGN

Many mailings work well in either one color (black ink on white stock) or two colors: typically black ink on white stock with the signature and other elements in blue or with the headlines, subheads, and key lines in red.

When doing a one-color mailing, consider using a light-colored paper stock other than white, such as canary yellow, robin's egg blue, or light green. This creates the effect of two-color without paying for a second color ink. Figure 6.1 on page 127 lists some of the most common colors used in direct mail and other marketing, the emotional attributes the color conveys, and the most common applications.

DESIGNING THE SALES LETTER

There is an old saying in direct mail: the letter sells, the brochure tells. The letter, because it looks and reads like a business or personal letter, is what conveys the primary sales argument. The brochure illustrates and expands on the letter with more detailed text and graphics supporting the letter copy.

Two popular typefaces for sales letters are Times New Roman and New Courier. Times New Roman is used in many Word documents and therefore is familiar and easy to read. I use 12-point unless I want to get more words per page, in which case I prefer 11-point.

Figure 6.1. **Uses and Attributes of Colors**

Color	Attributes/Usage
Yellow	Optimistic and youthful
	Often used to grab a viewer's attention
Orange	Aggressiveness
	Used as a call to action and attention grabber
Red	Energy
	Increases heart rate and creates urgency
	Often seen with clearance sales and references to food
	Eye-catching
Pink	Romantic and feminine
	Used to market products and services for women and young girls
Blue	Creates the sensation of trust and security
	Often used by banks and businesses
Purple	Soothing and calm
	Often relates to beauty or anti-aging products and services
Green	Associated with wealth
	The easiest color for the eye to process; used with finance or entertainment websites and for eco-friendly products
Black	Powerful and sleek
	Seen as luxurious and sophisticated

When you want the letter to look typewritten, New Courier conveys that feel. It looks the right size in 10-point type. So does Prestige Elite, though it has fallen out of favor today.

The graphic appearance of the letter is very important. It should be easy to scan through and easy to read. How do you achieve this?

✉ Use short paragraphs and sentences.

✉ Use arrows, bullets, asterisks, and other symbols to set off key paragraphs or phrases.

✉ Use underlining, italics, and boldface for emphasis.

✉ If a paragraph is especially important, put a box around it.

✉ Add marginal notes that look handwritten using a script font in blue.

✉ Make key copy stand out with a yellow highlight.

✉ Use subheads to break up the letter into sections and make it easy to scan.

✉ Indented paragraphs also help readability.

✉ Use long dashes (—) and ellipses (. . .) to separate phrases and paragraphs—like this—because it breaks long sentences into short sections . . . and adds a welcome change of pace.

✉ Letters are generally typed single space, but you can double-space an occasional paragraph or bump it up a point size or two to make it stand out.

✉ Avoid long paragraphs and pages where all paragraphs are the same length and design. Variety makes the page more appealing to the eye.

✉ Use the computer keyboard as a design device. Experiment with symbols, indentations, and spacing to breathe life into your sales letters.

✉ Always end the first page of the letter in the middle of a sentence. This forces the reader to turn to the next page.

✉ In a form letter, use a headline to grab attention.

✉ An alternative to the headline is to type a short summary of your offer or a key sales theme at the top of the letter and surround it with a border.

✉ Don't put your letterhead at the top of the first page—you don't want your logo to compete with your letter opening. In a direct-mail letter, put your logo and address at the bottom of the last page, after the signature and P.S.

THE OUTER ENVELOPE

In consumer mail, the envelope design should be appropriate for the product and the audience. Teaser copy and graphics effectively create a favorable expectation for what's inside the envelope. I generally dislike cluttered envelope designs, vivid artwork, and long teaser copy when mailing to business and professional audiences. I prefer a short, punchy, powerful teaser, printed in large, bold type on the front of the envelope. But that's my personal preference, not a hard and fast rule, and I will break it when I feel it's appropriate.

For instance, when doing a mailing from a bank to its customer list, I avoid all teaser copy and use the bank's regular stationery because practically everyone will open an envelope from their bank. The same goes for mailings from doctors and lawyers.

A sweepstakes mailing, on the other hand, should probably be plastered with loud, colorful messages to create excitement. A mailing for a children's book club should have lots of colorful drawings and photos to attract interest and show that the material is geared to a young audience.

The most popular envelope sizes are Monarch (3⅞-by-7½-inch), #10 (standard business size), 6-by-9-inch, and jumbo (9-by-12-inch). Other sizes are available.

Some mailers create envelopes that look like official notices, such as bills, invoices, or a letter from the IRS. The theory is that such an envelope is always opened. But I am against such scare tactics because they invariably anger and upset the recipient.

Envelopes don't have to be all paper. A paper envelope can have plastic windows that reveal the recipient's address label, which has been imprinted on the reply card or order form to make it easier to respond. Or you can use a clear all-plastic ("poly") envelope that lets everything show through.

If you are enclosing a premium, product sample or other 3-D object, use a paper envelope without windows. The bulging envelope creates curiosity, and you want the prospect to have to open it to find out what's inside.

I have never seen any conclusive data on whether it's better to use a brightly

> ✉ **TIP**
>
> A/B split test your outer envelope. (You'll learn more about these tests in Chapter 8.) Specifically, test an envelope with a teaser vs. a plain envelope. Sometimes the plain envelope wins.

colored envelope or a plain white, brown, or gray one. For a more low-key look, I prefer a white, off-white, or cream envelope. As with everything else for your mailing, you have to test.

REPLY ELEMENT

Don't disguise the reply element or make it hard to find. The reply element should literally fall onto the table when the reader opens the envelope or unfolds the letter. Ideally, it should not be attached to the letter or brochure. However, it is easier to personalize both if the reply element and letter are on the same sheet of paper. If you choose to go that route, add a perforation and a dashed line to separate them and make the response element easy to tear off.

Some direct-marketing experts say that a "busy" reply element (see Figure 6.2, on page 131)—one that is crammed with copy and visuals—will out pull a simple one. The theory is that the busy element looks important, while the simple one does not. Others report that in recent tests, less cluttered reply elements (for example, those with copy and graphics on one side only) are doing better than cluttered reply elements with printing on both sides.

My opinion is that you have to strike a balance. The reply element should be easy to find, easy to understand, and easy to complete. But it should not be so minimalist that it lacks vital information. It should repeat the offer, restate the guarantee, and explain what the buyer is getting for their money. And it should either have some eye appeal (bright colors, bold graphics) or look valuable and important, like official government, business, or personal mail.

People think of the reply element almost as a contract. If you graphically highlight the phrase "Money-Back Guarantee," they feel confident that the offer is risk-free. But if you fail to include the guarantee on your reply element, they are afraid to sign because your "contract" is not complete—even though you discussed the guarantee in your letter. Remember, you are asking them to mail back the reply element, not the letter. So the reply element must include everything of importance you have promised them.

Figure 6.2. **Order Form Layout**

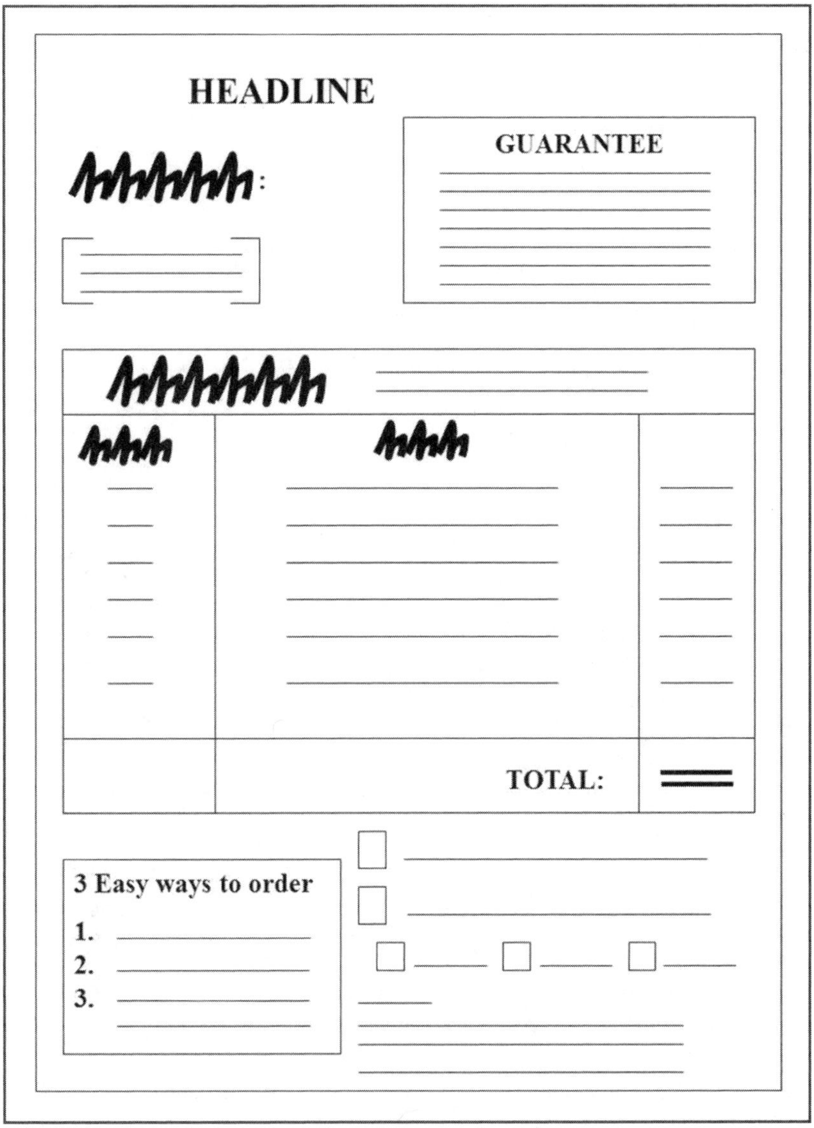

A reply element should have a bold headline identifying it as an order form or reply card. Of course, you can give it a fancier name, but there should be no mistaking its purpose. One of my favorite headers is "Risk-Free Trial Request Certificate."

I prefer to print the reply element on a different color and texture of paper stock than the letter and brochure. If, for example, the letter and flier are printed on off-white paper, I will print the reply element on light blue or yellow or hot pink . . . and on heavier stock. This makes the reply element immediately stand out from the rest of the package. In my copy, I say, "Just complete and return the yellow certificate enclosed."

I like to put a certificate-style border around either the entire reply element or just the guarantee copy. Anything that draws attention to the reply element is good.

A texture change is another way of separating the reply element from the rest of the package. If you print your letter and brochure on rag stock, for example, print the reply element on card stock. People separate things by feel as well as by sight.

DOES DIRECT MAIL STILL NEED A BUSINESS REPLY CARD?

Even though prospects can now respond to your direct mail and complete the reply form by going to your landing page online, you should still include a traditional reply element. When the recipient opens your mailing, the various elements fall out of the envelope, and each in turn is noticed and examined, even if only briefly. Having a separate reply element is a visual indicator to recipients that tells them, "This is one of those letters you are supposed to reply to." Even in the digital era, including a reply card in your DM package increases response rates. Not only do some people still complete and return paper reply elements, but just having a separate reply element in the package increases online and phone responses as well.

Put all your contact information on your reply element. Under the area where you ask the prospect to fill in their name and address, add in bold-face this copy: "For faster service, call toll-free 800-XXX-XXX. Or reply online at www.XXX.com/XX." This gives you yet another opportunity to bring your phone number and URL to the prospect's attention, which in turn gets more phone calls and increases online conversions. ✉

As you design your reply element, make your contact information big and bold. Throughout all elements of the direct-mail package—including the sales letter, brochure, and reply element—put your phone number and landing page URL in bold type that is a couple of point sizes larger than the rest of the text. Also experiment with adding your call to action to the headline at the top of page one of your sales letters and even on the outer envelope. You may find it further boosts conversion rates.

BROCHURE

The brochure is usually made from a single piece of paper folded to form pages and panels. Don't use a stapled or bound brochure in your direct-mail package. The reader's tendency is to view a folded piece as something of temporary value to be read immediately and then acted on or trashed. A stapled brochure is seen as something to be filed for later reading or permanent reference. You want immediate action, so use a folded design.

There is virtually no limit to the number of sizes, shapes, and formats you can use in your literature. Choose a format appropriate for your message and the amount of copy and visuals you have.

However, if your design gets too complicated, you can confuse yourself as well as your reader. You might want to stick to a simple, standard format:

- ✉ *For a #10 mailing*, I usually fold a letter-size sheet (8½ by 11 inches) twice to form six panels. If I need more room, I'll fold a legal-size sheet (8½ by 14 inches) three times to form eight panels.
- ✉ *For a 6-by-9-inch mailing*, I fold a letter-size sheet once horizontally to form a four-panel brochure (each panel measuring 8½ by 5½ inches). Or I can start with a larger sheet if I need more room.
- ✉ *For a 9-by-12-inch mailing*, I like to fold an 11-by-17-inch sheet once vertically to form a four-panel brochure (each panel measuring 8½ by 11 inches).

Brochures should be typeset to set them apart from the letter. They should also be printed on a different stock. They need not be elaborate. The format depends on what you're selling.

The outer panels of your brochure—the ones that show before the brochure is unfolded—should highlight, in large, bold lettering, a provocative headline that lures the reader into the body of the piece.

Once you unfold the brochure, the inside spread is where you do your real selling and product demonstrating. Use plenty of subheads to break your copy up into logical units. Many readers prefer to skim brochures, so they should be able to get the gist of the story just by reading the subheads. Use typography to make the subheads and headlines stand out.

Typography should be inviting to the eye and easy to read. Avoid reverse type (white type on a black background) or low-contrast tint colors (for example, black type on a dark gray or brown background). Do nothing in design that makes copy difficult to read.

Consider incorporating some useful content into the brochure. For instance, a casino brochure could have a sidebar giving the rules of blackjack or Texas Hold'em.

> ✉ **TIP**
>
> You can save money by eliminating the brochure, but test it first. When you know your package is a winner, do an A/B split test of the package (see Chapter 8) with and without the brochure. Surprisingly, the version without the brochure sometimes wins. I have found this to be true in certain categories, for example, mortgage direct mail.

BUCK SLIP

If you are offering a free gift with every order, you can highlight the gift in a buck slip. The *buck slip* is a separate piece enclosed in the direct-mail package. In a #10 DM package, the buck slip is usually a 4-by-9-inch sheet often printed in four-color (meaning full color) on glossy stock, the same as photos in magazines. By putting the premium (the free gift) in a separate color insert, the offer stands out more in the mailing, thereby gaining attention and increasing response. Figure 6.3 on page 135 shows a simple buck slip layout.

Figure 6.3. **This 4-by-9-Inch Buck Slip Fits in a #10 Envelope**

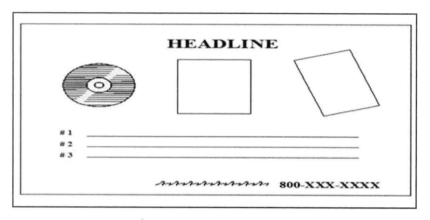

In a larger envelope, especially in a package offering multiple premiums, the buck slip is expanded into a full letter-size page known as a premium sheet. Sometimes the order form is integrated into the premium sheet.

LIFT NOTE

A *lift note* is a second letter in the DM package, usually printed on Monarch-size paper (7¼ by 10½ inches). It is used either to communicate a secondary message or sales benefit or to reinforce and expand on a benefit or idea in the main letter. It is called a *lift* note for its ability to lift response rates.

The lift note is often folded, with a teaser headline printed on the outer flap to gain attention, and a brief letter printed inside.

Chapter 7

DIRECT-MAIL PRODUCTION

O nce you have written and laid out the direct-mail package, you have to print and fold the mailing, stuff and seal the envelope, affix postage, take it to the post office, and mail it. These activities all fall under the umbrella of "direct-mail production."

SETTING YOUR PRODUCTION SCHEDULE

Your production schedule depends largely on the complexity of the format you have selected for your mailing. A one-page form letter can be printed, inserted, and mailed within a week. An elaborate four-color package with multiple inserts and personalization might take a couple of months to produce, especially in a larger organization with many layers of approval or committee oversight.

Warning: Unlike many digital promotions, which don't require printing and can therefore be done fairly rapidly, direct-mail production is labor-intensive and has multiple steps usually requiring several different vendors, including a copywriter, graphic designer, printer, and letter shop. Therefore, it can easily take two or even three months to plan, create, produce, and mail a DM package. So if you want to mail in January, you should start working on your promotion in early November.

CALCULATING COST PER THOUSAND

Direct-mail costs are usually estimated based on the recurring expense of mailing the package. These costs are represented by the formula $CPM = L1 + L2 + P1 + P2$, where all numbers are based on cost per thousand, as follows:

> ✉ **TIP**
> Proofread carefully. Typos in online promotions can be easily fixed, but once a direct-mail package is printed and in the mail, you can do nothing about any typos you discover. So proofread your DM pieces with great care before printing them.

- ✉ *CPM* = total cost per thousand pieces mailed
- ✉ *L1* = mailing list rental per thousand names
- ✉ *L2* = letter shop charges per thousand pieces to collate, assemble, insert components into the envelope, apply mailing labels, and affix postage
- ✉ *P1* = printing costs for all elements per thousand pieces
- ✉ *P2* = postage per thousand pieces

These are the physical costs to mail the piece. They are recurring, which means you pay the CPM every time you mail the package. For a package with a letter and a brochure in an envelope send bulk rate, a CPM of $500 to $700 is typical. The CPM for a small test is usually higher than for a large rollout mainly because when you print in larger quantities, you receive a volume discount.

The "creative" costs, which cover copywriting and graphic design, are one-time charges and are traditionally not amortized or included in the CPM calculation.

CALCULATING BREAK-EVEN

Break-even is when the sales generated by the DM package are equal to the CPM. So if your CPM is $700 and the mailing produces $700 in net revenue, you are at break-even.

When you know the percentage response required to achieve break-even, you have a realistic assessment of whether the package will be profitable. If a 0.5-percent response produces break-even, then you double your money with a 1-percent response. And a 1-percent response is a realistic target. On the other hand, if you need a 10-percent response just to break even, getting that is unlikely, so your chances of a successful mailing are slim.

Rather than walking you through the calculation to determine the percentage response needed for break-even, I have provided a free online tool that can calculate it for you here: https://www.dmresponsecalculator.com/.

AFFIXING POSTAGE TO THE MAIL PIECE

Postage can be applied in one of three ways: indicia, meter, or stamp. Here's a quick look at each:

- ✉ *Indicia*. An indicia is a postage permit printed directly on the envelope. This indicia design is reproduced on an offset press when the envelopes are printed, eliminating the need to apply a stamp or postage meter to each envelope individually.[1] But they do signal to savvy recipients that your mailing may be advertising.
- ✉ *Postage meter*. Applying postage with a meter makes your package look more like business mail than advertising.
- ✉ *Stamp*. A stamp on the outer envelope looks most like personal or "real" mail. Some mailers swear that using a stamp increases response. Others experiment with commemorative stamps or multiple small-denomination stamps.

THIRD-CLASS VS. FIRST-CLASS MAIL

Because of the high price of postage, third-class bulk-rate mail is often the optimal choice for marketers mailing large quantities of modestly priced one-step offers. First-class postage adds so much to the cost that it makes it difficult to get the package to break-even.

---

[1] https://bizfluent.com/info-8727173-third-class-mail.html

First class does work well when mailing to high-level executives at larger organizations since mailroom personnel and assistants at these firms routinely screen and destroy third-class bulk-rate metered and indicia mail. Assistants do it to spare the boss from having to read advertising material. Mailrooms do it to save themselves the time and expense of circulating your ads for you. In this environment, computer-personalized envelopes mailed with a first-class stamp may help you get past the mailroom and front-office barricade.

Corporate mailrooms often toss out catalogs delivered in bulk because they are obviously sales literature. One way to get around this: Target your most important prospects with a copy of your catalog in a gray or Kraft envelope sent first class, and mail only a few per day so they don't arrive in bulk.

Third class is slower, taking an average of two weeks or longer to reach its destination rather than just a few days for first class. And if you have a very large third-class mailing, it might take two or three weeks before it all arrives.

Currently it costs around $0.47 to send a letter first class, as opposed to about $0.29 for third-class bulk rate. That's a difference of $180 per thousand pieces mailed.

You should learn the ins and outs of third-class bulk mail because you'll be using it for most of your mailings. Your local post office can provide you with publications explaining all about third-class mail—what it costs, how it works, and what you have to do to use it. Your consultant, letter shop, or ad agency can also guide you. The USPS also has its postage rates posted online at https://www.usps.com/business/prices.htm.

BUSINESS REPLY MAIL

The post office can also provide you with a booklet explaining business reply mail. The booklet includes a drawing and specifications you can follow to create the proper business reply imprint on your reply envelopes and postcards.

Before you can use business reply mail, you will need to get a permit number from your local post office. This number must appear on all your business reply cards and envelopes. The current annual fee is $225 for the permit, plus a $690 annual account maintenance fee.

With the account, you are leaving money on deposit with the post office. They will subtract the cost of postage for incoming reply mail from the deposit rather than require you to pay cash every time the mail carrier delivers a fresh batch of reply cards and envelopes to your door. You don't pay postage for any business reply cards or envelopes not returned to you, but for every card or envelope mailed back to you, you pay the appropriate first-class postage plus an additional business reply fee.

Is business reply mail worth the extra money and hassle? Absolutely. Tests show that in consumer mail, postage-free business reply cards generally bring in higher responses than those for which the respondent must pay postage. One reason may be that many people simply don't keep stamps on hand.

PRINTING AND LETTER SHOP

After the copy is written and laid out, the components of the DM package must be printed and inserted in the envelope in the proper order, the postage and label must be affixed, the envelope must be sealed, and the mailings must be taken to the post office and sent out. You have several options here:

- *Commercial printers.* Unless you have an extremely small volume of personalized mail you intend to run off on your printer, the components of the package are printed, as other marketing materials usually are, at a commercial print shop. You may have one you already use for letterhead, business cards, posters, sales sheets, and so on. But for this, you should work with a printer who is experienced in printing direct-mail pieces. For one thing, once the separate components have been printed, they must be folded and inserted into the envelope, either by hand or by machine. A direct-mail printer knows how to print the pieces so they can be handled by the automated machinery. They are also familiar with the correct postal regulations for outer envelopes, business reply mail, postcards, and self-mailers. Sizing and other printing mistakes in these areas can result in a piece that cannot be mailed.

- ✉ *Letter shops.* A letter shop folds and inserts the various pieces into the envelope, affixes postage and labels, and takes the DM package to the post office for mailing. Many letter shops also handle the printing to give you one-stop service.

- ✉ *DIY.* For small mailings, you can always do the letter shop tasks yourself. But that is really not the best use of your time, space, and resources. Do-it-yourself is an option for a mailing of hundreds of pieces, but when you get into the thousands, you are better off outsourcing the job.

- ✉ *Graphic designers.* While many graphic design studios stick to their specialty, some will also handle other elements of direct-mail production, such as printing, collating, and mailing.

> ✉ **TIP**
>
> Before your direct-mail piece is printed, make up a dummy of the package and take it to the post office to get their approval on everything from the correct reply envelope bar codes to making sure you have sufficient postage for the package weight. Then be at the printer or letter shop when the first components of your package roll off the production line. Check them for errors and any color correction issues, and make sure the elements are inserted into the outer envelope in the correct order.

- ✉ *Direct-response ad agencies.* Direct-response ad agencies act as a one-stop resource for the entire direct-mail package, including strategy, copy, design, printing, letter shop, mailing lists, postage, mailing, tracking, and testing.

- ✉ *Consultants.* There are a number of direct-mail consultants out there. Most of them advise clients on strategies, offers, and lists, but a few also handle production similar to the direct-response ad agencies.

National advertising for major brands, especially TV ads, is often handled by Madison Avenue ad agencies. Direct-mail marketers often prefer to work with freelance copywriters and graphic designers who specialize in direct mail—something large ad agencies are often inexperienced at.

Chapter 8

DIRECT-MAIL TESTING

In direct mail, *testing* is the process of putting a letter or package in the mail, counting the replies, and coming to a conclusion based on the results.

Testing is a huge advantage direct marketers have over branding and general advertisers: We first do a small test to determine whether our direct-mail package works. If it does, we can gradually expand the campaign. On the other hand, if the test bombs, we know early on that the package doesn't work. The test costs only a few hundred or a few thousand dollars, and it saves us many more thousands of dollars by not continuing to mail a DM package that consistently loses money.

However, marketing coach Terry Dean cautions, "You can waste a lot of time testing little things that produce little or no results." In direct mail, the most important things to test are outer-envelope teaser vs. no teaser, the first page of the sales letter, the price, and the terms.

Testing is one of the central ideas of direct-mail marketing: Test small, then roll out in larger quantities once the tests show you which is the winning package.

A/B SPLIT TESTS

When two mailings or mailing factors are tested against each other, it is called an A/B split test, with one version labeled as test cell A and the second as test cell B.

For instance, you might test letter A against letter B to see which pulls more orders. Or you might take letter A and mail it to two different lists, to see which list produces the better response. Or you might mail a control as test cell A against a new test package as test cell B.

A *control* is the current best-performing DM package. For instance, a marketer may be mailing thousands or hundreds of thousands of the same direct-mail package month after month because it is profitable. But how do they know another package, with different graphics, size, colors, and copy, won't generate even better results? They can't, unless they test it. So they periodically commission a new direct-mail package or put one together in-house and then mail it against their control in an A/B split test.

If the test wins, it becomes the new control. If it loses, the marketer has renewed confidence that they are mailing a strong package. If the two packages tie, then they now have two controls. That is also a useful result because controls eventually grow tired, meaning response drops off. When control A gets tired, they can switch to mailing the equally strong control B and restore their response to its previously high levels.

You are not limited to doing A/B tests. You can test three or more packages or variables at one time. Figure 8.1 below shows a test grid with nine test cells. This allows you to test six variables simultaneously: three mailing lists and three offers. X is the number of pieces mailed per test cell, which is covered in the next section.

Figure 8.1. **Grid for A/B/C Test**

Mailing List	Offer 1	Offer 2	Offer 3
A	X	X	X
B	X	X	X
C	X	X	X

NUMBER OF DM PIECES PER TEST CELL

Some mailing-list brokers have a minimum order requirement of 5,000 names per list, which has resulted in the average test cell being 5,000 names. But statistical analysis shows that you can get a valid test result with 2,000 names per cell. The validity is determined not by the number of pieces mailed but rather the number of replies received per cell.

Experience and statistical analysis indicates that 14 responses per test cell give you a fairly reliable reading of each cell's performance. If your average response is 1 percent, then 1,400 names per test cell is an adequate size. However, because response is unpredictable, I would go with 2,000 per cell to give yourself some wiggle room.

PACKAGE AND ELEMENT TESTING

There are two approaches to testing, and each has its place.

The first approach is to test two completely different DM packages and see which one is the winner. The winner beats the current control and becomes the new control, increasing your ROI. However, if the new test package is completely different from the control (different graphics, copy, price offer, guarantee, package format, etc.), you won't know which of these elements made the difference.

The second approach is to test multiple versions of the control where just a single element is different; for example, the envelope teaser, copy theme, size of envelope, price, premium, or first-class vs. third-class postage. By testing just one variable at a time, you can determine how each factor influences response.

TRACKING RESPONSES

To test, you must be able to track response. That is, when you receive a reply, you must be able to identify that reply as coming from a specific mailing or from a recipient whose name was on a specific mailing list.

There are several ways to do this. The simplest is to put a key code on the reply element. This code can be a series of numbers and letters in fine print tucked away in the corner of the reply card, or it can be worked into the address. Your list broker can handle this for you.

If you are affixing or imprinting the recipient's address on your reply card or order form, the mailing-list owner can, if you wish, add a key code to the order form. The charge for this service is nominal.

The same coding can be done for telephone responses. For catalogs, when you call to order, the customer service representative typically asks for a code printed in a blue or yellow box on the back cover near the recipient's address.

ROLLOUT

After a successful test, a winning direct-mail package is "rolled out," meaning it is mailed to more names on the profitable lists. But can the results of a small test mailing remain statistically valid regardless of how many additional names we mail to? The answer is no. The rule of thumb for rollouts is that the total quantity you mail to should be no more than ten times the number of names you tested. Therefore, if you got a 5-percent response in a test of 5,000 names, you can mail to as many as 50,000 additional names on the list and be confident that you will get a similar response (see Figure 8.2 on page 147 for guidelines on the percentile range you can expect in a rollout response).

No matter how sorely you may be tempted, never do a rollout to more than ten times the test. The results may not be valid over those amounts.

Let's say you have a list of 80,000 names. If you ran a test of 2,000, you can roll out up to 20,000 and expect the percentages to hold. Should results prove profitable on the rollout, you can then safely mail to the remainder of the list.

THE THREE MOST IMPORTANT FACTORS TO TEST

What are the three most significant factors you can test—the ones that can have the greatest influence on response?

Number one is the mailing list. As discussed in Chapter 4, there could be a half-dozen mailing lists suitable for your offer—or even more. You can't assume you know which one is best based on your personal biases. The only way to know for certain which list will pull best with your package is through a test mailing.

Figure 8.2. **Guidelines for Rollouts After a Successful Test**
Reprinted with permission from "444 Begged, Borrowed, Stolen, & Even a Few Original Direct Response Marketing Ideas" from Rockingham/Jutkins Marketing.

Response Probabilities		
Size of Test Mailing	Response of Test Mailing	Anticipated Rollout Response (95% Accurate)
2,000	1%	0.55% to 1.45%
2,000	2%	1.37% to 2.63%
2,000	3%	2.24% to 3.76%
2,000	4%	3.12% to 4.88%
2,000	5%	4.03% to 5.97%
2,000	10%	8.66% to 11.34%
2,000	20%	18.21% to 21.70%
10,000	1%	0.80% to 1.20%
10,000	2%	1.72% to 2.28%
10,000	3%	2.66% to 3.34%
10,000	4%	3.61% to 4.39%
10,000	5%	4.56% to 5.44%
10,000	10%	9.40% to 10.60%
10,000	20%	19.20% to 20.80%

The second most important factor to test is the price. This applies mainly to mail-order selling. For instance, let's say you've published a thousand-page market-research report on broadband internet. How much will people pay for it? $195? $495? $1,200? You simply don't know until you test. And frequently you will be amazed at how many people place orders at prices you think are sky-high.

The third most important factor to test is the offer. Should you try for mail orders or leads? Should you offer a premium? If you do, will you get better response offering a gift item such as a digital watch or free information such as a booklet or special report? You won't know which works better unless you test.

When choosing names for a test mailing, ask your list broker to supply you with an *nth name selection*. How does this work? Let's say the list has 50,000 names and you are going to test-mail to 5,000 of them. In this example, 50,000 divided by 5,000 equals an *n* of ten. So for your test mailing, the computer will select every tenth name as it goes through the list.

A random *n*th name selection ensures that you get an unbiased sample that represents a typical cross-section of the list. This is much better than ordering the entire list and picking the test names by hand. The danger of doing it that way is that you subconsciously select the names that will give you the best results (because you want your mailing to be a success). Test responses are therefore artificially elevated, and rollouts don't bring the results you expect.

This applies only if you have the budget to mail all 50,000 names on the list. If you can only afford to mail 5,000 altogether, cherry-pick the best names, the ones that fit your target market closest.

OTHER TEST VARIABLES

Be selective. Don't test everything, and don't overtest. Use tests only to ensure success or determine key information you really want or need to know. The following, in no particular order, are factors that can be tested via direct mail:

- Products
- Premiums
- Formats
- Sizes
- Copy
- Personalization
- Brochure vs. no brochure
- Themes or sales appeals
- Envelope teasers
- Colors

- ✉ First-class vs. third-class mail
- ✉ Business reply vs. "place stamp here"
- ✉ 800 number vs. regular phone number
- ✉ Personalized URL
- ✉ QR code
- ✉ Online form vs. paper reply element

TEN RULES FOR DIRECT-MAIL TESTING

Here are ten more suggestions to make your testing more productive and useful. Follow these rules and testing will yield actionable data you can use to improve your direct-mail package and results.

1. Make every mailing a test.
2. Establish goals for each test. Determine what information you want to get out of the test, the degree of reliability needed in your data, and how much money you can afford to spend.
3. Test significant factors that make a substantial difference in direct-mail results, including the list, the offer, and the price.
4. Also test to find out things you need or want to know. There may be issues specific to your industry, product, or market that have never been tested in direct mail before. If there is no reliable data from other sources, you have to be the pioneer in your field.
5. Use direct-mail tests to settle questions and disagreements concerning strategy, format, lists, design, and copy. Instead of arguing about theory, put ideas to the test.
6. Test even if you are using a small list with minimal or no rollout. Try to split the list for an A/B test of a mailing package or a direct-mail element, such as letter length or offer.
7. Be consistent in your testing. For example, if you are testing a single factor, such as an envelope teaser, all other factors in the two test packages must be identical—including the mailing list and the price.
8. Don't assume you know what will work. Test to find out. More often than not, the results will shock you. Direct-mail tests are

great for shaking up so-called marketing and advertising experts who think they know it all.

9. Even if you don't have enough money or names for a statistically valid test, test anyway. Some information is better than no information. Just remember that the test is not statistically valid and act on the results accordingly.

10. To learn more from a direct-mail test, make a list of questions you want answered. Call up some of the people who did not respond and ask them your questions. In addition to learning a great deal about why your mailing failed to motivate these people, you may be able to turn nonresponders into responders and generate additional inquiries or orders.

PART III

DIRECT-MAIL COMPONENTS AND FORMATS

SPECIAL OFFER INSIDE

In the following chapters, you will discover how to create the various components of a direct-mail package, including an outer envelope, a sales letter, an insert such as a brochure or a buck slip, a reply form, and a business reply envelope.

Chapter 9

SALES LETTERS

There is an old saying in direct mail: The letter sells; the brochure tells. In any direct-mail package, the letter has the toughest job because it does most of the selling. The outer envelope carries the package and may be designed to stimulate interest in its contents through teaser copy, illustrations, or see-through windows. The brochure gives descriptive information. The order form encourages readers to respond and gives them an easy way to do so. Figure 9.1 on page 154 shows a standard direct-mail package with all the basic elements: outer envelope, sales letter, brochure or other sales insert, and reply element. The reply element may be a business reply postcard or an order form. If you use a form, you must also include a business reply envelope the recipient can use to mail the completed form back to you along with payment.

But the direct-mail writer uses the letter to make their sales pitch. The letter must grab attention with a powerful, relevant, engaging lead paragraph. It must stimulate readers' interest in the product or what the product can do

Figure 9.1. **Elements of a Direct-Mail Package**

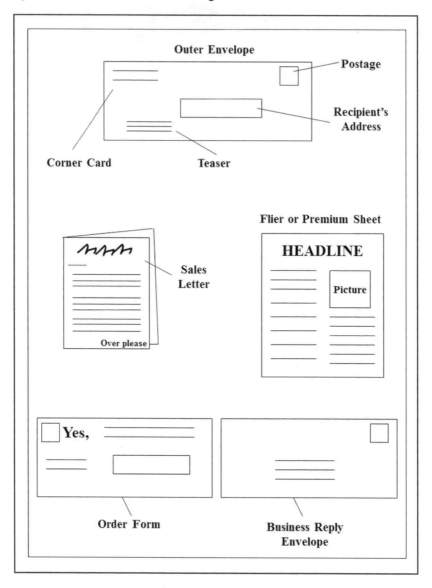

for them. It must create desire for the product by describing its benefits in an enticing fashion. And it must ask the readers to act by giving them reasons they should buy now—not tomorrow.

HOW TO WRITE A WINNING SALES LETTER

Here are some things to keep in mind when sitting down to write your next direct-mail letter:

- ✉ *Make your direct-mail letter look like a regular letter.* Use a typewriter-style typeface such as New Courier or Prestige Elite, not Arial or Garamond.

- ✉ *Write in a friendly, natural, conversational tone.* Use personal pronouns—I, the letter writer, am talking directly to you, the reader. Avoid the pompous business-memo style or the overly puffy "advertising" style. Just write naturally.

- ✉ *Think about how the letter looks on the page.* Readers are turned off by long blocks of text. Use short paragraphs and sentences. Align text on the left edge, not justified (even on the left and right edges). The first two paragraphs should be especially inviting in their brevity—just one or two sentences each—to pull the reader into the letter.

- ✉ *Underline phrases and indent paragraphs for emphasis.* Use symbols as graphic devices. These can include asterisks (*), bullets (•), ellipses (. . .), and dashes (—).

- ✉ *Put a box around important copy that you want to stand out.* Or put a blue bracket or notes in the margin in simulated blue handwriting to draw attention to key information.

- ✉ *Make your letter lively and personable, not dull and boring.* Be "up" and enthusiastic about your product. Let your enthusiasm and personality shine through in the copy.

- ✉ *Focus on the readers and their needs rather than your product and your own interests.* For example, instead of "Our new phone system" say "Your telecommunications needs . . ." or "Are your phone bills too high?"

- ✉ *Use a hook.* Extremely short paragraphs and sentences in the beginning of the letter help hook readers and draw them into the body. They work best when presenting a compelling reason to keep reading the letter (e.g., a discount offer with an expiration date).

✉ *Talk about their most important problem.* The best thing to talk about in the lead paragraph is the reader's most important problem or most pressing concern (health, security, money, happiness)—the one thing that is keeping them up at night. Then you can tell them how you're going to help them solve this problem or address this concern.

✉ *Be concise.* Most people would rather read a short letter than a long one. If you need to tell a complicated story or make a complete sales pitch, make sure every sentence adds to the message and cut all unnecessary words.

✉ *Be clear.* If readers have to struggle to figure out what you're talking about, they will quickly throw your letter away.

✉ *Be direct.* Get to the point right away.

✉ *Be specific.* Explain exactly what you're selling and what it can do. Some writers try to arouse curiosity by being deliberately vague and masking the nature of the product. Sometimes this works. But more often, it flops because it annoys people.

✉ *Be simple.* Take pains to explain your product and your offer in terms the reader will understand. If you need to elaborate on a principle, theory, or technical point, consider using a brochure. The letter's job is to sell, not tell.

✉ *Be personal.* If you have affinity with the prospects, use that. For instance, if you are writing a subscription package for a dog magazine and you have a dog, the salutation could read: "Dear Fellow Dog Lover." The copy can reveal some personal information showing the love between you and your dog.

See Figures 9.2 through 9.4 on pages 157 to 160 for some sample direct-mail letters.

Figure 9.2. **Letter to Secure an Appointment**

Date

Dear Mr. Bly:

You know how difficult it is to look your best if dental problems are causing discomfort and pain or if the appearance of your teeth needs improvement.

Have you been putting off a dental checkup or consultation on an existing problem? This note may encourage you to take the important step to help yourself feel better by making a dental appointment.

In our spacious comfortable dental offices, our patients receive skilled and concerned care. Our equipment and techniques are among the most advanced. You will find us competent and understanding, whether you need a simple filling, cleaning, or require a crown, bridge or complete dental restoration.

We are expert in the modern "bonding technique," which enables us to whiten discolored teeth, repair chipped teeth, or reshape your teeth usually without injections or drilling.

You will find that our fees are very fair for fine complete dentistry with convenient appointment schedules.

My card is enclosed—please keep it. If you require high-quality dental care now or just want a checkup, please call 555-5555.

Sincerely,

John Smith, D.D.S.

P.S. Neglecting your teeth and gums can create many problems. With this note as a reminder, why not call today for an appointment?

1234 Main Street • Somewhere, SW • 555-555-5555 • jsmith@ukw.com

Figure 9.3. **Letter Selling Shoes by Mail**

They said it couldn't be done.
Yet here they are . . .
Luxurious "rich men's" shoes—
AT YOUR PRICE.
Try a pair for 30 days AT NO RISK.

Dear Friend,

Ever eased your feet into luxury? Shoes with LEATHER uppers . . . LEATHER linings . . . even LEATHER insoles?

Never all three? Most men haven't. After all, these luxuries cost you an arm and a leg in stores these days.

Take leather insoles. 95% of American men have never felt the luxurious difference they make.

Leather insoles bend easily—right out of the box.

Leather insoles soak up perspiration, "breathe" naturally.

Leather insoles add SOFTNESS.

Why don't ALL shoes have them? They cost too much. In stores, you'll pay $85, $95, even more for shoes with this "extra."

But not if you buy DIRECT—from Ortho-Vent.

See for yourself. Order at no risk. I'll rush you ON APPROVAL shoes with all the style, comfort, and craftsmanship rich men pay $95 for. All at YOUR price.

They have genuine LEATHER uppers—shaped on true-to-your-size combination lasts for guaranteed perfect fit.

They have glove-soft LEATHER linings—often combined with cotton twill at the toe for even greater absorbency.

They even have LEATHER insoles—an "extra" offered by less than 5% of the shoes made today.

On top of that, they offer a luxury you won't find in ANY other shoes at ANY price . . .

OUR EXCLUSIVE SPRING-STEP® CUSHION.

Figure 9.3. **Letter Selling Shoes by Mail,** continued

I know the statement I'm about to make is pretty daring—especially in these days of grand juries, the FTC and all. But I've got millions of repeat customers who agree that SPRING-STEP® SHOES ARE THE MOST COMFORTABLE YOU CAN WEAR.

ORDINARY SHOES have an asphalt/cork "filler" between the outer sole and insole. It's hot, stiff. Resists every step, even after long wear.

SPRING-STEPS® have no stiff "filler." We've replaced it with a layer of bubbly foam cushion from heel to toe. It's 80% AIR!

Thanks to Spring-Step®, your feet no longer feel the pounding shock of each step. Instead, they're cradled by our supple leather insole and the resilient cushion beneath it. You've got to feel it yourself to believe the comfort.

PLUS—Spring-Step® makes our shoes so soft, so flexible, they need no "breaking in." Just order your usual size, and PRESTO! Right out of the box they feel as natural as your shadow.

How can we do it? All this leather luxury, all this comfort, AND guaranteed fit—at your price?

By dealing with you DIRECT. From one central warehouse. You pay NO middleman's markup. NO costly store overhead. We've been saving customers money this way for over 80 years now.

YOU RISK NOTHING by trying a pair. Wear them a full 30 days. Compare looks, comfort, and fit with ANY other shoe at ANY price. If ours aren't the most comfortable, the best value, I'll buy them back. No questions asked. Regardless of wear.

Order today—so I can rush your shoes by return mail. If you like, just say "charge it" to your favorite credit card.

Sincerely,

Pat Thomas

P.S.: To encourage you to give us a try, I've enclosed a special coupon that gives you $10 off your first order—in addition to the 30% to 40% we already save you off store prices. But it's only good for the next 10 days—so redeem it right away!

Figure 9.4. **Mail Order Letter From New Process Company (now called Blair)**

Date

Dear Mr. Bly:

A memo recently crossed my desk that said I would have to RAISE MY PRICES—NOW—to offset our spiraling operating costs!

But I said, "No! Not Yet!"

I know that customers like you, Mr. Bly, expect the BEST VALUE for their money when they shop at NPC. And that's why I'm going to hold the line on higher prices just as long as I possibly can!

So, in the next few minutes, while you're looking through the enclosed group of Bargain Slips, please keep in mind that I may not be able to guarantee such terrific low prices in the future.

Now, my only problem is keeping enough of these fantastic Bargains in stock to handle the avalanche of orders we'll be receiving.

You see, Mr. Bly, my supplies are not unlimited, and those I do have on hand are going to go F-A-S-T!

To be sure of your selections for a WEEK'S FREE TRIAL, mail your order TODAY in the postage-paid envelope attached.

Sincerely,

John L. Blair, President

P.S. Please remember to fill in and sign the Preferred Customer Certificate above. Then, detach and return it along with your selected Bargain Slips.

1234 Main Street • Somewhere, SW • 555-555-5555 • jsmith@ukw.com

---

A CHECKLIST FOR WRITING SALES LETTERS

Here is a useful checklist of some sales-letter writing tips and techniques you can use to make your letters easier to read while generating higher response rates:

- [ ] Shift your letterhead to the bottom of the letter to avoid distraction.
- [ ] Lead with a benefit or promise headline.
- [ ] Use the salutation to target your primary audience.
- [ ] The first sentence should make the recipient want to read more.
- [ ] Write in a natural, conversational style.
- [ ] Use small words, short sentences, short paragraphs, and short sections divided by subheads to make the copy easy to read.
- [ ] Use lots of benefit-loaded subheads.
- [ ] Place the basics of your offer upfront on page one if it is strong.
- [ ] Focus on the perception of believability.
- [ ] Always write from a "you" orientation.
- [ ] Use emotional copy in the sales letter.
- [ ] Justify the desire to buy with proof of your promise.
- [ ] Choose one primary copy theme and wrap others around it.
- [ ] Include precise user benefits by audience type to increase sales.
- [ ] Remember that specifics are much more potent than generalizations.
- [ ] Prompt action in the last paragraph and sentence.
- [ ] Use command/suggestion copy throughout the letter.
- [ ] Keep words and sentences short and vary paragraph length.
- [ ] Add some sell to the closing.
- [ ] Always use a postscript.
- [ ] Choose a logical spokesperson as the signatory.
- [ ] Print the signature in blue.

LONG COPY VS. SHORT COPY

For decades, copywriters have argued over the ideal length of a sales letter. Some—mainly mail order copywriters—observed that the more they tell, the more they sell. But in many other mailings (for instance, to announce

HIGHLIGHT IMPORTANT COPY IN YOUR LETTER
WITH GRAPHIC DEVICES

There are a number of graphic devices you can use to call the reader's attention to specific sentences or paragraphs in your letter—the ones you most want them to read. These devices can include:

- Underlining
- Italics
- Boldface
- All caps
- Indented paragraphs
- A second color
- Highlighting in yellow
- Handwritten notes in the margins
- Putting a key paragraph in a box

a storewide sale or an update to a smartphone), shorter copy often works better. So which should you choose?

Here are a few simple guidelines for determining the best length for your letter:

- Letters to generate sales leads can be one or two pages. You are not trying to sell a product with your letter, so you don't have to include every last fact. You only have to say enough to whet the prospect's appetite so that they raise their and say, "Tell me more."
- Letters to generate a direct sale are typically three or four pages for two reasons. First, they must provide a lot of proof for the advantages you promise in your copy. Second, they must anticipate and answer the most common objections since this is the only chance you will have to make the sale.

- Business-to-business lead-generating sales letters have gotten progressively shorter over the years—many are just a single page today—due to the belief that B2B prospects are extremely busy. The details are relegated to the white paper, article reprint, or brochure you offer to send the prospects.
- Consumer letters for simple, price-driven offers are shorter, while consumer letters on products that are sold with emotional appeals are often four pages or even longer.
- Low-priced items can be sold with shorter copy, while high-priced items often work best with longer copy and enclosures such as a DVD or brochure.

OUTER ENVELOPE TEASERS

One way to get your reader's attention is with teaser copy on the outside of the envelope. Teaser copy is exactly what it sounds like—it teases, or entices, readers to open the envelope. Most mailings use short teasers set in large, heavy type. Others use lengthy teaser messages that involve headlines, subheads, body copy, and notes written in fake handwriting. You can even use photos, drawings, or graphics to illustrate your teaser and draw more attention to your envelope.

Your goal, of course, is to get a good response rate on your mailing. Teaser copy can help, though test results reveal that its usefulness varies depending on the product, the offer, the mailing, and the teaser itself. Sometimes adding a teaser increases response dramatically because it makes the recipient curious about the contents. Other times, a blank envelope does much better than a teaser envelope because the recipient may not identify it immediately as direct mail and be more inclined to open it.

Some recipients may see teaser copy as saying, "This envelope contains an advertising pitch, not important business or personal mail, so feel free to throw it away." And many people do.

But successful teaser copy says, in effect, "Hey, this is something you'll really be interested in!" If the material inside delivers what the teaser promises, you'll have your reader hooked.

Here are some examples of effective teasers:

Geico Life Insurance

THE INVITATION INSIDE COULD HELP SAVE YOU
HUNDREDS OF DOLLARS . . . and provide better financial security for
your family. Please open and respond.

IBM

Announcing great savings on the IBM Personal Computer.
Plus convenient financing . . .

Mutual of Omaha Accident Protection Insurance

If You Think $2.00 Doesn't Buy Much Anymore, Look Inside—
You'll Be Amazed!

Here are a few rules for writing good teaser copy:

- ✉ Identify the target audience: "A money-saving tool for the plant engineer," "An announcement of unprecedented importance to Windows users who want to be Apple users".
- ✉ Talk about the reader's problems. Then say that the solution to the problem is inside the envelope: "COMPUTER CRASHES. Now you can end them—forever. How? See inside . . .".
- ✉ Tell the reader that something free or valuable is inside the envelope—or at least hint at it: "INSIDE: Free Gift Worth $25," "TEAM UP, AMERICA! Your official decal of the 2018 Winter Olympics is enclosed," "Your temporary AAA membership card and AAA bumper sticker are inside."
- ✉ Use language that refers to the contents of the envelope: "See inside," "For details, see inside," "Here's your invitation," "Enclosed is your . . .".
- ✉ Promise the reader a benefit: "INSIDE: A new way to save time and money on X."
- ✉ Mention that the envelope contains something new or exclusive.
- ✉ Use the word FREE on the envelope. This never fails to get attention: "HERE'S AN OPPORTUNITY TO GET FREE SOFTWARE," "Your FREE BOOK is enclosed."

- Make a provocative statement. This arouses curiosity and gets the reader to tear open the envelope. For example, political fundraisers might write on their envelope: "Donald Trump doesn't want you to read this."
- Create a sense of urgency: "LAST CHANCE to renew your Membership and receive a FREE gift."
- Don't mislead the reader with the teaser or make the teaser sound so great that the contents of the envelope can't live up to it. If you do, the reader will be disappointed when they get into your letter and throw the package away in disgust.

AVOID THE PERSONAL PREFERENCE TRAP WHEN CREATING AND EVALUATING DIRECT MAIL

Some people say common direct-mail techniques irk them. They frequently object to tactics like using long sales letters, initial caps, or all caps in headlines and subheads, and writing that violates the strict rules of grammar. These people will tell their friends who work in direct marketing, "These things put me off and signal that it's a sales pitch."

The answer to "I don't like letters that do these things" is, frankly: So what? What you or anyone else likes or doesn't like in direct-mail marketing doesn't matter. As a 1993 article in the *Journal of Direct Marketing* by Bush et al. stated, "Liking the advertisement is by no means a guaranteed link to sales or persuasion."

The only thing that matters to direct marketers is what works: what generates the highest response and the most orders and sales. There is no correlation between consumers liking a direct-mail package (or any other marketing campaign, such as TV commercials) and whether they will buy a product from it.

BLIND ENVELOPES

A *blind envelope* is an outer envelope with no teaser and often with no company logo on it. One advantage of blind envelopes is that they hide the fact that they contain direct mail.

"A perfectly blank white envelope with no teaser and a blind return address is bound to be opened," said freelance copywriter Bob Matheo. "Does anybody throw away a piece of mail without at least finding out who it's from or what it's about?"

The key to using a nonteaser envelope is to maximize its resemblance to personal mail. Here's how to do it:

- Don't use even a single word of teaser copy, graphics, or illustrations. The envelope should be 100 percent teaser-free.
- Don't use your regular letterhead, which is imprinted with your corporate logo and identifies the mail as coming from your company.
- Instead make the return address (printed in the upper left corner of the envelope, which is called a "corner card") a plain street address or box number, or use the name of an individual rather than your company. And have this printed in black in a plain typeface.
- Better still, if you're not worried about returns, omit the return address and mail a completely blank white envelope. This type of mailing never fails to get opened.
- Use a closed-face envelope, not a window envelope.
- Don't affix a mailing label. Use a printer to imprint the recipient's name and address on the front.
- Use a live stamp or postage meter, not an indicia.
- Some mailers have had great success with envelopes that resemble invoices, bills, bank statements, or legal notices, but this can backfire. Many people get scared by official-looking envelopes and become annoyed when they realize they've been tricked. And the post office is increasingly not approving envelopes that are too official-looking.
- The same goes for envelopes that look like official correspondence or overnight-delivery packages.

USING SALES LETTERS TO GENERATE LEADS

For many organizations, a primary objective of advertising and promotion is to generate inquiries, and direct mail is one of the best ways to do this.

One of the biggest differences between letters that generate leads vs. letters that seek to generate orders is length. In mail order, there is an old saying: "The more you tell, the more you sell." But in lead generation, things are different. The lead-generating direct-mail package does not have to do the whole job of selling the customer and bringing back the order. Rather, the goal of the lead-generating package is to get a prospect to raise their hand and say, "Yes, your product sounds like something that might be able to help me. Tell me more!"

However, if you tell your whole story in the mailing, there is nothing left for the reader to inquire about. The prospect may feel that they know everything there is to know about your product or service and there is no reason to respond—unless they are ready to buy.

For this reason, lead-generating packages *don't* tell the whole story. Rather, they provide just enough facts to whet the reader's appetite for further details. The interested reader is invited to send for more information—which might be a brochure, a presentation, a demonstration of the product, a DVD, or a price list.

Exactly how much information should your package include? Enough to give the prospect a good idea of 1) what you are selling, 2) the problem it solves or the key advantage your product holds over similar products, and 3) how the reader can personally benefit from the product. You should also specify, in detail, the action you expect on the part of the reader—and provide an incentive for immediate response, if possible.

Lead Quality vs. Quantity

In some situations, you may be after the best leads possible. If, for example, each lead must be followed up by a salesperson, you don't want them wasting their valuable travel or telephone time chasing after nonviable prospects. Thus, you would be willing to sacrifice quantity to improve quality. In his book *Direct Marketing: Strategy, Planning, Execution* (McGraw-Hill Education, 2000), Edward Nash gives seven ways to get better-quality sales leads:

1. Mention the price.
2. Say that a salesperson will call.
3. Give a lot of information about the product, including any potential negatives.
4. Ask the prospect to give you a lot of information on the reply card, such as phone number, best time to call, number of employees, and annual sales.
5. Charge something. Even a small amount for a booklet or sample will eliminate the freeloaders.
6. Require a stamp. Don't use a business reply card or business reply envelope.
7. Make the offer specific and relevant to the product or service you are selling.

All these rules are really common sense. Take rule 7, for example. Imagine how many replies you would get if you offered a free framed motivational poster to everyone who responded to your mailing! But how many of these people, do you think, would respond just to get the framed art, without having any real interest in your company or your product?

On the other hand, if you changed your offer to a free booklet entitled "Seven Ways to Protect Your Computer Equipment Against Power Surges," only people interested in protecting their computers would be inclined to send for the booklet. Thus, you would be attracting the right type of prospect for a surge protection device.

In other situations, you might want to increase the number of leads your mailing generates. For instance, I had a client tell me, "We have a new product, no prospects, and three new salespeople sitting around twiddling their thumbs. I need leads and lots of them—FAST!"

As a rule, the more leads you get, the lower their overall quality. In his book, Nash also gives seven ways to get more leads:

1. Tell less. Leave something to curiosity.
2. Personalize the response device so the prospect doesn't have to write in their name and address.
3. Add convenience. Supply the stamp, the envelope, maybe even a pencil.

Figure 9.5. **Quantity vs. Quality Comparison Lead-Getting Offers**

Offer	Quantity of Leads Produced	Quality of Leads Produced
Free gift by mail	10	2
Free information report by mail	9	3-6
Free brochure	8	5
More information	7	5
Demonstration	5–6	5–6
Sales presentation/consultation	4	7
Salesperson will call	3	7-8
Write on your letterhead to request information	1	8
Complete questionnaire or spec sheet	2	9

Key: 1 = low   5 = average   10 = high

4. Give a gift or a premium—one that is valuable and not necessarily related to your product. The more valuable, the more leads you'll get (see Figure 9.5 above for offer ideas).
5. Make the entire offer FREE.
6. Ask less on the reply card—the fewer questions, the better.
7. Add a prize. Sweepstakes can really boost response.

Figure 9.5 provides additional guidelines on which techniques produce more leads vs. which generate better-quality leads.

50 POINTS TO PONDER WHEN CREATING A LEAD-GENERATING DM CAMPAIGN

What should you know when planning a lead-generating direct-mail program? Here, from copywriter Milt Pierce, are 50 questions to ask yourself, the answers to which will guide you in the right direction:

1. How many steps are there in the buying process for this product? Where in this process does my mailing fit?

2. What can I tell my prospect that will get them to take the next step in the buying process?

3. Can I reduce selling costs by creating a mailing designed to produce a direct sale (a mail order) instead of an inquiry?

4. How many leads do I want to generate? Do we want a large quantity of "soft" leads? Or are we better off getting a smaller number of more highly qualified leads?

5. What happens if the mailing produces too many leads? Too few?

6. Is there a geographic region that my sales force or distribution system does not cover? How can I respond to inquiries from this region?

7. What is the primary market for my product or service? (Which industry needs it most?)

8. Are there any secondary markets for the product large enough to justify a custom-tailored version of the mailing?

9. Who is my primary prospect within the target industry? What is their job title/function?

10. Who are the other people (by job title) involved in the purchase decision for this product? What are their roles? (Who recommends the product? Who specifies it? Who has authority to approve the purchase?)

11. Must we reach all these prospects? Or can we generate the desired sales result by targeting only one or two key decision-makers at each organization?

12. If we don't know to whom we should be mailing, how can we find out? From our sales representatives? Market research? Direct mail?

13. If we don't know what we should be telling our potential customers about our product, how can we find out?

14. Should we tailor versions of our sales letter either to vertical markets or various job titles—or both?

15. Should we tailor our brochure to specific job titles?

16. What offer are we using in our current mailing? Is there a way to make the offer stronger or better?

17. Is the prospect in need of information about our product or the problem it solves? Can we package this information in a booklet or report and offer it as a response piece in our mailing?

18. Does our sales process involve a face-to-face meeting with the prospect? Can we legitimately call this sales meeting a "free consultation" and feature it as the offer in our mailing?

19. Do we allow the user to sample our product on a free trial basis? Should we be stressing this free trial offer in our mailing?

20. Do we offer our customers a free gift, price discount, free shipping and handling, or other money-saving incentive for responding to our mailing? If not, why not?

21. What reason or incentive can we give the reader to respond now and not later?

22. Can we use telemarketing to qualify sales leads generated by our direct-mail program?

23. Can we use an email autoresponder series to convert nonresponders into responders?

24. Can we use telemarketing to identify and presell prospects before we send them our mailing package? Can we follow up with respondents to set appointments or close sales?

25. What format is best for our mailing? Full-blown direct-mail package (letter, brochure, reply card)? Or sales letter only?

26. Is there any benefit to personalizing the mailing?

27. What graphic treatment is appropriate for our audience? Should it be businesslike or bright and loud? Should it be "disguised" as personal correspondence or clearly marked (by use of teaser and graphics) as direct mail?

28. What copy approach should I use? Serious or breezy? Educational and informative or hard sell?

29. Does my reader want or need a lot of information?

30. Can I use a self-mailer format?

31. Is a postcard appropriate for my offer?

32. Should I use a single mailing or a series of mailings?

33. How many mailings should I send to my list before giving up on people who don't respond?

34. In a series of mailings, am I using a variety of sizes and formats to gain attention for my message?

35. Are requests for more information fulfilled within 48 hours?

36. Are hot sales leads separated for immediate follow-up by sales representatives or telephone salespeople?

37. What is the conversion ratio (the percentage of mail-generated inquiries that result in a sale)?

38. Are our salespeople competent? If not, what can we do to ensure better handling of sales leads?

39. Do salespeople follow up on all leads provided? If not, why not?

40. Do salespeople welcome direct-mail leads or do they grumble about them? Why?

41. Are there qualifying questions we can add to our reply form to help salespeople separate genuine prospects from "brochure collectors"?

42. Can we afford to send a brochure, catalog, or product sample to everyone who requests one?

43. Do we have a sufficient quantity of sales brochures on hand to fulfill all requests for more information—assuming we get a 10 percent response to our mailing?

44. Do we get a better quality lead by requiring the prospect to put a stamp on the reply card than by offering a postage-paid business reply card?

45. Do we get better sales results from prospects who respond by telephone vs. those who mail in reply cards?

46. Does our fulfillment package or sales brochure provide the prospect with the information he asked for? And does it do a good job of selling our product or service?

47. Do we include a cover letter with the brochures and data sheets we send in response to mail-generated inquiries?

48. Do we include a questionnaire, spec sheet, or some other type of reply form with our inquiry-fulfillment package?

49. Do we automatically send follow-up emails to prospects who don't respond to the inquiry-fulfillment package?

50. Should we be more vigorous in our program of follow-up mailings, emails, and phone calls?

A successful lead-generation letter I created for a corporate-training seminar is shown in Figure 9.6 below.

As you can see in Figure 9.6, this lead-gen sales letter includes many of the go-to techniques you've read about so far, including a statement

Figure 9.6. **Lead-Generating Sales Letter**

THE CENTER FOR TECHNICAL COMMUNICATION
22 EAST QUACKENBUSH AVENUE, DUMONT, NJ 07628 · (201) 385-1220 · FAX (201) 385-1138

If waiting for FDA approval costs you money...
...here's one way to get them to move more quickly.

Dear Marketing Director:

Are you sick and tired of waiting for the FDA to get around to approving your products?

You can't force them into faster action. But you can take an important step toward ensuring that the documents you submit to the FDA—and other regulatory agencies—aren't contributing to the delay of new-product launches. How? With our popular in-house seminar...

**"Effective Technical Writing for Pharmaceutical Firms,
Biotechnology Companies, and Medical Equipment Manufacturers."**

As a marketing professional, you know that clear writing has become increasingly important in our industry.

Regulatory agencies demand that the documents you submit for approval be understandable, accurate, and unambiguous.

Submissions that are confusing, inaccurate, vague, or misleading irritate the bureaucrats. And can dramatically slow the approval process.

The result is missed deadlines...and missed marketing opportunities...that can cost you revenue, profits, and market share.

Our "Effective Technical Writing" program teaches your employees how to write better and faster. So the documents they produce are clear, well-organized, and easy to read. Since they learn to write with greater confidence and enjoyment, productivity increases as well.

"Effective Technical Writing" is available as a one- or two-day on-site seminar. Because the program is privately sponsored by your company, we can totally customize it to your objectives and needs—at no extra cost to you.

For complete details on our "Effective Technical Writing" training program, just complete and mail the enclosed reply card. Or call me at (201) 385-1220. The information is free. And there is no obligation of any kind.

Regards,

Bob Bly

P.S. When you call or mail the reply card, be sure to request a free copy of our informative special report, "10 Ways to Improve Your Technical Writing." It can help your employees avoid the most common writing mistakes that managers, executives, scientists, engineers, and other professionals make.

of substance, strong call-to-action, and a P.S. that includes the magic word "free." As you'll see in the next section, many of these must-include elements differ slightly when it comes to writing B2B sales letters.

23 TIPS FOR WRITING BUSINESS-TO-BUSINESS SALES LETTERS THAT WORK

There are many similarities between business-to-consumer (B2C) and business-to-business (B2B) direct mail. But there are also some differences. Here's what works best for B2B DM:

1. Short letters—one or two pages—are usually best. Executives don't have time to wade through a lengthy sales pitch. Exceptions are subscriptions, seminars, and some other mail order offers.

2. If you can personalize, great! But form letters addressed to "Dear Executive" or "Dear Engineer" can also pull well.

3. Should business mailings take a "consumer approach"? Some mailers argue that executives are human beings before they are businesspeople, so all consumer DM techniques can apply to business mail. But remember that executives have professional responsibilities, and they take their work seriously. So business mailings must address their needs *as professionals*. Not every consumer gimmick is appropriate for business mail.

4. In particular, avoid "busy" graphics (for example, look at Publishers Clearing House mailings). Use graphics that make your mailing immediately clear, easy to follow, and easy to read. For an executive audience, use a clean and professional design. When mailing to field workers with "boots on the ground," less upscale mail can often work better. For one DM campaign, the marketer imprinted the outer envelope with brown ink that looked like mud—and it worked.

5. If an envelope is filled with too many inserts, a busy executive will be more inclined to throw the whole thing away. A standard package with a letter, brochure, and reply card seems to work best.

6. The biggest mistake you can make in writing B2B DM is to assume that the reader is as interested in your product or industry as you are.

When writing copy, assume your product is the *last* thing on your readers' minds. They may never have given a second thought to the issues, technology, and competing products that you worry about every day.

7. Another major error is writing copy that speaks on a layman's level when your mailing is targeted to industry professionals. For example: IT professionals are very familiar with Java, CSS, Python, and XTML. You aren't—so the natural tendency is to explain them in your copy. But being too elementary turns readers off and signals that you're not really in touch with their business. How would you respond to a mailing that began, "Direct mail is an exciting way to sell products?" Yawn.

8. Make your mailing look professional—a business communication from one executive to another. A letter crammed with fake handwriting, arrows, pop-ups, and other gimmicks strikes many business readers as undignified and unprofessional.

9. One rule that applies equally to business and consumer mail: *Sell your offer.* If you offer a 30-day trial, sell the reader on asking for the trial. Explain the benefits and assure them there is no risk or obligation. If it is an invitation to a seminar, sell the knowledge to be gained at the seminar.

10. A corollary to the previous point is that there must be an appealing offer. A lead-generating package should never sell just the product. It should also push the offer. And there is *always* an offer. The best offer is some type of free trial, analysis, consultation, or sample. Premiums can also work well. At minimum, offer a brochure of "free information." "Free information" is still an offer, and it does work. If you fulfill inquiries with multiple items (a brochure, a map, a DVD), call it a "free information kit."

11. Write copy that enhances the perceived value of your offer. For example, a product catalog becomes a product guide. A software catalog becomes an international software directory. A collection of brochures becomes a free information kit. A checklist becomes a convention planner's guide. An article reprinted in

pamphlet form becomes "our new, informative booklet: HOW TO PREVENT COMPUTER FAILURES." And so on.

12. Many clients begin planning by sitting around a table and saying, "We want to do a mailing on product X. Should we use a mailing tube? A box? A message in a fortune cookie? What gimmick works best?" In my opinion, they are asking the wrong question. The *right* way to get started is to ask, "What is the key sales appeal of this product?" Ideally, this is something the product does better than other products, which solves a major problem or addresses a key concern of the customer.

13. Clients often ask, "Shouldn't we do some market research and focus-group testing to uncover key sales points and appeals before we do the mailing?" They probably don't realize that direct mail is a good research tool in itself. For a few thousand dollars, you can test an offer and, within weeks, know whether prospects will respond.

14. Postcard decks generate a high number of responses at low cost. Direct-mail packages are more costly and time-consuming to produce, but generate a better-quality lead. The only way to know which will work better for you is to set up a lead-tracking system and test both types of mailings.

15. Self-mailers generally don't usually pull as well as packages with separate letters, brochures, and reply cards. They work well, however, for seminars and can add an attention-grabbing change of pace to a series of mailings. One ad agency I know has used self-mailers for years to generate new business with great success. One reason self-mailers do poorly is that most are not given the same level of attention that businesses put into their regular DM packages.

16. About gimmicks, such as pop-ups, fancy folds, 3-D objects, and so on: They generally work only if there is a strong, logical tie-in to the product or offer and to the sales appeal. Enclosing a pair of sunglasses doesn't make much sense for a valve manufacturer, but it might work for a travel agent offering a package cruise to the Caribbean or for a tanning salon prospecting for new clients.

17. Another mistake is to make the copywriter base your package around some artificial theme or slogan. A company selling industrial pumps, for instance, insists that the theme of its mailings be *quality*. A manufacturer of metal buildings wants a futuristic image with the copy full of references to outer space and science fiction. This is a costly error. Perhaps their advertising can be tied effectively to such weak themes. But response-getting mail *can't*. Mailings that get results push product benefits, cost savings, free gifts, and no-risk guarantees—not images or themes. Forcing a mailing to fit some predetermined concept is difficult, tricky, and often fatal to results.

18. A business reply card (BRC) that restates the offer and asks for the order is doing only half the job. Reply elements should also be used to gather information that helps qualify prospects. For instance, if you're selling accounts receivable software, the BRC should ask respondents what type of computer they have, what operating system they use, and how many invoices they write per month. If you are seeking detailed facts, use a separate questionnaire or "specification sheet." And include a business reply envelope (BRE) as well as your landing page URL.

19. "Is there any advantage to using business-reply cards and envelopes in industrial mailings?" asks one client. "After all, the businessperson doesn't care about a few cents postage, and their assistant has plenty of stamps handy." True— but use them anyway. Why? Because such cards and envelopes *look* like response devices. They signal the reader that a response is required.

20. The same holds true for 800 numbers. Sure, the executive isn't paying for the call out of their own pocket, so they're less motivated by a free call than a consumer is. But the 800 number leaps off the page and says, "Hey, pick up the phone—we want you to *respond* to this offer!" Regular phone numbers don't have this effect.

21. A popular technique is to add to the perceived value of the order form or BRC by calling it an "information request form," "trial

request form," or "needs analysis." This still works but is losing impact as more and more mailers use the technique.

22. Response goes up when you give the reader choices. For instance, include both a BRC and a toll-free number. And allow for multiple responses, such as:

[ ] Reserve my free 30-day trial

[ ] Have a sales representative call

[ ] Send brochure by mail

[ ] Not interested right now, but add me to your mailing list

23. Tell the reader there is no cost or obligation or that no salesperson will call . . . *if* these statements are true.

DIRECT MAIL TO INVITE PROSPECTS TO YOUR TRADE-SHOW BOOTH

Direct mail in the hands of a knowledgeable pro can be a powerful promotion that builds traffic, targets key prospects, generates sales leads, fills conference rooms, creates awareness of an event and your participation in it, or just gets the word out about your products and services.

GETTING PAST THE MAILROOM

In large corporations, mail is often screened by mailroom employees. When you send a mailing piece to a large company, there may be dozens of people on your mailing list who all work there. If the mailroom gets multiple copies of the same mailing piece addressed to different employees, the clerk can more easily identify it as "junk mail"—and instead of delivering it, choose to save some time by just throwing out the entire pile.

So when you mail to multiple individuals at a single company, instead of mailing them all at once, send just a couple of pieces each day. That way, they will arrive in dribs and drabs rather than one big pile and escape the notice of mailroom personnel. ✉

Unfortunately, most trade-show direct mail I see violates the fundamentals of successful direct marketing. For this reason, few of these mailings generate anywhere near the desired response.

The rest of this section covers proven techniques for creating trade show direct mail that gets the attention of trade show audiences. Try them on your next letter or invitation and watch your response rates soar.

The Importance of the List

Even the most brilliant package will flop if it is mailed to the wrong people. Selecting the right mailing list is the single most important step in ensuring direct-mail success. According to Freeman Gosden, Jr., author of *Direct Marketing Success* (Wiley), list selection is twice as important as copy, graphics, and printing combined.

For a trade-show invitation, the best list is key prospects and current customers within a 100-mile radius of the exhibit hall. Invite only those people who are genuine prospects for the products you are featuring in your display. One good source of names might be a list of people who have responded to ads about the product within the past six months.

Executive Seminars

An even more select list of key prospects can be targeted to receive special invitations to hospitality suites, executive briefings, presentations of papers, seminars, and other special events held in conjunction with your exhibit. If the event is relatively minor, you can include a notice about it in the invitation to the exhibit. But if the event is major (such as the opportunity to see a new product introduction), you can play it up in a separate mailing.

Carry Cards

A *carry card*, mailed with the invitation, is a printed card the prospect can present at your booth to receive a small gift or perhaps to enter a sweepstakes or drawing. I call it a "carry card" because the prospect must carry it with them to receive whatever is offered in the mailing.

By printing your booth number on the card, you remind the prospect to visit you; the offer of the gift provides the incentive to do so. The gift need not be expensive or elaborate—perhaps free information, such as a special report, or an inexpensive item, such as a pen or key chain.

Be Personal

The more personal a mailing piece, the greater the response. One effective technique is to personalize each mailing with the prospect's name. A form letter, for example, can be made to look personal if produced on a computer using a program that inserts the prospect's name and address.

There are other ways of individualizing the mailings. Carry cards or invitations can be numbered in sequence so that each person receives a unique number, which may be used to qualify them to receive a prize or other gift.

Another technique is for salespeople to include brief handwritten notes to each prospect. The note, written in the margin of a preprinted form letter or on the flap of a formal invitation, adds a human touch to the mailing.

Urgency

Direct mail is designed to generate an immediate response, so your mailing must give the reader reason to read and act now.

A teaser on the outer envelope is often used to urge the reader to open the mailing right away. For example, it can tell the reader that the envelope contains dated materials. It can stress the importance of attending the show or emphasize its benefits. Or it can tell the recipient to take action. For example, the teaser copy could read, "Urgent: open by November 15." Time your mailing so that it arrives a few days earlier.

If you want the reader to RSVP, you should create a sense of urgency for this, too. The close of an invitation to a seminar might say, "But hurry. Attendance is limited. Reserve your seat at this important briefing today."

Give Them a Choice

Years ago, direct marketers discovered they received greater response when they gave the reader a choice. This holds true in trade-show promotion as well.

For example, many of the people you invite will be unable to attend, even if they are genuinely interested in the products being displayed. Why not have your mailing do double duty by offering information or further action to those people? You could offer to send them a brochure or a newsletter or to call on them in person and tell them what they missed. One exhibitor even offered to send a DVD of their exhibit! This technique can dramatically boost response.

Always include a business reply card or envelope in mailings designed to elicit a response.

Create an Event

Although it is difficult for our egos to accept, your next trade show is not a major event in the lives of your customers. Your challenge, then, is to change their reaction from boredom to excitement.

How? There are many possibilities. One exhibitor featured the Dallas Cowboy Cheerleaders in their booth. Another had an exciting multimedia presentation on a revolutionary new type of technology. An instrumentation manufacturer hired a magician to perform at their display. A major defense manufacturer hired a quick-draw fighter to teach people how to use a six-shooter (with blanks, of course!).

Once you've come up with an event that generates real excitement but also ties in with your product or theme, make this the featured subject of your mailing. Just as publishers win subscribers by featuring a free gift or a discount, a successful trade-show mailing features the "gimmick" rather than the exhibit itself. For example, a mailing designed to draw people to the defense manufacturer exhibit might read, "MEET THE WEST'S FASTEST GUNFIGHTER AT HIGH NOON AT THE AMCOM AIR SHOW—AND WIN A GENUINE, OLD WEST TEN-GALLON HAT." Sell the sizzle rather than the steak.

Exclusivity

A powerful appeal of direct mail—and of trade shows—is exclusivity. Many trade show visitors go specifically to see new products and services that have not been shown before.

If you're introducing a new technology, a new product, or an improved version of an old product, play this up in your mailing. Emphasize both the importance of the product as well as the fact that the reader is having an opportunity to see it first—an opportunity not extended to other people in the business. This sense of being exclusive, of being first, is flattering, and it can do wonders for your response rate.

Gimmicks

People love getting free stuff, and it doesn't have to be expensive. Small items have the potential to amuse, entertain, communicate a message, and grab attention. An automobile manufacturer, for example, could mail keychains to important customers and enroll them in a drawing for a brand-new car. But to win, they must bring the keychain to the drawing. The mailing would stress how you can add a key to your chain (and the car that goes with it) by visiting the show.

In another variation on this theme, Omron Electronics mailed a box containing a fortune cookie. The fortune inside the cookie predicted "A fortune in your future!" at the ISA show in Philadelphia. Copy on a carry card enclosed with the cookie reinforced the message: "Bring this ticket to Omron's Booth #R631 to collect a fortune."

Note that the nature of the "fortune" was never specified. In direct mail, you can often boost response by leaving part of your story untold. This creates a sense of mystery, and many people respond simply to satisfy their curiosity.

Use a Series of Mailings

A series of mailings can generate more response than just one mailer. So it may pay to mail more than once to the same list of people. Many exhibitors have used the following three-part mailing format with success:

1. The first mailing is a simple postcard that "previews" the show. It is used to pique the reader's curiosity but demands no response.
2. The second mailing is the full invitation package. It can consist of a letter, an invitation, a carry card, a reply card, a booklet or brochure, or any combination of these elements. The theory is that more people will read the full invitation if they are "warmed up" with the postcard first.

3. The third mailing can be either a reminder or, if the reader has responded to the invitation, a letter confirming the time, date, and location of the event.

Telemarketing

The use of telephone calls to follow up direct mail can dramatically raise response levels, but it is expensive: A phone call generally costs about three to five times more than a mailing piece.

You might want to save the phone for targeting a small, exclusive list—say, your top 20 or 30 clients. Call after the second or third mailing to repeat the offer of the mailings and urge them to attend your display.

Include a Free Show Admission Ticket

Even if you design your own invitation, it's a good idea to include an official show pass or registration form in the envelope as well. Having a show pass gives your prospects the security of knowing they have the necessary paperwork to get them into the exhibit hall. You should print your company name and booth number on the show passes so prospects will be reminded to visit you even if they throw away the rest of your mailing.

Chapter 10

DIRECT-MAIL BROCHURES

In direct mail, we have something called the *classic #10 package*. It consists of a business-size outer envelope, a sales letter, a brochure, and a reply element. There may be additional elements, such as a buck slip, lift letter, or even a second brochure.

Although this is the standard in direct mail because of its superior pulling power, we have seen a curious phenomenon: In some cases, when we omit the brochure and mail the letter and reply element only, it actually raises rather than depresses response. One theory is that the presence of a slick color brochure signals that it is advertising.

But for many mailings, having a strong brochure does in fact improve results. So our standard methodology is to start with the full package, and if that is successful, send out a small test cell without the brochure to see whether response goes up, down, or stays the same. If mailing without the sales brochure lowers response, we put it back into subsequent mailings with the confidence that the brochure is in fact a response-booster. But you don't know unless you test.

The converse—boosting response by removing the letter and mailing only the brochure inside the envelope—virtually never works. The lesson is that, as stated earlier, the letter does the primary selling job: It gets attention, draws the prospect into the copy, asks for the order, and makes the sale. The letter sells.

The brochure helps by illustrating, explaining, proving, and expanding on key sales points discussed in the letter. But it plays only a supporting role: The letter sells, and the brochure tells.

Figure 10.1 on page 187 shows a layout for a typical direct-mail brochure. This brochure is an 11-by-17-inch sheet folded once vertically to form four pages, and then folded twice horizontally, like a letter, for insertion in a #10 outer envelope.

> ✉ **TIP**
>
> To save money when printing your DM brochure, instruct your graphic artist to design it to fit on one piece of paper. A brochure printed on multiple sheets that have to be bound together doesn't usually work as an enclosure in a DM package, mainly because it is more expensive than a single-sheet brochure, driving up your mailing costs. Multipage brochures usually work best as self-mailers.

WHAT TO PUT INTO YOUR DIRECT-MAIL BROCHURE

In general, the brochure contains written information too detailed or lengthy to include in the sales letter. It can also show photos, drawings, diagrams, charts, graphs, and tables—something a letter usually cannot do. For instance, in a mailing selling industrial equipment, a table of technical features and specifications might be printed on a separate sheet of paper because it is too much information to include in a letter.

Your brochure can include any of the following:

- ✉ Testimonials of satisfied clients and customers
- ✉ List of clients and customers
- ✉ Photos of clients and customers
- ✉ Photos of your staff
- ✉ Capsule biographies of key company personnel

Figure 10.1. **Brochure Layout**

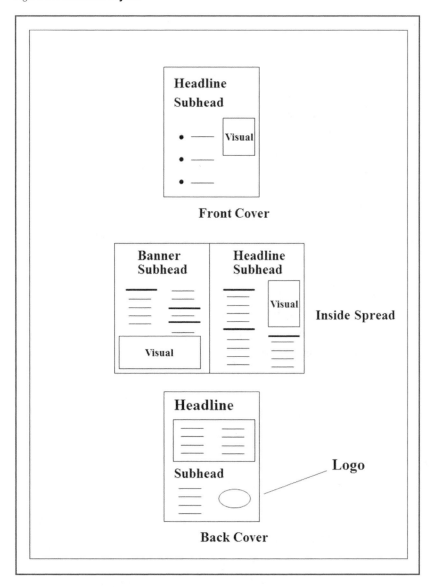

- ✉ Photo series demonstrating how your product works
- ✉ Product photos
- ✉ Photos of people using your product
- ✉ Photos of people enjoying the benefits or end results of your product or service

- ⊠ Typical applications for your product
- ⊠ Certificate of warranty or guarantee
- ⊠ Order blank
- ⊠ Toll-free number and web URL
- ⊠ List of local offices or sales representatives
- ⊠ List of product features
- ⊠ Descriptions of related products or services
- ⊠ Descriptions of accessories and supplies
- ⊠ Brief description of your company
- ⊠ Sample news clips from articles about you in the press
- ⊠ Diagram of the product with call-outs pointing to specific features
- ⊠ Quiz or other checklist the reader can fill out to demonstrate a need for the product
- ⊠ Graph showing product performance
- ⊠ Bar chart or pie chart
- ⊠ Map showing location of plants, offices, customers
- ⊠ Table of data or information
- ⊠ List of product specifications including dimensions and weight
- ⊠ Photos of facilities (manufacturing plant, offices, etc.)
- ⊠ List of key benefits
- ⊠ Picture of premium or free gift offer
- ⊠ Cover of booklet, brochure, report, or other information sent in response to inquiry

In a mailing I sent to dentists, the letter asked them to request a sample of a new type of dental post. The problem was that the procedure for using this post was slightly different from the standard method, which made some dentists hesitant to adopt it.

The solution was to include a small illustrated flier showing, in simple words and pictures, the new technique. When the dentists saw that the procedure was easy to learn and very similar to current practices, it overcame their resistance to the product.

An illustrated brochure can sometimes make a point more dramatically than an all-text letter. For example, a brochure for a hair-replacement center shows before-and-after photos of men who have had hair transplants, demonstrating how much better they look after the procedure. A brochure for a diet center shows a picture of a 200-pound woman. Next to this is another photo of the woman at 130 pounds six months after starting the program. A fundraising brochure for an animal welfare society could show photos of animals abused in laboratory research. A mailing for a foster-parents program could show a heart-rending photo of a hungry, poverty-stricken child.

DIRECT-MAIL BROCHURE DESIGN

Following these simple rules for direct-mail brochure design can keep you on the right track, reduce costs, prevent mailing difficulties, and improve results:

- Pick a size that fits the envelopes you will be using in your mailing.
- Be sure to use a standard size. Custom envelopes are expensive.
- Make a dummy, also called a mock-up. This makes it easier to visualize what the final piece will look like. Also make sure the dummy fits easily in your envelope so that automated letter-shop equipment can insert it.
- Keep cost in mind. A two-color printing job is about 15 percent more expensive than one color. Four colors can add 50 percent or more to the cost.
- Using a professional photographer to take new photos or commissioning an illustrator to do a drawing is also expensive. Are there existing stock photos and illustrations you can use in your brochure, most of which can be found online?
- You can often save money by reusing photos and drawings created for other mailings, ads, presentations, or brochures.
- You'll get a better response by designing the brochure as a separate piece from the letter rather than combining letter and brochure into a single piece.
- It's also better to keep the reply card or form separate from the brochure rather than have a reply form you have to tear off or cut out of the brochure. However, if there's room, you might consider having two reply forms—one separate and one as part of the brochure.

- ✉ Guarantee and warranty statements should be surrounded by a certificate-like border to make them look more "official" and valuable.

- ✉ Pop-ups, die-cuts, engraving, and embossing can add visual appeal, but they also add cost. Use with caution.

- ✉ Use full color only if your budget permits or when your product must be illustrated in color—for instance, collectibles, clothing, gourmet food, floral arrangements, or fine art.

- ✉ You can still be creative with one-color and two-color jobs. For example, instead of printing with black ink on white stock, print with black on yellow, blue on gray, or dark brown on light beige paper.

- ✉ Unless you're striving for a dignified approach or you're image building, it's best to use bold, "hot" colors. Red is very good as a second color in hard-sell direct mail.

- ✉ Use borders, boxes, tints, and other graphic devices to break the copy up into short sections. Arrows, bursts, asterisks, and handwritten notes can help draw the reader's eye to a particularly important message.

- ✉ Readability is vital. Don't use a creative color scheme or complex design if it makes the copy difficult to read.

- ✉ Make headlines and subheads big and bold.

- ✉ Underlining, tints, and printing in a second color can help highlight phrases or paragraphs. But tints should be high-contrast; don't print with black ink on a dark gray tint, for instance.

- ✉ If there's a toll-free number, put it in large type and place an icon of a telephone to the left of the number. Also use large, bold type for your landing page URL.

WRITING DIRECT-MAIL BROCHURES

The first thing readers see when they look at your brochure is the front panel or cover. For this reason, it pays to start selling right on the cover with a strong headline and copy. Just putting your company name on the cover doesn't cut it!

One technique is to use a cover headline that gives the reader a self-contained message. For example: "THIS NEW ENERGY-EFFICIENT CHILLER-HEATER CAN CUT YOUR HEATING AND COOLING COSTS UP TO 50% OR MORE."

The thinking behind this technique is that many people will glance at the cover but never open the brochure. And those who do get past the cover may only skim the rest of the brochure. So headlines, especially cover headlines, should present the key benefit upfront.

A second technique is to use the headline to lure the reader inside. For example: "HOW ARE COMPANIES IN YOUR AREA PAYING UP TO 50% LESS IN HEATING AND COOLING COSTS THAN YOU ARE? See inside for details. . . ."

The logic behind this method is that people who just skim the cover aren't really interested anyway and real prospects will want the information in the brochure. The cover headline is used to grab the attention of those prospects and direct them toward your detailed sales pitch.

Here are some examples of strong selling headlines taken from the covers of direct-mail brochures I've received over the years:

Palmer House Conference Center
Here's the free cup of coffee you missed
[packet of instant coffee was attached to front of brochure]

Lettershop Service
HOW TO PRINT, STUFF, SEAL, STAMP AND
SEND 100,000 LETTERS OVERNIGHT

Citibank
In a comparison test, which card do you think would win?
[VISUAL: side-by-side photos of Citibank Visa card and
American Express card]

Sandler Training
SELL MORE . . . SELL MORE EASILY. "I don't care how hot, cold,
or lukewarm you are now. If you are selling, you can do much better—
the easy way!"

Home Study Course

THE HARDEST THING ABOUT BECOMING A MILLIONAIRE
IS BELIEVING YOU CAN DO IT.
The next hardest is getting started
We'll help you do both . . .

Audio Home Study Courses

GREAT IDEAS THAT SHAPED OUR WORLD
The classic thinkers you always intended to read (but never had
time for) are now available on audio CDs

Here are some other tips for writing effective direct-mail brochures:

- *Cluster your thoughts.* For example, when using testimonials, put them all on the same page rather than spreading them throughout the brochure. Put all biographies of key personnel in the same section. Keeping similar thoughts in a cluster makes a much greater impression on the reader.
- *Use plenty of headlines and subheads.* Many readers will only scan your brochure quickly without reading the copy. A glance at headlines and subheads should give them the gist of your story.
- *Make headlines and subheads sales-oriented, not just descriptive.* For instance, instead of "Here's how it works," say, "Here's how the Financial Advisory Service increases investment income by 20 percent or more." Put benefits in every headline and subhead. Make them persuasive, not just informative.
- *Use short sections of copy.* Readers would rather read many short sections than one long one. (This is why books are divided into chapters and chapters into sections.)
- *Separate important elements.* If you want to highlight a particular section, have the layout artist put it in a box surrounded by a border and printed on a light color tint. For example, you may want to emphasize a special service (such as a Facebook group) or a premium (such as a free gift or report).
- *Use a two-part headline to lure the reader inside the brochure.* The first half of the headline is printed on the front cover and the second half on the inside spread. For example: "Here's the free cup of

coffee you missed . . . if yours wasn't one of the 2,513 meetings held at Conference Center 7 in its first year."

- ✉ *Numbered lists.* If you have a lot of benefits or sales points to discuss, list them in 1-2-3 order. The headline of such a brochure might be "10 Reasons to Buy Universal Life Insurance" or "6 Steps to a Secure Retirement."

- ✉ *Bulleted lists.* If you have a number of miscellaneous features, sales points, or technical specifications, put them in a separate part of the brochure and list them in table or "bullet" form rather than as straight text. This makes the brochure easier to read.

- ✉ *Q&A.* If you have a lot of explaining to do, consider a question-and-answer format where each subhead is a question and the answer is in the body copy below.

- ✉ *Contact information.* Be sure to put your company name, address, and phone number on every piece in the direct-mail package including the brochure. Highlight toll-free numbers and URLs by setting them in large, bold type.

Employing these tips can help take your brochure copy to the next level and increase your conversion rate. The power is in your words—use them wisely.

Chapter 11

REPLY ELEMENTS

Effective direct mail always tells the readers what the next step is—and urges them to take it.

A good direct-mail package doesn't just ask for a response; it makes readers feel they would be making a mistake by not responding. It also creates a sense of urgency, or gives a compelling reason why a response is required today, not tomorrow or next week.

It boldly asks for the order or some other response, such as a request for information. The focal point at that stage becomes the reply element: the part of the package the reader mails back to the advertiser to place an order or request more information. This is usually a reply card in the case of lead generation or an order form and reply envelope in the case of one-step marketing.

HAS THE WEB MADE REPLY FORMS OBSOLETE?

In the digital age, many marketers wonder whether they even need a paper reply element. After all, why not just provide a URL to a form the prospects can fill out online or a QR code they can scan with their smartphones?

Here's why: Having a paper response element, even if it isn't used, is a visual indicator that the mailer has an offer for the recipient and a response is required to get it. The response form can be a traditional reply card or just a 4-by-9-inch slip with the response URL and toll-free phone number printed in large, bold type. The separate reply element in effect says, "This is direct-response mail, and we would appreciate a reply from you." This increases overall response, both from people who use the reply element and those who prefer to respond by phone or online.

Given that I strongly advise you to include a reply element in your DM package, the rest of this section explores some basic rules that apply to all types of reply elements including reply cards and order forms.

Easy to Fill Out

The reply form should be clear, never confusing. Tell the reader what to do in simple 1-2-3 language. The form should be designed so that anyone can follow your directions without assistance. If the form is complicated, unclear, or difficult to complete, people will throw it away.

For a one-step promotion, make it crystal clear how much should be added for sales tax, shipping, and postage. If the recipient isn't sure, they will throw out the form rather than ask for help. Complex order forms can lose orders for you!

GET THE POSTAL SERVICE'S OK BEFORE MAILING

Show your business reply card or envelope to your local postmaster to make sure it meets USPS guidelines. If you make an error, the cards or envelopes may not reach you when your recipients mail them back. While you are at it, get the entire DM package checked, especially the outer envelope, to ensure that the post office won't have any trouble handling it. ✉

A Clean Design

The design should be simple, clean, and uncluttered. Don't try to cram too much into a limited space. If you have a lot of information, use a larger form (see Figure 11.1). A cluttered design turns readers off. And you don't want an order form that repels potential customers.

Figure 11.1. **Order Form Layout Example**

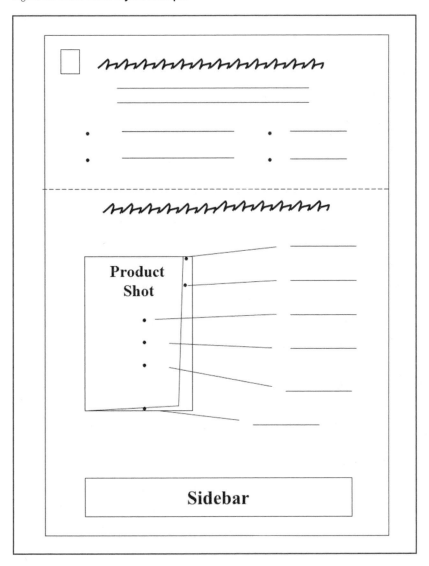

Enough Room to Fill Out the Form

This rule seems obvious, but I see it ignored in hundreds of mailings every year. I'm sure you've been frustrated by forms that ask for your full name and then give you a quarter-inch of space to write it or that force you to cram your address, apartment number, city, state, zip code, and phone number on a single line.

When designing your order form, give the reader plenty of room to write. A good test is to fill out your reply card or order blank yourself. Do you find yourself writing in tiny, cramped letters to make it all fit? If so, rework it to give your prospects more breathing room.

Fewer Steps

The less work the reader has to do to complete your order form and get it in the mail to you, the better. Remember, the more time it takes to fill out a form, the less likely people are to bother.

There are a number of things you can do to make it easier for them. A self-addressed, postage-paid business reply envelope (BRE) saves readers the trouble of addressing and stamping their own envelopes. A toll-free phone number and URL printed on the order blank gives people the option of phoning in their order or going online rather than mailing in the form.

If you're mailing to businesspeople, tell them they can attach their business card to the reply form, eliminating the need to fill in their name, company, address, and phone number. Better still, if you use an envelope with a transparent window, the mailing label can be affixed to the reply form (which shows through the window) rather than the outer envelope. Thus, the readers don't need to fill in their name and address on the reply card because you've already done it for them.

Headline Your Offer

The first sentence of the reply form should be a headline that restates the offer and rekindles the reader's desire to take advantage of it. Here are some examples:

Thomas Securities

YES, I would like to receive a complimentary information kit about
the Thomas Securities Investment Trust

Humane Society

YES! I want to help bring an end to this vile sport and stop
the suffering for thousands of loyal pets!

American Museum of Natural History

I accept your invitation to become an Associate Member of the
American Museum of Natural History at the low introductory rate. . . .

Entrepreneur Magazine

YES, enter my trial subscription to *Entrepreneur* as checked below.

GBC Binding Machines

YES, show me how SureBind will make
my Plastic Binding System even better . . .

Short Sales Pitch

In the most concise language possible, your reply form should restate the nature and terms of the offer and highlight the key benefits stressed in the letter and brochure. You want to summarize your whole sales pitch in a few sentences so the reader can get the essence of your story just by reading the reply form.

Although it's important to be concise, it's even more important to be complete. Don't leave out information the reader must have to make a proper response. For example, if your minimum order is $100, the form should specify that: "Minimum order—$100." Otherwise, you will have a lot of explaining to do to people who send you checks for $25 or $50 or $75.

No Risk, No Obligation, No Sales Calls

People who might otherwise send in an order or a request for more information are sometimes reluctant to do so because they think either you will somehow trick them into buying merchandise they didn't order or your salespeople will put pressure on them in person or over the phone.

Reply copy should reassure prospects that this isn't so. It should make the ordering process as painless, pressure-free, and nonthreatening as possible. If there is no obligation for requesting free information or a free gift, say so. If you offer a money-back guarantee, say so. If the customer has 30 days to return the merchandise for a full refund, say so. If no salesperson will call them, say so. These messages go a long way toward putting them at ease.

Of course, you shouldn't make these statements if they aren't true. If you do plan to call prospects, you can always say, "No salesperson will visit."

Make It Look Valuable

People are reluctant to throw away anything that looks valuable. The more important your order form looks, the more likely people will be to stop, examine, and use it. There are two ways to make your order form seem more valuable.

First, never call it an order form. The word *order* is a negative one because it implies spending money. Instead, give it a title that connotes value and, if possible, savings (if yours is a money-saving offer) or some other benefit. Here are some examples:

- If your reply form entitles the user to a discount, call it a CERTIFICATE OF SAVINGS.
- If the form opens an account or credit line, call it an ACCOUNT OPENER FORM.
- If it entitles the user to a money-back trial, call it a NO-RISK TRIAL REQUEST FORM.
- If it brings the reader a free gift, call it a FREE GIFT CHECK.
- If it brings the reader free information, such as a brochure or report, call it a FREE INFORMATION REQUEST FORM.
- If it is used to set up an appointment for a product demonstration, call it a FREE DEMONSTRATION RESERVATION FORM.
- If the prospect will receive a brochure, DVD, and order form, call it a FREE INFORMATION KIT FORM.

These are only suggestions. Be imaginative!

Second, design the form so that its appearance gives the impression of importance and value. A common technique is to put an ornate border around it similar to that of a stock certificate or other valuable document.

Use Visuals

If you are offering a free color brochure, illustrate your reply card with a picture of the brochure's front cover. If you are giving away a free gift, show a picture of the gift. Illustrations and photos catch the eye and enhance the form's appeal.

In cases where the reply form is small enough to fit on a postcard, you can use a postage-paid business reply card (BRC), eliminating the need for a separate reply envelope. The reader just fills in the back of the card and drops it in the mail.

However, if the reply form asks for confidential or sensitive information, it's best to include a reply envelope to ensure the prospect's privacy. For example, let's say you ask prospects to indicate their annual income on the reply form. Most people would not want the postal carrier or others to see this information. By mailing back the card in a sealed reply envelope, they can respond to your questions while maintaining their privacy.

QR CODE

A Quick Response (QR) code (shown in Figure 11.2 on page 202) is a smartphone-readable bar code that can store website URLs, plain text, phone numbers, email addresses, and most other alphanumeric data. In use since 2012, QR codes are a relatively new response mechanism that integrate print advertising with the digital world. When you scan the QR code with your phone, you are immediately taken to the landing page for the offer being made in the direct-mail piece, postcard, or ad. One-third of QR code scanners did so in response to a coupon or offer.

Storing up to 4,296 alphanumeric characters, QR codes are internationally standardized under ISO 18004, which means they work with smartphones all over the world. They can be coded so you know

Figure 11.2. **QR Code**

which of your customers used one to get to the landing page vs. those who just typed in the URL.

The QR code must be printed clearly in black ink on a white background. To scan it, you usually need the original mail piece. If you try to scan a fax or photocopy, it will usually not succeed.

In direct mail, the QR code is typically printed on the front or back of the outer envelope. This enables the recipient to respond without even opening up the package. It is again reprinted on one or more the elements inside the package, most often on the reply card or brochure.

Chapter 12

SELF-MAILERS

A *self-mailer* is a direct-mail piece that is not mailed in an envelope. Years ago, many old-school direct-mail pros believed that traditional envelope packages would always outperform self-mailers. Whether it was true then, it isn't now. Self-mailers are a popular and proven format in today's multichannel marketing world. Also, it depends on what you're marketing. For instance, self-mailers have consistently worked better than DM packages for selling seminars.

Simple, short self-mailers are less expensive to produce and mail than standard direct-mail packages. These mailers are made by folding a single sheet, so you have only one piece of paper to print.

However, other self-mailers, such as tabloids and digests, which we'll discuss in a minute, are made of multiple sheets of paper. Some are 12 to 16 pages or even longer and printed in full color. These can be quite expensive.

One of the biggest advantages of self-mailers is that, by definition, they are mailed as printed, without being stuffed and sealed in an envelope. Some people toss the direct mail they receive into the recycling without even opening the envelope, so they never see the contents at all.

With a self-mailer, the copy and graphics are visible on the front and back panels even when it has not been opened, which helps get the recipient's attention. Another advantage is that you can prominently display your call-to-action, including your URL and toll-free phone number, in big, bold type; people see it immediately without even opening the mailing

In addition, when the self-mailer is unfolded, you can use the bottom panel as a reply element. I have also gotten good results designing part of the other inside panels as a small sales letter.

SELF-MAILER FORMATS

There are many formats to choose from. Here are just a few of the most popular.

Single-Sheet Self-Mailers

As the name implies, these self-mailers are made by folding a single sheet of paper, which makes them the most economical self-mailer format. Here are the most common sizes:

- 11-by-17-inch sheet folded once to form four panels (shown in Figure 12.1 on page 205).
- 11-by-25-inch sheet folded twice to form six panels
- 8½-by-11-inch letter-size sheet folded twice to form six panels (shown in Figure 12.2 on page 206); this configuration is called a *trifold* or *slim jim*
- 8½-by-14-inch legal-size sheet folded three times to form eight panels
- Broadsides—an oversize sheet of paper printed in color on one or both sides and folded for mailing
- Faux newsletter—a four-page direct-mail piece designed to look like an informational newsletter

Figure 12.1. **Front Cover of Four-Page Self-Mailer**

"Learning how to write procedures and work instructions taught me about ISO 9000 and how powerful it really is."
—Operations analyst

"Handouts were specific examples of what to do and what not to do. The exercises made understanding the material easy and comfortable. Excellent."
—QA Engineer

"The specifics were great. The most frustrating part of ISO documentation is vagueness. Also, where does a company begin? You covered this very well."
—Technical Writer

A comprehensive 2-day seminar
WRITING FOR ISO 9000

How to write quality manuals, procedures, work instructions, and other documentation required for ISO 9000 certification

Led by Gary Blake and Robert W. Bly, co-authors of the best-selling writing books, *The Elements of Technical Writing* and *The Elements of Business Writing*.

Getting ISO certified can produce dramatic improvements in quality while giving your company a competitive edge in today's global marketplace. But getting ISO certified isn't easy.

When it comes to the quality, clarity, and context of your writing, ISO 9000 auditors hold your company to a strict standard.

Since 1982, Blake and Bly have helped more than 45,000 managers, engineers, and professionals nationwide improve their writing. Now your team members can learn how to write clear, concise, accurate documentation to ensure that your company gets ISO certified.

Program includes:

- The 4 key ingredients of successful ISO documentation
- How to organize and prepare ISO quality manuals
- Making your ISO 9000 documents "auditor friendly"
- The worst mistake you can make in writing quality documents
- Real-life examples of quality manuals, procedures, and work instructions
- How to edit and improve your company's documentation

Locations and dates:

- Fort Lee, NJ   *Days Inn*   October 26 - 27,
- Chicago, IL   *The Palmer House*   November 15 - 16,
- San Jose, CA   *Le Baron*   January 25 - 26,

"Writing for ISO 9000" is jointly sponsored by: THE CENTER FOR TECHNICAL COMMUNICATION

**THE
COMMUNICATION WORKSHOP**

Multipage Self-Mailers

Multipage self-mailers are made by stapling or gluing more than one sheet of paper to form the mailing. They include magalogs, digests, snap packs, tabloids, and catalogs:

Figure 12.2. **Slim Jim Self-Mailer**

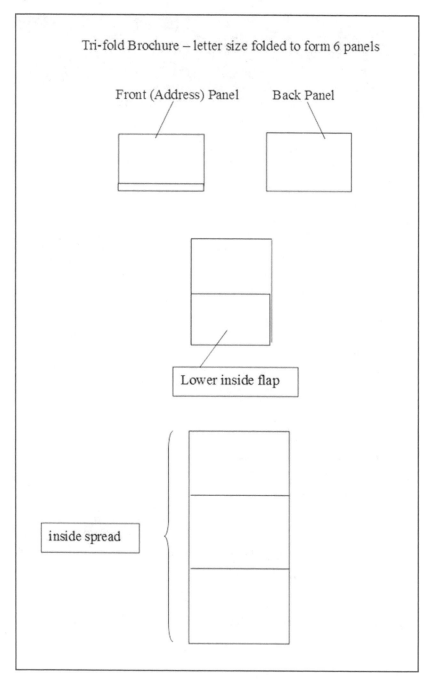

Tri-fold Brochure – letter size folded to form 6 panels

Front (Address) Panel   Back Panel

Lower inside flap

inside spread

☒ *Magalogs.* A direct-mail piece designed to look like a magazine, a magalog is typically 8 to 16 pages long with a 7-by-10-inch page size, the same as you find in magazines. The magalog is made by binding multiple 11-by-17-inch sheets. The sheets are saddle-stitched (stapled) through the spine and folded once vertically to form four pages per sheet. Magalogs are long-copy mailings used to sell mail-order products, including subscription newsletters and vitamin supplements. Figure 12.3 shows a rough layout for a typical

Figure 12.3. **Magalog Cover Layout**

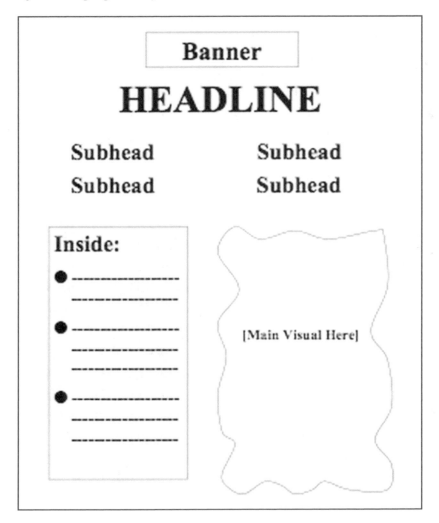

magalog front cover. Notice that there is a table of contents on this particular cover. Though this is optional, it can help entice readers to open the magalog and look inside.

- ⊠ *Digests.* Similar to magalogs, the pages in digests are half the size made by folding 8½-by-11-inch sheets of paper once vertically and saddle-stitching them.

- ⊠ *Snap packs.* Mailers that are made of multiple plies or pages and sealed at the edges and at the top are called snap packs. You have to tear off the perforated seals before you can open the pack and leaf through the pages.

- ⊠ *Tabloids.* These are similar to magalogs but larger with the pages approximately the same size as a newspaper.

- ⊠ *Catalogs.* Catalogs are a type of self-mailer in that they are usually mailed without an outer envelope. Some catalogs stand alone as a primary promotion from which products can be ordered via toll-free phone number or online: According to the USPS, supporting your website with a print catalog increases revenue an average of 163 percent compared to sites that are not augmented by a print catalog. And nearly one out of three online shoppers has a print catalog in hand when making an online purchase.

Quick Tips for Writing Catalog Copy That Sells

Before you approve your catalog copy and send it to the printer, be sure that it's *right*. Getting it right involves more than spelling and punctuation. Here's a handy checklist of questions to help you review your copy. As you put your prose to the test, look for ways to incorporate these "rules" into your personal writing style:

- ⊠ *Is your copy in the right order?* Is there a logical scheme to how you present the points about your merchandise? Have you been faithful to this organizational principle throughout? Is this the best way to organize the items in your catalog? Or would another method make more sense?

- ⊠ *Is it persuasive?* Does your copy begin with a strong selling message? Have you indicated your sales message on the catalog cover?

Do individual headlines promise solutions to reader problems and draw them into the product descriptions? Does the body copy stress user benefits as well as features such as available sizes and colors?

- *Is it complete?* If the catalog is designed to generate direct sales, does it include all the information the reader needs to make a buying decision? Have you described the products fully? Is it easy for the customer to specify and order the product?

- *Is it clear?* Is the copy understandable and easy to read?

- *Is it consistent?* Have you been consistent in your use of logos, trademarks, spellings, abbreviations, punctuation, grammar, capitalization, layouts, copy style, and visuals?

- *Is it accurate?* If you are selling electronics, motors, laboratory supplies, or other technical products, is the copy technically accurate? Has an engineer checked all numbers, specifications, and calculations to make sure they are correct? Have you carefully proofread tables, lists, and other fine print? Do the photos show the current models or versions of your product? Have you matched the right photo to each item description?

- *Is it interesting?* Is your catalog attractive, lively, and informative? Or is it boring? The typeface and the style of layout encourage (or discourage) the viewer's desire to read the copy. And let's face it, for some products, like swimwear or lingerie, pictures of attractive people wearing the merchandise help attract the eye.

- *Is it believable?* Is the copy sincere or full of hot air? Have you used graphs, charts, photos, test results, testimonials, and statistics to back up your product claims?

- *Have you included all necessary "boilerplate" copy?* This includes areas such as effective and expiration dates of prices, "how to order" info, notification of possible price changes, payment terms and methods, shipping and handling information, returns policy, quantity discounts, credit terms, sales tax, trademark information, copyright line, disclaimers, guarantees, warranties, and limits of vendor liability.

- *Is it easy to place an order?* Does your copy explain how to order? Is there an order form? Is it easy to fill out? Is there enough space to write in the required information? Is a business reply envelope enclosed or attached to the order form? Is the toll-free number prominent? Is your website URL in large type and printed on multiple pages?

EIGHT WAYS TO PRODUCE SELF-MAILERS THAT SELL

The following sections offer advice on producing self-mailers that really sell.

1. Use a Strong Headline on the Cover or Outer Panel

The headline on the outside panel is usually what decides whether the reader will open your self-mailer or throw it away. Make sure your headline delivers the most powerful selling proposition possible. The headline should be immediately clear and in no way confusing or vague. And it should give the reader a powerful reason to look inside either by stating a benefit or arousing curiosity. Check out the examples in Figure 12.4 on page 211.

2. Set the Headline on the Outer Panels in Large, Bold Type

Draw attention to your headline. Make it bold. A headline in large letters catches the eye of people who see your self-mailer on a table, desk, or the top of someone's inbox.

Also put the headline on both the front and back panel. This way the selling proposition is visible no matter which side is showing. You should also place a headline above the copy in the interior spread when the self-mailer is opened.

3. Break the Copy Up Into Short Sections on Different Panels of the Self-Mailer

The total length of the self-mailer can vary depending on product and offer. But each section of copy should be brief. Each block of copy should cover only one sales point or feature. When you want to discuss another point, insert a subhead and start a new section.

Figure 12.4. **Self-Mailer Headline Explanations**

Headline	Comment
HERE'S A SIMPLE BUT POWERFUL INVESTING TECHNIQUE THAT ANYONE CAN UNDERSTAND	Some people will believe it; others will be immediately skeptical. But don't you at least want to open the mailer to find out what the story is?
NEED CHEMICAL OR BIOCHEMICAL INFORMATION IN A HURRY? START YOUR SEARCH HERE ...	If I needed this type of information, I would read further.
STOP WATER DAMAGE IN YOUR BASEMENT *BEFORE IT'S TOO LATE!*	Fear is always a powerful motivator. Basement water damage is a concern for homeowners. And the phrase "before it's too late" adds a real sense of urgency.
RECEIVE VALUABLE FREE PRESENTATION TIPS WHEN YOU REQUEST INFORMATION ON ABC'S COMPLETE LINE OF PRODUCTS AND SERVICES. Offer expires December 31, 20XX	"Free" is still the most powerful weapon in the direct-mail copywriter's arsenal. More people respond to free offers than any other kind. Having an expiration date also helps boost response.
INSIDE! FIND WHAT COULD BE YOUR KEYS TO SUCCESS ...	Borders on too vague and general, but somehow manages to make a strong enough promise and arouse enough curiosity to get you to take a look inside.

4. Use Bullets, Boxes, and Other Graphics to Make the Copy Easy to Scan

Use subheads, bullets, borders, boxes, color tints, numbered points, and checklists to make your copy easy to scan. Don't bury key points in long-winded paragraphs. Experience shows most people only skim self-mailers; few read them thoroughly. The reader should be able to tell at a glance what you are selling and the key benefits of your offer.

5. Make Important Information Stand Out

Illustrate the self-mailer with visuals to identify the product or service. If you're selling computer training, show pictures of people sitting at computer terminals. If you're selling a lawn-care service, include photographs of lush, green lawns. The pictures are a visual device that help the reader instantly identify the nature of your offer and prepare them to listen to a sales pitch on the subject.

Don't forget to list the features of your product or service in a separate copy block. You don't need to elaborate on them—a simple listing of the facts in bullet form will suffice. This is especially important when selling books, seminars, or technical equipment. You never know which feature of your product or which chapter in your book will appeal to a particular reader. By including a comprehensive list, you know you have mentioned everything a potential buyer might be looking for.

Also include testimonials from satisfied customers. These can be grouped together or sprinkled throughout the margins of the self-mailer. I prefer to put them all in one section because I think it makes a greater impact.

6. Highlight the Offer

Unless your mailing is designed merely to build awareness or make an announcement, you should tell readers exactly what you want them to do and what will happen when they do it. Are you offering more information, a free product sample, or a free analysis or consultation? Make your offer clear and highlight it both in the closing paragraphs of your copy and again in the reply card.

Make bargains apparent. Highlight sale prices and discounts. Provide an incentive for immediate response, such as a cash discount or free gift. This discourages the readers from their natural inclination, which is to put the mailing aside and think about it later—something that seldom results in a sale for you.

Also emphasize free offers. If you are offering something free to people who respond, highlight that offer in a separate block of copy. Use a subhead that says, "Yours FREE" or "Special FREE offer." Show a picture of the item you are giving away.

SELF-MAILERS VS. ENVELOPE PACKAGES

Marketers continually argue over which is better, a self-mailer or a traditional direct-mail package enclosed in an envelope. In the 20th century, most top DM experts stated unequivocally that a package with a sales letter would always out pull a self-mailer. Their reasoning:

- The letter gave the mailing the feel of personal correspondence rather than advertising material.

- The envelope could be designed to look like important business, a personal note, or official mail.

- The full DM package could contain separate response mechanisms, most notably a reply card, form, and envelope.

- You could enclose 3-D objects including product samples.

However, in the 21st century, there is no hard-and-fast rule saying letter packages always outperform self-mailers because in many instances, the opposite is true.

In a few product categories, most notably in the promotion of public seminars, self-mailers almost always outperform traditional DM packages.

In other categories where full DM packages were once the standard, they are increasingly outperformed by self-mailers. Magazine subscriptions were traditionally marketed with a four-page sales letter in a #10 envelope. Those packages were beaten by double postcards (see Chapter 13).

We can no longer assume that the traditional direct-mail package is the default format for winning direct mail. Testing formats has become as important as testing offers, mailing lists, and sales copy.

7. Make It Easy to Respond

Use a toll-free telephone number and a URL. Highlight the phone number and URL on the reply element and throughout the body of the self-mailer. You might even consider putting it on the cover; this may prompt calls from "impulse buyers" who are too busy or impatient to read through your mailing.

Emphasize the reply element by using graphics that draw attention to it. For example, print a heavy dashed line along the border where the reply card is to be torn off or cut out. Show a little picture of a pair of scissors along the dashed border. Use a certificate border or other design element to make it look official and important. Give it a title that implies value, such as "FREE TRIAL RESERVATION CARD," "FREE INFORMATION REQUEST FORM," or "EXECUTIVE VIP INVITATION RESPONSE FORM." (See Chapter 11 for more information on designing a reply element.)

The point is to make the reply element leap off the page when the reader opens your mailing. Unlike regular direct-mail packages where the reply element is a separate piece, in most self-mailers it is attached to the main selling piece so you must take extra pains to make it stand out. A reply card that isn't begging to be clipped and mailed won't generate a lot of replies for you.

8. Highlight Your Guarantee

As with the reply element, make the guarantee stand out. Put a certificate-style border around it, use a different color, or have arrows or other graphics pointing to it.

State the guarantee so it is clear and easy to understand. For example: "This is our promise to you: If for any reason you are not pleased with the results of the treatment, simply notify us and we will re-treat your lawn at no extra cost. So you have nothing to lose and a better lawn to gain."

Chapter 13

POSTCARDS

For many products and offers, especially complicated ones, either a full direct-mail package or a self-mailer is needed to tell the story, present the facts, answer objections, and allow the consumer to place an order.

On a postcard the space for graphics, copy, and the reply mechanism is much more limited. Postcards work best under these conditions:

- The product is familiar to the reader or simple and easy to explain.
- The marketing objective is to generate a lead or inquiry rather than to generate orders accompanied by checks and credit card payments.
- The offer features a premium or other free item the prospect can send for, such as a demo disk, CD, catalog, or brochure.
- The primary response mechanism is a phone call via a toll-free 800 number or a URL for a landing page (see Chapter 14) that gives the prospect more detailed information on the product or offer.

Postcards get their message across at a glance. That's because the copy and graphics are immediately visible with no envelopes to open. Postcards stand out in the mail with a brief, to-the-point message. Even when someone is sorting incoming mail over the trash can, the postcard will get noticed and read—even if it's on its way to getting tossed.

ADVANTAGES OF POSTCARDS

Many marketers, especially small businesses on a budget, prefer using postcards for their direct-mail campaigns. Here are some of the advantages of using postcards in direct-mail marketing:

- *Postcards don't need to be opened.* The headline, copy, and graphics are all right there for the viewing unlike other marketing that comes in an envelope and requires the prospect to at least open it. This gives your marketing piece more opportunities to catch the prospect's attention before being tossed.
- *Postcards are short.* This appeals to readers or skimmers with a short attention span because they can get to the point quickly without wading through what they see as a bunch of unnecessary filler material.
- *Printing and postage costs are cheaper.* Traditional sales letters or direct-mail packages often cost twice as much as postcards if not more. So if you're working with a small budget, want to reach thousands of people you couldn't afford to mail to otherwise, or simply want to test the waters, postcards can be a cost-effective means of doing just that. Creative and printing costs for postcards are much less than for a full-blown direct-mail package because there are no envelopes, letters, brochures, buck slips, or other inserts.
- *Writing and designing postcards is easier and less costly.* If you choose to write your own copy and do your own design, postcards take a fraction of the time you'd invest in a typical direct-mail package. Alternatively, if you hire out the writing and design to a third party, you'll spend a bit more than doing

it yourself but still not nearly as much as you would with a full DM package.

- ✉ *Postcard mailings are simpler to produce than full DM packages.* There's no folding, bindery, insertion, or packaging. Postcards have only two sides to worry about—the front and the back.
- ✉ *Postcards work for many businesses.* Whether you're a retailer, an information marketer, a direct marketer, or any other type of vendor, postcards have worked for a wide variety of businesses.

POSTCARD COPY

This section offers some guidelines for writing effective postcard copy. Many of these are dictated by the limited space on a postcard as opposed to the almost unlimited space in a direct-mail package or the even more unlimited space on the web.

Keep It Short

You don't have much room on a 3½-by-5³/₈-inch or 4¼-by-6-inch postcard. Copy must be brief and to the point. Maximum length is approximately 100 to 150 words.

Don't use an overly verbose or descriptive style. Write in terse, almost clipped prose. Make sure each sentence gives the reader a new piece of information; you don't have room to repeat yourself. Avoid transitional phrases, warm-up paragraphs, and other stylistic habits that waste words. List key features or benefits with bullets.

Do a Copywriter's Rough

Sketch a rough layout showing how your copy should be positioned on the card. Figure 13.1 on page 218 shows an example of a copywriter's rough for a postcard.

Don't just write copy in ordinary paragraph format. Use headlines, subheads, captions, bullets, bursts, arrows, underlines, boldface type, and other graphic devices to highlight various components of your copy.

Figure 13.1. **Copywriter's Rough Layout for Postcard**

Make the Headline Pay Off Right Upfront

The promise of the headline should be fulfilled in the body copy—immediately. Your first few sentences should explain, elaborate on, and support the promise made in the headline.

Here's an example from a classic postcard selling a $69.95 book, *The Complete Portfolio of Tests for Hiring Office Personnel:*

HIRING THE WRONG PERSON
CAN BE A VERY EXPENSIVE MISTAKE!

Now you can avoid it with
The Complete Portfolio of Tests for Hiring Office Personnel.
Be sure the person you hire has the *right skills* for the job.

Stress Benefits

Highlight the benefits of what you are selling. For example, if you are selling a machine that folds paper into booklets, don't just say, "Stainless steel hopper, 10 inches wide." Add, "Makes up to 600 booklets per hour."

Postcards are inadequate for explaining complex products and concepts. If the reader needs a basic education in your product before they can make a buying decision, postcards may not work well for you. Of course, you can write a booklet or report presenting the background information and then offer it free through a postcard.

Tell the Prospect What to Do

Even though it may seem obvious, don't assume the reader knows what to do with your card. Include instructions on what to do next. Your copy should tell the reader, "For a free decorating guide, call toll-free 800-XXX-XXXX or visit www.XXX.com today." A card that doesn't ask for action is often just looked at and then thrown away.

DESIGN

Postcards today are colorful and illustrated with photos and drawings. Typically one larger photo, usually a shot of the product, draws the eye in and clearly shows what you are offering. Showing another object next to the product gives the reader an idea of its scale and size.

Because you need room for a headline, copy, and name-and-address block, the space for your visual is extremely limited: usually no more than 2½ inches wide by 1½ inches high.

Most postcards are illustrated with either a picture of the product or, if you are offering free information, a picture of the front cover of your free booklet, catalog, or brochure.

Take a look at some postcards. The quality of photo reproduction may not match a glossy magazine or annual report, but it's much sharper than a newspaper. So it pays to use high-quality photographs.

Detailed diagrams, charts, graphs, schematics, and other complex visuals often don't work well on postcards. The original must be reduced in size to fit the space, rendering fine detail unreadable.

If you are advertising a book and the author is well-known to people in the field, you might increase response by showing a photo of the author in addition to the cover of the book.

Although some advertisers are successful with all-copy postcards, I recommend you include a visual. A picture will catch the reader's eye as they rapidly flip through the day's mail.

Product photos already taken for PowerPoint® presentations, print ads, catalogs, or press releases can work well in postcards. Many advertisers routinely create postcard versions of all their product ads using the same visual plus an abbreviated version of the ad headline and copy.

As for size, nine times out of ten, bigger is better. If you can spring for the extra postage and printing costs, you're better off doing an oversized postcard. These generally measure 6 by 9 inches but can be as large as 6 by 11 inches.

What about color? The more the merrier, but it's not essential. Color postcards tend to pull better than black-and-white ones, but that doesn't mean black and white doesn't work.

If you are sending a postcard that is designed to look like an official mailing from the DMV, the state treasurer, IRS, or some other agency, black and white is the best choice and the layout should be as simple and no-nonsense as possible. Show the layout to your local postmaster before you print the card to make sure they find the design acceptable. If it looks too much like a real government notice, the SEC may give you a warning or even a penalty for deceptive marketing practices.

Where appropriate and applicable, pictures can be a huge asset. Whether it's a full-body picture of you, a headshot, a picture of the product, pictures of the people whose testimonials are featured, or some other image, pictures not only draw the eye in but also lend credibility to your offer.

Having said that, there are instances where you don't want to use a picture. Again, I reference the "official government notice" example where you want the piece to look like a government agency sent it. Check the layout of these "official" cards with your compliance officer, attorney, or postmaster to make sure you are not violating any laws.

After completing your layout, review the card for ease of scanning. Why? Because more than 30 percent of the U.S. population classifies themselves as "scanners," which means they won't be reading your copy word for word. This number surges even higher when reading online, newspapers, magazines, and direct mail.

So how do you check for this? By making sure you can understand all the important points of your message, the offer, and the call to action even if you only read the words and phrases printed in bold, italics, or some other identifying characteristic. Additional tricks for improving readability include the following:

- ⊠ Using bullets
- ⊠ More white space
- ⊠ Creating anchors for the reader's eyes by using pictures or bold subheads
- ⊠ Using screened boxes to highlight important points or testimonials
- ⊠ Yellow highlighting
- ⊠ Circling, underlining, or using arrows pointing to important information
- ⊠ Crossing out text: for example, ~~$19.95~~ $9.95
- ⊠ Simulated handwriting in the margin
- ⊠ Short photo captions

Headlines

Unlike an advertisement, which seeks to build image or awareness over an extended period of time, the postcard headline's main mission is to make the reader pause long enough to remove the card from the pile of mail, for immediate response. Here are some examples from postcards that worked:

Charles Schwab

UP TO 75% DISCOUNT ON COMMISSIONS WHEN YOU TRADE
WITH CHARLES SCHWAB . . .

Quill

HOW TO SAVE MONEY ON OFFICE SUPPLIES

Paper Shredders

HOW LONG MUST YOU KEEP IMPORTANT PAPERS?

Seton Identification Products

PROTECT YOUR COMPANY'S VALUABLE ASSETS

American Management Association

DEVELOP A WINNING BUSINESS PLAN WITH THIS
EASY-TO-FOLLOW GUIDE

***Esquire* Magazine**

Save 50% on ESQUIRE and get this important book—
A MAN'S BODY—FREE!

Art Poly Bags

16-CENT CUSTOM TOTE BAGS. FAST DELIVERY. LOW QUANTITIES.
For trade shows, meetings, promotion, retail—any occasion

Postcard Sizes

The USPS gives you a special discount rate for mailing postcards as first-class mail. To qualify, your postcard must be no more than $4^{1}/_{4}$ inches high by 6 inches long. For a slightly higher rate, you can mail first-class postcards as large as $6^{1}/_{8}$ inches high by $11^{1}/_{2}$ inches long.

Double Postcards

A double postcard (shown in Figure 13.2 on page 223) consists of two postcards printed from one sheet with a perforation between the two cards. One card is filled with advertising copy and graphics promoting

Figure 13.2. **Layout for a Double Postcard**

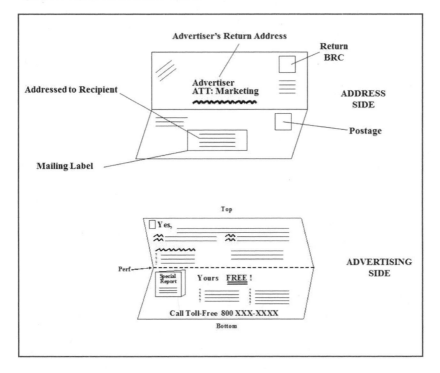

TEAR ON THE DOTTED LINE

Print a line of dashes where the double postcard is physically per-forated. A dashed or dotted line is a visual indicator that something should be torn off and will get more prospects to do so. Some graphic designers also put a small icon of a pair of open scissors left of the perforation as a graphic representation of "cut here." ✉

the product. The other is a business reply card the prospect can fill out, tear off, and drop in the mail to respond to the mailing. Once widely used, double postcards have fallen out of favor. Thanks to toll-free 800 numbers and online response forms, paying the extra cost for a double postcard is largely unnecessary and not the response booster it once was.

PART IV

INTEGRATING DIRECT MAIL AND DIGITAL MARKETING

SPECIAL OFFER INSIDE

A common mistake marketers make, which you can exploit to your advantage, is that many don't even consider including direct mail as part of a multi-channel campaign. This is to their detriment, because direct mail stands out and gets noticed in a digital-dominated world. Many people like going through their mail each day to see what awaits. Direct mail has a tactile element: You can hold it in your hands, tear open the envelope like wrapping paper, discover something new in every element in the package, and even order without going online if you want to. In addition, inserting one or two nondigital elements in a series of largely online promotions serves as a "pattern interruption." It's unexpected, which increases its attention-getting power. These final chapters look at the three elements needed to integrate direct mail with digital: landing pages, emails, and strategic integration of online with offline.

Chapter 14

LANDING PAGES

In most of the 20th century, the primary response mechanisms for direct mail were the phone and the mailed reply card. Faxing back an order form to the marketer was also common.

All these are still used today, but another option has been added: responding via the web. Yes, you can give your prospect an email address for them to reply to you. But the primary online response mechanism today is the landing page, and many marketers aggressively use direct mail to drive prospects to a landing page as they pass through the sales funnel (see Chapter 17).

HOW LANDING PAGES WORK

A *landing page* is a web page designed to either capture a prospect's name and email address, generate a lead, or make a direct sale.

It is *not* your homepage. The landing page is a separate, stand-alone web page with a unique URL. This URL allows your direct mail and other promotions to drive traffic directly to the landing page rather than to your homepage or another page on your main website. Landing pages are used as the online responses mechanism for most solo mailings offering a single product. The only ecommerce marketers to routinely send traffic to their home page instead of a landing page are catalog mailers.

The sole purpose of a landing page is to facilitate a call to action (CTA): for example, to get the visitor to opt into your email list, download your lead magnet, make an inquiry, request a cost estimate or conversation with you, or purchase a product. The landing page is strictly an online response form that enables prospects to respond to your CTA on the web.

For the landing page's URL, you have two options. The first is to make it an extension of the URL for your main website. For instance, my website's URL is www.bly.com. But I have a landing page where visitors can get four free special reports and a free subscription to my online newsletter at www.bly.com/reports. Because this is an extension of my main domain name, I don't pay anything extra for it.

BUY DOMAIN NAME MISSPELLINGS

Many people do not know how to spell, so they search for the wrong spelling and may not find your site or page. You should buy not only the correctly spelled domain name, but also common misspellings. For instance, let's say you sell a health product that clears up excess phlegm and mucus in your throat. You should reserve www.clearphlegmnow.com as well as www.clearflemnow .com, as "flem" is how many people tend to misspell "phlegm." When someone types in www.clearflemnow.com, they are automatically redirected to your page at www.clearphlegmnow.com instead. Similarly, if you sell stuffed monkeys and your main domain is www.stuffedmonkeys.com, also buy www.stuffedmonkies.com and www.stuffedmonkey.com. Domain names are cheap (typically around $10 per year), so the expense of buying these extra names is nominal. ✉

You can also register and use a separate domain name for your landing pages. For instance, for an audio course I have on building an opt-in email list, my domain is www.buildyourlistfast.net.

Whichever option you choose, the landing page is a separate page from your homepage. When the recipient types the URL on your direct-mail piece into their browser, they go to the landing page and nowhere else. Note that, unlike your homepage, the landing page does not link to the other pages on your site. When the prospect is on your landing page, the only thing they can do is respond or leave; there are no other choices. If you had a menu, the prospect would naturally start clicking to explore your other pages and content and be unlikely to return to the landing page. Conversion rates would plummet.

THE PRINCIPLE OF COPY CONNECTIVITY

The copy on the landing page, particularly the headline, must match the copy in your direct-mail promotion and any other marketing used to drive traffic to the page. For instance, say you have a standard landing page describing a product, and it lists the regular retail price—say, $50. Now you send out a postcard with the URL advertising a 50-percent-off sale, making the price $25.

But if the prospects go to the standard landing page, it will say nothing about a half-off sale, and when they click to order, the price will still be $50. The prospects will feel duped. The correct way to handle this is to create a URL with a new version of the landing page, and one that reflects the sale price in the mailing. For instance, if the regular landing page is at www.gymshoes.com, for the direct-mail promotion and sale, use the URL www.gymshoes.com/halfoff.

Then place a duplicate of the regular landing page at that URL but modify the copy and shopping cart to reflect the 50 percent discount. Make the special offer prominent in the headline and elsewhere on the page. Say in large, bold type: "Sale—50% off!" If there is a time limit on the special deal, make that prominent, too; for example, "This week only" or "Mother's Day one-day sale."

Yes, you could just make these changes on the regular landing page during the sale and change it back when the sale is over. But the custom

URL makes it easier to track orders generated by the direct-mail promotion vs. organic search and other sources.

ATTRIBUTION

Attribution is the term marketers use for being able to track the sources of all opt-ins, leads, and sales. In today's multichannel world, it is arguably more complex than in the pre-internet era.

For instance, a health blogger might get your mailing, write about the gym shoes, and include in their post a link to www.gymshoes.com/halfoff. In one sense, this gives the direct-mail promotion a viral marketing effect, getting orders from many people who never got the direct-mail piece. When you want to determine the exact response rate of the DM package, the viral marketing makes attribution more difficult.

Why does this matter? Well, let's say you do a test mailing and it goes viral in the way I just described, and the results are through the roof—say, 3 percent.

Based on this response, you then mail thousands more of the same package. Only this time, the health bloggers don't give you any more coverage.

Now, though the test mailing generated a profitable 3 percent response, you were unaware that most of it was viral. To your shock and dismay, the much larger rollout produces a dismal 0.5 percent response rate, and you lose a lot of money on the mailing. The reason is the difficulty of pinpointing proper attribution.

In direct mail, we use custom URLs, key codes on the order device, and extensions on the toll-free phone number to track response. But these days, attribution is not quite as precise as it once was.

LEAD MAGNETS

As discussed in Chapter 3, direct mail usually generates a higher response rate when the prospect gets some kind of free bonus for ordering or inquiring. For instance, a numismatic dealer selling an expensive gold coin might offer a free display case or a free booklet on the history of that particular coin or perhaps a guide to investing in gold through coins.

Any free gift given to the consumer in response to the mailing is called a *premium*. If the mailing is designed to generate leads rather than direct sales and the free gift is a special report, newsletter, booklet, or other content rather than merchandise, it is called a *lead magnet*.

Landing pages designed to capture prospect names and email addresses, or to otherwise generate an inquiry, almost always work better if a lead magnet (see Figure 3.3 on page 63) is prominently offered on the page.

Featuring lead magnets, blog posts, newsletters, white papers, special reports, and other information as offers in your direct mail and other promotions is called *content marketing*. So how well does content marketing work in a multichannel campaign with a direct-mail piece driving traffic to a landing page? Is it good, bad, or terrible?

ELECTRONIC VS. PHYSICAL LEAD MAGNETS

Marketers who grew up with the internet seem to prefer digital lead magnets: PDF special reports and white papers, ebooks, streaming video, and downloadable MP3 audio files. And there are good reasons to prefer electronic over physical lead magnet fulfillment: Electronic lead magnets can be almost instantly received by the prospect, and they cost the marketer virtually nothing to give away.

But for a variety of reasons, some marketers want to capture not only the prospect's email address but their physical address as well. For instance, if you operate a chain of auto-service centers, it helps to know how close your prospects are to your shops.

When you offer a physical lead magnet—such as a printed white paper, a bound book, a product sample, a DVD, or a free gift like a pen or keychain—the prospect must give you their postal address to get it. So getting the mailing address is one advantage of offering physical lead magnets. The other is that, in a digital world, paper and merchandise stand out more, have higher perceived value, get more attention, and are more likely to be filed, displayed, or otherwise kept on hand. ✉

DOWNLOADS VS. QUALIFIED LEADS

The positive side of offering a lead magnet on a landing page is that it almost always increases conversion rates, often significantly so.

The drawback is that it brings in unqualified leads: If you emphasize the lead magnet instead of the product or service you are selling, you risk getting a lot of unqualified responses from people who just like getting free information and are not serious prospects for what you are selling.

In the pre-internet era, marketers called these people "brochure collectors" because when attending trade shows, they took a brochure from every booth they passed. Some exhibitors gave away plastic bags imprinted with their company logo so these collectors could carry all their brochures.

But companies and marketers gradually realized that these brochure collectors would fill up the bag with every brochure they could take, put the bag in a corner or closet or file cabinet in their office, never even look at any of the brochures, and a few months later set out the entire bag for recycling. In other words, they were worthless leads.

There is a danger of meeting up with these brochure collectors in direct mail, too. But with a multichannel campaign involving direct mail driving recipients to a landing page, there is a way to avoid this problem. It can help you increase response rates while attracting not just brochure collectors but also qualified prospects for your product or service.

The first part of this lead-qualification process is to feature the product as the primary topic and offer in your direct-mail package. Use the direct-mail piece to sell the product and focus on that. Your primary offer is more information on the product or an opportunity to talk with a salesperson.

The lead magnet is your secondary offer. Often I place this in the P.S. of the letter. The lead magnet therefore is not the focus of the sales letter, but it serves as extra incentive to respond, especially for prospects who may be on the fence about calling, mailing, or visiting the landing page.

The second part of this lead-qualification process is the landing page. The next section discusses a type of landing page that gets high conversion rates while generating qualified leads.

CREATING A LEAD-QUALIFYING LANDING PAGE

Figure 14.1 is an example of a landing-page format I think I invented, but it's possible someone else came up with it first. At any rate, it is extremely effective; let me explain why and how it works. There are three aspects of my model you should note and adapt for your own landing pages.

First, the page is in two columns, not one. The reason for this is simple: If the page were a single column, you would have to scroll down to find

Figure 14.1. **Landing Page Offering a Lead Magnet**

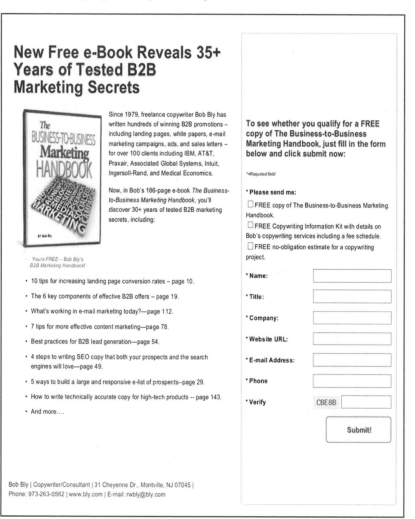

New Free e-Book Reveals 35+ Years of Tested B2B Marketing Secrets

Since 1979, freelance copywriter Bob Bly has written hundreds of winning B2B promotions – including landing pages, white papers, e-mail marketing campaigns, ads, and sales letters – for over 100 clients including IBM, AT&T, Praxair, Associated Global Systems, Intuit, Ingersoll-Rand, and Medical Economics.

Now, in Bob's 186-page e-book *The Business-to-Business Marketing Handbook*, you'll discover 30+ years of tested B2B marketing secrets, including:

Yours FREE – Bob Bly's B2B Marketing Handbook!

- 10 tips for increasing landing page conversion rates – page 10.
- The 6 key components of effective B2B offers – page 19.
- What's working in e-mail marketing today?—page 112.
- 7 tips for more effective content marketing—page 78.
- Best practices for B2B lead generation—page 54.
- 4 steps to writing SEO copy that both your prospects and the search engines will love—page 49.
- 5 ways to build a large and responsive e-list of prospects--page 29.
- How to write technically accurate copy for high-tech products -- page 143.
- And more....

To see whether you qualify for a FREE copy of The Business-to-Business Marketing Handbook, just fill in the form below and click submit now:

*Required field

* Please send me:

☐ FREE copy of The Business-to-Business Marketing Handbook.
☐ FREE Copywriting Information Kit with details on Bob's copywriting services including a fee schedule.
☐ FREE no-obligation estimate for a copywriting project.

* Name:

* Title:

* Company:

* Website URL:

* E-mail Address:

* Phone

* Verify   CBE8B

Submit!

Bob Bly | Copywriter/Consultant | 31 Cheyenne Dr., Montville, NJ 07045 |
Phone: 973-263-0562 | www.bly.com | E-mail: rwbly@bly.com

the submission form. Forcing the visitor to do that results in an abysmal conversion rate. By using a two-column layout with the response form in the right column, the visitor immediately sees the submission form at the top of the screen, which raises conversion rates significantly.

Note that the left column advertises not my services, but the lead magnet. I have created many pages in this format and often make the headline "New Free Report [on topic] gives you [benefits]." It's a proven formula, and in direct response, if something works, don't reinvent the wheel.

The submission form on the right qualifies the lead in two ways. One way is by making the fields requesting the information I need to determine whether a prospect is qualified mandatory; for example, email address, phone number, and company name. If you don't fill in those fields, you cannot submit the form. Even more important, I also require the prospect to specify what they want from me. There are three choices; they can select one, two, or all three:

1. *The first option is to request the lead magnet.* A visitor who does this is only mildly qualified at best. You could argue that the person wouldn't download it unless they were interested in direct marketing, my specialty and the subject of the ebook. But a large number of people like to download white papers even though they never read them. Why? Because it's human nature to want free stuff.

2. *The second option is to request information on my freelance copywriting services.* The person who checks this is somewhat more qualified. Yes, many are just curious, but others want this because they use copywriters, are looking for another copywriter, and want to know more about who I am, what I have done, and what I can do for them.

3. *The third option is to request a free estimate on a specific copywriting project.* These are the most qualified leads and convert better to paying clients than the other two options.

Most landing pages offering white papers or other lead magnets just require you to give some basic information, including name and email address. Some ask for more. But they do nothing to determine whether the visitor has any real interest in the marketer's product or service. These

---

SHOW A PICTURE OF THE LEAD MAGNET

Whether on your landing page or on the reply card in your direct-mail package, showing an image of the lead magnet or other giveaway typically increases response. Even if the lead magnet is a PDF, the more "real" it looks, the higher the response. Have your webmaster make a 3-D image of your report or white paper. Graphic-design techniques to make the object seem physical include a drop shadow (shading behind the cover) and showing it at an angle where it appears to have multiple pages. ✉

---

pages tend to generate loads of inquiries from freebie seekers but not much else.

In sharp contrast, the model landing page in Figure 14.1 does much more than give away free content; it also produces qualified leads that turn into customers. This is why I urge you to use it or some variation of it instead of the standard white paper download landing page.

LIST-BUILDING SQUEEZE PAGES

The primary objective of the landing page in Figure 14.1 is to generate sales leads, but not all landing pages have that objective. Other pages are designed simply to capture names and email addresses to build an opt-in email list. Such lists have great value for a couple of reasons. First, you "own" the name and can email the person as often as you like at very little cost and with no list-rental fee. Second, many people on your list become customers, which is why the expression among internet marketers is "the money is in the list." It's the same with paper direct mail: Your own list or "house file" will generate more revenue than any rental list.

To build an opt-in email list, you drive traffic to a *squeeze page*, also called a *name squeeze page*, which is a landing page optimized for list-building. You can see an example in Figure 14.2 on page 236. A few features go into its design:

Figure 14.2. **Free-on-Free Squeeze Page**

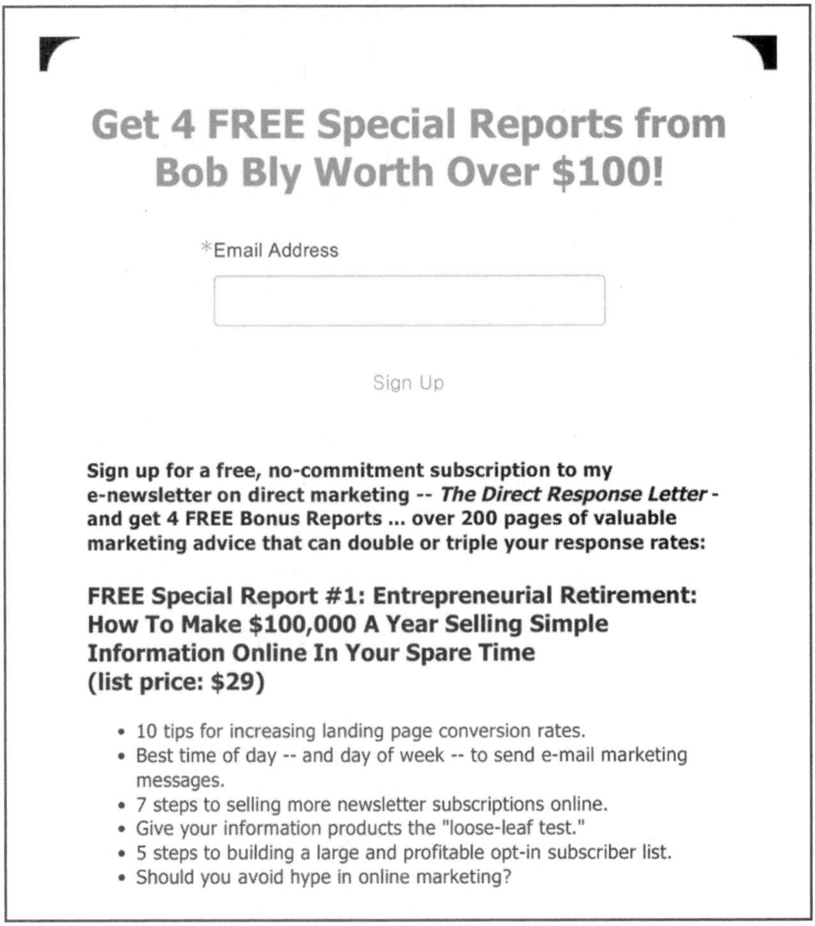

Get 4 FREE Special Reports from Bob Bly Worth Over $100!

*Email Address

[   ]

Sign Up

Sign up for a free, no-commitment subscription to my e-newsletter on direct marketing -- *The Direct Response Letter* - and get 4 FREE Bonus Reports ... over 200 pages of valuable marketing advice that can double or triple your response rates:

FREE Special Report #1: Entrepreneurial Retirement: How To Make $100,000 A Year Selling Simple Information Online In Your Spare Time (list price: $29)

- 10 tips for increasing landing page conversion rates.
- Best time of day -- and day of week -- to send e-mail marketing messages.
- 7 steps to selling more newsletter subscriptions online.
- Give your information products the "loose-leaf test."
- 5 steps to building a large and profitable opt-in subscriber list.
- Should you avoid hype in online marketing?

- The field for entering email and address is right up top. Again, if you force the user to scroll down to find them, your conversion rate will plummet.
- Registrants are signing up for a free online newsletter. This is ideal because it allows you to communicate with them regularly and, over time, build a relationship with them. They come to trust and like you, and people who trust and like you will buy from you.
- It is not enough just to offer a free online newsletter today because there are so many of them. My page offers a bribe—four free special reports when you subscribe. It may seem odd to have to offer a free

gift to get people to subscribe to a free enewsletter. But that's what it takes. We refer to pages that use this method as *free-on-free squeeze pages*.

The special reports I am offering sell on my site for $29 each. The reason I offer four here is that four times $29 is $116. This allows me to say the gift has a retail value of over $100. As soon as I did this, my conversion rate on the page more than doubled, jumping to 49 percent.

TEN TIPS FOR WRITING HIGH-CONVERSION LANDING PAGES

Once you have squeeze pages in place, you can focus more on sharpening up your content to create a higher conversion rate. Here are a few suggestions for increasing conversion rates on your landing pages:

1. Build Credibility Early

People have always been skeptical of advertising, and with the proliferation of spam and shady operators, they are even more skeptical of what they read online. Therefore, your landing-page copy must immediately overcome that skepticism.

One way to do that is to make sure you clearly display one or more *credibility builders* on the first screen the visitor sees. In the banner at the top of the page, use your logo and company name if you are well-known; the official seal of universities, associations, and other institutions (if that's what you are) can go in the upper left of the screen.

Within or immediately under the banner, put a strong testimonial or three above the headline on the first screen. Consider adding a pre-head or subhead that summarizes your company's mission statement or credentials.

2. Capture the Email Addresses of Nonbuyers

There are a number of mechanisms available for capturing the email addresses of visitors who come to your landing page but don't buy the product. One is to use a window offering a free report or online course in exchange for their email address. This window can be served to the visitor as a *pop-up* (it appears when the visitor arrives at the landing page) or a *pop-under* (a window that appears when the visitor attempts to leave the landing page without making an inquiry or purchase).

The problem with pop-ups and pop-unders is that if the user has a pop-up blocker installed on their browser, they won't ever see them. The solution is to use a *floater*—a window that slides onto the screen from the side or top. Unlike the pop-up and pop-under, the floater is part of the website HTML code, so it is not stopped by the pop-up blocker.

3. Use Lots of Testimonials

Testimonials build credibility and overcome skepticism, as do case studies and white papers posted on the website. If you invite customers to a live event, ask if they would be willing to give you a brief testimonial on video. Have a professional videographer tape it, get a signed release from the customer, and post the testimonial on your landing page as streaming video. The visitor must click a button to play the video testimonial.

For written testimonials, customers may suggest that you write what you want them to say and just run it by them for approval. Politely ask that they give you their opinion of your product in their own words. What they come up with will likely be more specific, believable, and detailed than your version, which might smack of puffery and promotion.

4. Use Lots of Bullets

Highlight key features and benefits in a list of short, easy-to-read bulleted items. I often use a format where the first part of the bullet is the feature and after a dash comes the benefit: for example, "**Quick-release adhesive system**—your graphics stay clean and don't stick together." Online buyers like to think they are getting a lot for their money, so when you are selling a product directly from your landing page, be sure you cover all major features and important benefits in a comprehensive bullet list on the page.

When generating leads by giving away white papers, you don't need a huge bulleted list of features and benefits. But using bullets to describe the contents of the paper and the benefits that information delivers can raise conversion rates for download requests.

5. Arouse Curiosity in the Headline

The headline should either arouse curiosity, make a powerful promise, or otherwise grab the reader's attention so they have no choice but to keep reading. The headline for a landing page selling a training program on how to become a professional property locator made a big promise: "Become a Property Locator Today—and Make $100,000 a Year in the Greatest Real Estate Career That Only a Few Insiders Know About."

6. Use a Conversational Copy Style

Most corporate websites are unemotional and sterile, offering just "information." But a landing page is a letter from one human being to another. Make it sound that way. Even if your product is highly technical and you are selling it to techies, remember that they are still human beings, and you cannot sell something by boring people to death.

7. Incorporate an Emotional Hook in the Lead Paragraph and Headline

Logical selling can work, but tapping into the prospect's emotions is much stronger, especially when you correctly assess how the prospect feels about your product or the problem he needs solved.

Another effective tactic for lead-generation landing pages is to stress your free offer in the headline and lead. Kaydon's landing page showed a picture of its catalog with the bold heading above it reading, "FREE Ceramic Bearings Product Selection Guide."

8. Solve the Reader's Problem

Once you hook the reader with emotional copy dramatizing their problem or a powerful free offer, show how your product—or your free information—can help solve that problem. For example: "Now there is a better, easier, and more effective solution to wobbly restaurant tables that can irritate customers and ruin their dining experience: Table Shox, the world's smallest shock absorber."

To maximize landing-page conversion rates, you have to convince the visitor that the quickest route to solving their problem is taking the action indicated on the landing page, and not—as you might be tempted to let them do—exploring the rest of your site. That's why I prefer that landing pages have no navigation—so the reader's only choice is to respond or not; there's no menu of links to other interesting pages to distract them.

9. Make It Timely and Current

The more your online copy ties in with current events and news, the higher your response rates will be. This is especially critical when selling financial and investment information as well as regulatory compliance products in fields where laws and rules change frequently. Periodically update your landing-page copy to reflect current business and economic conditions, challenges, and trends. This shows that your company is on top of what's happening in your industry.

10. Stress the Money-Back Guarantee or Lack of User Commitment

If you allow customers to order products directly from the landing page, make sure you clearly state a money-back guarantee on that page. All your competitors give strong money-back guarantees, so you must do the same. If your product is good and your copy accurate, your refund rates can be as low as 1 percent or less.

If you are generating leads, stress that your offer—whether a white paper, online demonstration, or webinar—is free. Say there is no obligation to buy and no salesperson will visit.

A WORD ON COPY LENGTH

Here is a practical guide to proper copy length on landing pages. For lead generation and free offers, such as a download of a free white paper, short copy usually works best.

For a landing page that seeks to generate an order and payment with PayPal or a credit card, the length can vary from medium to long depending on how much copy is required to adequately explain and sell the product.

Chapter 15

CONTENT MARKETING

The term *content marketing* appears to have been coined by John F. Oppedahl in 1996 at a roundtable for journalists held at the American Society of Newspaper Editors. That would mean it's about 20 years old. But in fact, content marketing has been used far longer than that. It's only the name that is of recent vintage, not the method.

For instance, I did my first content-marketing campaign in 1980. At the time, I was advertising manager of Koch Engineering, an industrial-manufacturing company owned and run by David Koch, who then was relatively unknown but today is a household name for his extreme libertarian views and being half of the infamous "billionaire Koch brothers."

Among the products we sold were various "tower internals," and one type of internal was the "tray": circular metal discs with capped openings on their surfaces. The trays are placed inside refinery towers to enhance the distillation of crude oil into kerosene, gasoline, heating oil, jet fuel, and other products.

SPECIAL OFFER INSIDE

Specifying the correct configuration of trays for a particular refinery is a highly technical task, and the engineers who were our customers needed help. We produced a technical guide, which we dubbed the "tray manual." It cost us several dollars per copy to print and bind. The manual had stiff covers, spiral binding, and fold-out blueprint-style drawings showing the configurations of various trays.

The tray manual was wildly popular—by far our most requested piece of literature. But back then, we didn't call it content marketing. We called it "giving away free information." The practice was the same; we just didn't have a name for it.

Back in those days, this content was simply called "free booklets." In the late 20th century, marketers referred to them as *bait pieces* because they helped "hook" prospects and turn them into leads.

Today the preferred term for free content is *lead magnet*, the idea being that the offer of valuable free information is like a magnet that draws people into your ad and gets them to respond.

There are all sorts of published opinions and tests on the effectiveness of content marketing. But let me sum up my experience in three simple points:

1. I can't remember the last time I did a B2B or B2C marketing campaign without a free content offer.
2. For B2B, the lead magnet is often the primary offer that drives prospects to respond. For B2C, it is often a bonus report given as an added gift with purchase of the product.
3. On average, adding the offer of a lead magnet to a B2B lead-generation campaign will double the number of inquiries (or more) over the same campaign without the free-content offer.

In the "good old days" of B2B marketing, our primary offer was a "free color brochure" filled with sales copy about the product. It worked then. But today prospects respond better if you promise to send them free information that will be useful to them in their job.

WHY CONTENT MARKETING WORKS SO WELL

Content marketing performs six functions that help marketers generate more leads and ultimately close more sales:

1. *Sets the specs.* Say you sell motionless mixers, another product I helped market at Koch Engineering. You offer in your ads a booklet, "7 Things to Look for When Specifying Motionless Mixers." Prospects read it and use your criteria when looking to purchase motionless mixers. And whose motionless mixer fits all seven criteria perfectly? Yours.

2. *Makes the prospect beholden.* This is the principle of reciprocity as described by marketing professor Robert Cialdini in his book *Influence: The Psychology of Persuasion* (Harper Business, 2006). When you give somebody something, they feel obligated to give you something in return. Giving a prospect free content does not make them feel obligated to buy your product. But it does make them more inclined to give you a little more of their time and attention than they otherwise might.

3. *Generates more inquiries.* As noted, a lead-generating promotion with a free content offer on average pulls double or more the response as the same campaign without the free offer.

4. *Establishes you as the expert.* Publishing content on your industry, niche, or area of specialization helps position you as a recognized authority in your field. And prospects would rather buy from knowledgeable experts than ordinary salespeople.

5. *Educates the market.* One marketer of content management software (CMS) was a pioneer in that they were the first to integrate the CMS with analytics, ecommerce, and other applications. But the market did not understand the benefits, so the marketer published a white paper explaining it with good results.

6. *Drives sales.* Content can be strategically disseminated at various steps in the buying cycle, accelerating each step and ultimately producing more sales.

But for your content to achieve these important objectives, you first have to get prospects to request and then read your lead magnet. And that's largely determined by the headline on the front cover.

CREATE A GREAT TITLE FOR YOUR LEAD MAGNET

Perhaps the biggest factor determining whether prospects will request your free content is the title. The title of a lead magnet is like the headline of an ad

Figure 15.1. **Lead Magnet Titles**

Type of Title	Example
List	"The Top 7 Security Problems of 802.11 Wireless Networks"
Active Verb ("ing")	"Managing Large UNIX Data Centers"
Why	"Why Six Sigma Doesn't Work"
Colon	"Defending the Remote Office: Which VPN Technology Is Best?"
How to	"How to Prevent Machine Parts From Failing Prematurely"
Dramatic	"The Death of Passwords"

or the subject line of an email. In fact, it often *is* the headline or the subject line. The purpose is the same: to grab the prospect's attention, generate interest and curiosity, and compel them to request the lead magnet.

There are a number of common title conventions for content, including "why" and "how to" titles. More are listed and examples given in Figure 15.1.

The cover of the lead magnet should have the title in large type. This way, when the cover image is reduced to fit in an HTML email or landing page, the title is still easily readable. For the same reason, the best cover is black type on a white background. Avoid color schemes like dark blue type on a black background, which make the title almost impossible to read.

CREATING YOUR CONTENT MARKETING PLAN

If you asked me to name the two biggest trends in marketing today, I'd have to say social media and content marketing. And social media seems to work best when it's based on content.

In a survey by *Target Marketing*, 71 percent of subscribers said content marketing complements and works in tandem with traditional marketing communications, and 12 percent stated that content is replacing traditional marketing as the primary selling tool. Only 15 percent of marketers said they don't really do content marketing. None of those surveyed agreed with the statement that content is a waste of time. Joe Pulizzi, founder of the Content Marketing Institute, says that the average business marketer spends 30 percent of their marketing budget on the creation and execution of content.

But content marketing isn't just publishing information. There's way too much information available today. Your prospects are drowning in it. But they are starved for *knowledge*: ideas on how to solve problems and methods for doing their jobs better.

In addition, you're not in business to publish and give away content; you're in business to sell your products and services. Unless publishing content helps you achieve that, it's a waste of your time and money.

The rest of this section discusses seven guidelines that can help make your content marketing plan more productive and effective so you can, in turn, seamlessly integrate your direct-mail program into it.

1. Narrow the Topic

There is no benefit to cramming every bit of information about a subject into your white paper or other content-marketing piece; the prospect can get all the same data using Google.

Content marketing works best when you narrow the topic. The narrower the topic, the more in-depth and useful your content can be. For instance, let's say you are an industrial-gas manufacturer creating a ten-page white paper on safety for plant managers. If the title is "Plant Safety," you cannot hope to cover that topic in even the most superficial way; entire books have been written on that subject.

On the other hand, you could produce a very useful white paper called "Safety Tips for Handling Compressed Gas Cylinders." It's a topic plant personnel want and need to know more about. And with your vast experience, you can probably offer some tips and methods that are new to the reader.

2. Target the Prospect

The more narrowly you target the audience for your white paper or other content-marketing piece, the better able you are to deliver content that is truly useful to them.

For our example of the white paper on tips for handling compressed cylinder gas, are you targeting plant managers or plant operators? Plant managers might be more interested in cylinder inventory and control, while plant operators want nuts-and-bolts tips for handling the cylinders. A CFO would want to look at reducing costly cylinder accidents, while the CEO might be concerned about liability. And what about the truck drivers who deliver the cylinders from the plant to the customers? What are their concerns?

3. Determine the Objective

Remember, we don't give away free information for fun. There has to be a purpose for the content we are spending time and money to produce.

For instance, a software publisher found that when they lost sales, it wasn't because prospects were buying a competitor's products with better features and benefits. It was because software in that category is expensive, and prospects, even though they wanted the functionality the software delivers, couldn't cost-justify its purchase.

To solve this problem, the marketer published a white paper titled "Calculating Return on Investment for Purchase of XYZ Software." It demonstrated that, even though the software was expensive, the time and labor savings it provided could pay back its cost in six to eight months. Salespeople used the paper to overcome the pricing objection.

4. Educate the Reader

Many years ago, Duncan Hines ran an ad in women's magazines about its chocolate cake mix. The headline was "The secret to moister, richer chocolate cake." Why was that headline so effective? Because it implied you would learn something useful just by reading the ad regardless of whether you bought the product. It sounded like a promise: Read this ad and learn how to bake a chocolate cake. But when you read the ad, the answer was to buy Duncan Hines chocolate cake mix; no other recipe was given.

That won't cut it in content marketing today. The prospect does not want to read the same old tips he's seen a dozen times before in your white paper. Chances are you possess proprietary knowledge about your product and its applications. Share some of this knowledge in your white paper. Give your reader specific advice and ideas they haven't already heard from everyone else.

Don't be afraid that by telling too much you'll eliminate the prospect's need for your product or service. It's quite the opposite: When they learn how much effort solving their problem entails and see that you clearly have the necessary expertise, they will turn to you for help.

5. Deliver Value

When you can, include some highly practical, actionable tips the prospect can implement immediately. The more valuable your content is to prospects, the more readily your content-marketing program will achieve its objective. It's like fast-food stands giving away free samples: The better the free food tastes, the more likely the consumer is to buy a snack or a meal.

6. Set the Specs

Outline the characteristics, features, and specifications the prospect should look for when shopping for products in your category. If you do this credibly, the prospect will turn your white paper into a shopping list. And of course, the requirements you outline fit your product to a T. For example, if your white paper is about ten things to look for when buying a shredder, your paper shredder naturally will have all ten characteristics while the competition's model won't.

7. Generate Action or Change Beliefs

Content marketing succeeds when it gets prospects to act or changes their opinions, attitudes, or beliefs about you and your product as it relates to their needs.

When writing white papers, I always ask my client, "What do you want to happen after the prospect is finished reading our white paper?" I often end the white paper with a final section titled "The next step" that tells the reader what to do and how to do it.

COPING WITH "CONTENT POLLUTION"

Futurist John Naisbitt in his book *Megatrends* (Warner Books, 1984) famously said, "We are drowning in information but starved for knowledge."

The web overwhelms us with more data than we could absorb in a hundred lifetimes. So in one sense, we are choking in an endless cloud of "content pollution."

But true knowledge, wisdom, actionable ideas, and proven solutions are desperately needed and still in short supply. Readers, including your prospects, are constantly searching for strategies that can help them overcome obstacles, achieve their goals, and gain a competitive edge. When your content delivers that kind of superior value, it will always be welcome and will always get you the sales results you want.

Chapter 16

EMAIL

When email became a dominant medium for business and personal communication, many marketers saw it as an alternative to or replacement for direct mail. After all, email cost less, was quick and easy to send, and got high response rates.

But the popularity and effectiveness of marketing tactics are cyclical. And as we discussed in the introduction, direct mail is having a resurgence while email response rates are declining.

In an integrated multichannel campaign, we use email *in addition to* direct mail and other touch points, rather than as a replacement for them. Email's low cost reduces the total campaign expense, and varying between paper and digital seems to boost response to the series as a whole.

SIMILARITIES AND DIFFERENCES OF POSTAL MAIL AND EMAIL

In one sense, postal sales letters and text emails are cousins. They both look like letters and are written in letter style. But there are a few significant differences you should be aware of:

- ✉ Email copy works best when it is shorter—anywhere from 100 to 400 words. (Of course, there are exceptions.) Postal letters, on the other hand, can go on for many pages.

- ✉ The response device for postal direct mail is a paper reply element, which naturally has limited space for copy and graphics. By comparison, the response device for email is often a landing page with almost unlimited space; you can therefore include much more detail on the page than in the short email that drove traffic to it.

- ✉ Increasingly, the offer and response mechanism are appearing at the beginning as well as the end of emails and direct-mail letters, though this is still more prevalent in email.

- ✉ Email should only be sent to prospects who have opted in to a list and therefore have agreed to receive it. Postal mail can be sent to anyone whose address you possess.

- ✉ Both work well when the writing style is informative, breezy, and conversational.

CREATING AN INTEGRATED CAMPAIGN WITH BOTH SNAIL MAIL AND EMAIL

In multichannel marketing campaigns, marketers can integrate all of the following: an envelope direct-mail package, self-mailers, postcards, emails, phone calls, blog posts, social media, print and online ads, and text messages. It may take a lot of testing to develop the optimal messaging, sequence, and media list. But the advantage is that multichannel campaigns have multiple touch points as opposed to solo direct-mail packages that have only one, and the repetition and frequency of the former can boost your results.

The Classic Three-Part Series: Postcard, DM Package, Email

The simplest multichannel campaign has three elements in this order:

1. A postcard telling the prospect to watch out for a coming direct-mail announcement of interest

2. The full direct-mail package giving the details and asking for the order

3. A follow-up email to capture interest from prospects who didn't respond to the first two efforts

Sometimes the sequence is reversed with the email first, then the DM package, and finally the postcard.

Autoresponders

An *autoresponder* is a piece of software or a service that automatically sends prewritten email messages to a select list of prospects or customers, either in response to an action taken by the prospect or at a predetermined, preset date or interval. Popular autoresponder services include AWeber and 1ShoppingCart.

For example, say you get a postcard offering you a free white paper, which you can download from a landing page at a URL given on the card. You download the paper and a few minutes later get an email from the company saying they noticed you requested their white paper on X, and now they would love to talk to you about the X services their company offers.

These automated emails are called autoresponders because they automatically respond to a given action (e.g., downloading a lead magnet or submitting an online response form), data (the anniversary of your car purchase from the auto dealership), or "triggered event" (completing a survey or downloading a coupon).

Logistically, autoresponders can be a great boon since they can handle requests that come in while you attend to other business (or sleep). You prewrite the autoresponder emails and then set a schedule for sequence and frequency of delivery. This automated inquiry fulfillment to your direct mail assures timely follow-up. Best of all, you make multiple contacts rather than the single contact of the original direct-mail piece.

While setting up your autoresponder is not rocket science, it will involve a time commitment: a week or so to become relatively fluent in the process, and some months to write all your autoresponder email series, which will vary with the product and offer.

Today I use autoresponders to follow up with direct mail–generated inquiries, build my mailing list, disseminate my newsletter, and in general to keep in touch with clients and prospects. Direct-mail results can be greatly enhanced by launching and sustaining follow-up autoresponder email campaigns over time. You decide the ultimate purpose of your campaign and set the parameters.

Let's take the example of a company that sells different types of flours and baking ingredients. The winter holiday season is a great time to sell those products. One campaign might send out recipes for Christmas cookies. I start to get these right after Halloween. They might begin with an email a week, but by the time the holidays draw closer, I could be receiving a recipe a day. These emails always feature links to buy a product used in the recipe, such as specialty molds or unusual ingredients like hard-to-find chestnut flour (a favorite in Italian Christmas cookies).

The owners of this company know we are apt to splurge during Christmas and New Year's. Often, I receive multiple emails for different holiday campaigns. For example, the New Year's campaign might overlap the Christmas campaign. They succeed because of the carefully timed delivery of interesting, helpful information and inherent follow-up.

26 TIPS FOR WRITING MORE EFFECTIVE EMAILS

Email generates open rates from 5 to 25 percent or more, with clickthrough rates of 2 percent to above 10 percent, although some do better and a few do worse. The copy in your message plays a big role in whether your email ends up at the bottom or the top of that range. Here are 26 proven techniques for maximizing the number of email recipients who click through to your website or other response mechanism:

1. At the beginning of the email are the "from" line and the "subject" line. The subject line should be constructed like a short, attention-grabbing, curiosity-arousing outer-envelope teaser, compelling recipients to read further—without being so blatantly promotional that it turns them off. For example: "Come on back to Idea Forum!"

2. The from line identifies you as the sender if you're emailing to your house file. If you're emailing to a rented list, the from line might identify the list owner as the sender. This is especially

effective with opt-in lists where the list owner (such as a website) has a good relationship with its users.

3. Some marketers think the from line is unimportant; others think it's critical. Internet copywriter Ivan Levison once told me, "I often use the word 'Team' in the from line. It makes it sound as if there's a group of bright, energetic, enthusiastic people standing behind the product." For instance, if you are in the marketing department at Microsoft and are sending an email to a rented list of computer people to promote a new software product, your from and subject lines might read: "FROM: The Microsoft Team / SUBJECT: Microsoft Access limited-time offer!"

4. Despite the fact that *free* is a proven, powerful response-booster in traditional direct marketing and internet culture is biased toward free offers, some marketers avoid FREE in the subject line. The reason is the spam filter software most ISPs and some individual internet users have installed to screen their email. These filters eliminate incoming email classified as junk mail, and many identify any message with FREE in the subject line as promotional. Despite that, FREE often works. But I wanted you to be forewarned.

5. Lead off the message copy with a killer headline or lead sentence. You need to get a terrific benefit upfront. Pretend you're writing envelope teaser copy or a headline for a sales letter.

6. In the first paragraph, deliver a brief version of your complete message. State the offer and provide an immediate response mechanism, such as clicking on a link to a web page. This appeals to prospects with short attention spans.

7. After the first paragraph, present expanded copy that covers the features, benefits, proof, and other information the buyer needs to make a decision. This appeals to prospects who need more details than a short paragraph can provide.

8. The offer and response mechanism should be repeated in the close of the email as in a traditional direct-mail letter. But they should almost always appear at the very beginning, too. That way, busy users who give each email only a second or two get the gist of the story.

9. If you put multiple response links within your email message, the vast majority of clickthrough responses will come from the first two links. Therefore, you should probably limit the number of response links in your email to three. An exception might be an enewsletter or ezine broken into five or six short items, where each item is on a different subject and therefore has its own link.

10. Use wide margins. You don't want to have weird wraps or breaks. Limit yourself to about 55 to 60 characters per line. If you think a line is going to be too long, insert a character return. Set your margins at 20 and 80, keeping sentence length to 60 characters and ensuring the whole line gets displayed on the screen without odd text breaks.

11. Take it easy on the all caps. You can use some WORDS IN ALL CAPS, but do so sparingly. They can be a little hard to read—and online, all caps give the impression that you're shouting.

12. In general, short is better. This is not the case in classic mail order selling, where the general rule is, "the more you tell, the more you sell." Email is a unique environment. Readers are quickly sorting through a bunch of messages and aren't disposed to stick with you for a long time.

13. Regardless of length, get your important points across quickly. If you want to give a lot of product information, add it lower down in your email. You might also consider a hyperlink to a page where people can find more information.

14. The tone should be helpful, friendly, informative, and educational, not promotional or a hard-sell. "Information is the gold in cyberspace," says online marketing expert Joe Vitale. Trying to sell readers with a traditional, hyped-up sales letter won't work. People online want information and lots of it. You'll have to add solid material to your puffed-up sales letter to make it work online. Refrain from saying your service is "the best" or that you offer "quality." Those are empty, meaningless phrases. Be specific. How are you the best? What exactly do you mean by quality? Who says it besides you? And even though information is gold, readers

don't want to be bored. They seek, like the rest of us, excitement. Give it to them.

15. Including an opt-out statement prevents flaming from recipients who feel they have been spammed. State that your intention is to respect their privacy, and make it easy for them to prevent further emails from being sent to them. Just have an unsubscribe button at the bottom of your email. When the recipient clicks it, they are taken to a page where they can quickly unsubscribe.

16. Short statements should tease the reader or arouse their curiosity. Ideally, these make you want to know more. For example, "Advice from Bill Gates" is better than "Bill Gates on innovation." Many people want free advice from a billionaire, but few want a sermon or lecture.

17. As with printed direct mail, offers that contain a bargain of some sort—a discount, free gift, free shipping and handling, BOGO (buy one, get one free)—are extremely effective in email marketing.

18. Free money is a powerful offer, and given the dynamics of online buying and the lifetime value of an internet customer, it can often be profitable. One marketer told potential registrants that one of the people who signed up on their website during a specified period would win $500 in cash. A major national emarketer offered an incredible $10 million drawing once a year as well as regular drawings with smaller cash prizes.

19. When you have a strong offer, put it in the subject line and the lead of your email. Don't bury it midway in the text.

20. Don't make the offer exclusive to the recipient as is sometimes done in traditional direct mail. Encourage the recipient to forward the email—and the offer—to friends and colleagues. For example: "Give this special gift offer to your friends by forwarding them this email now. They'll be glad you did!" This tactic is known as *viral marketing*.

21. People on opt-in email lists overwhelmingly prefer to respond to email online rather than by calling a toll-free number or printing

THE DIRECT MAIL REVOLUTION

out a reply form that has to be faxed or mailed. That doesn't mean you shouldn't offer those other response options as well. But you should always have a link to a response website in your email. For example, one marketer decided to offer an upgraded version of their software only on CD-ROM with no option to download it from their website. When they sent out an email with this offer, many recipients went to the website and downloaded the old, outdated version. That's how strong their preference was to conduct the entire transaction online.

22. Most people think of an email marketing campaign as having only one part: the email. But it actually has two parts: the email the prospect receives and the web-based response form they go to when they click on the link in the message. The headline and copy at the top of the response page should reflect the theme of the email and motivate the reader to complete and submit the form.

23. Long copy often works best in certain segments of the direct-marketing industry, particularly when marketing newsletters, magazines, and other information products. But for most online offers, short copy works best in emails.

24. One marketing manager observed, "People don't always hate email, but they are often bored, indifferent, or annoyed by it." One way to overcome this is through personalization: adding customized information based on the prospect's buying habits, preferences, web browsing, or other data. For example, some retail sites suggest merchandise for you based on things you have ordered in the past.

25. When emailing to your house file, the ideal frequency seems to be twice a month. Make one of these emails an informative ezine (a short newsletter); the other can be a special offer or promotion. Space them two weeks apart. Ezines should be at least 80 percent news and useful information and the other 20 percent or so of the content should be promotional.

26. Before you begin emailing to your house file, send them an email notifying them of your intention and stating the benefits (for example, they will get special discounts available only through

these emails). Tell them if they would rather not get these emails, they can click the UNSUBSCRIBE hyperlink in your email; doing so takes them to a page where they can remove their name from your list. On subsequent emails, always include opt-out instructions. Never send any email marketing message without an opt-out option.

Avoiding Spam

The legal requirements governing email marketing are explicitly defined in the CAN-SPAM act. Here are some things you can do to make sure you are not spamming those who get your emails and therefore stay out of trouble:

- Don't use false headers that deceive recipients as to the source of the email.
- Don't use misleading sender or subject lines.
- Add your postal address to all emails. The signature or .sig file is ideal for this. Your email provider almost certainly allows you to create and then automatically add to all your outgoing emails a .sig file with your name, address, and any other information you wish.
- Include an easy-to-find unsubscribe mechanism in every email. This mechanism must be simple: a link they can click or a simple reply email. Remove from your email list anyone who unsubscribes within 10 days.
- Offer recipients a way to receive some types of email from you while blocking others along with a "global unsubscribe" option to stop all future emails from your organization. All quality email-marketing services offer these options.
- Don't share the address of anyone who has subscribed to the list or who has unsubscribed.
- Don't harvest (collect) email addresses or use automated means to randomly generate addresses.
- Remove any sexually oriented material from your messages. The law requires such material be identified in the subject line as "SEXUALLY EXPLICIT" in all caps. When initially viewed, the message body should include only instructions on *how to access*

the sexually oriented material, not the *actual* material. It must also include your postal address, a notice that the message is an advertisement or solicitation, and an unsubscribe mechanism. You can ignore this if the message is sent to someone who opted in.

HYPERLINKS IN YOUR EMAILS

Hyperlinks, when clicked, take prospects to the landing page, order page, shopping cart, or wherever else you want to send them.

The *clickthrough rate* is the percentage of email recipients who click on a link within the email. You can have multiple links in your email, but, with rare exception, they should all link to the same URL. If you have multiple links with each going to a different web page, confusion and lower conversion rates usually result. There are three ways to present links in your email copy:

- ✉ *Give the actual URL*: To download a free sample chapter of my new book on digital marketing, visit www.bly.digital.
- ✉ *Put the link in words that are underlined and in blue*: Click here to download your free sample chapter now.
- ✉ *Make the linked words more graphically prominent*: To download your free sample chapter, **click here now.**

Chapter 17

INTEGRATED CAMPAIGNS AND SALES FUNNELS

So how do we integrate all the elements discussed in this book—direct mail, email, and landing pages—into an effective multichannel campaign?

The model used to orchestrate such campaigns is called the *sales funnel*. The funnel begins at the top by collecting leads from people who respond to your first promotion. It then qualifies those leads and takes the qualified prospects along a preplanned sequence of marketing touch points. At the bottom of the funnel emerge those prospects who have made a purchase and are now customers.

A typical funnel for a multichannel marketing campaign in which direct mail is one of the elements is shown in Figure 17.1 on page 260. Let's go through it step by step.

THE TOP OF THE FUNNEL: DIRECT MAIL

The first step in the funnel sequence, which starts at the top of the funnel, is to get people who might be good prospects for what we are selling to contact us,

Figure 17.1. **Multichannel Marketing Campaign Sales Funnel**

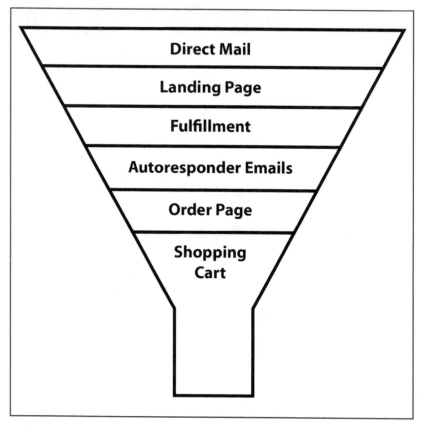

in essence getting them to raise their hands and say, "Tell me a little more about who you are, what you do, and what you want to sell me."

In a multichannel campaign, you accomplish this by driving traffic to a specific web page. You can drive this traffic using a variety of methods, both off-line and online, as shown in Figure 17.2 on page 261. This example sends traffic to the sign-up page for a free subscription to the marketer's online newsletter. But the page could just as well offer a white paper, a special report, or even a discount on a product.

As you can see, one of the traffic drivers available to you in this part of the funnel is direct mail. To make it work, the mailing piece should prominently feature, in large, bold type, the URL of the web page you want the prospects to go to. As the diagram illustrates, many other marketing

Figure 17.2. **Traffic-Driving Methods for Multichannel Marketing**

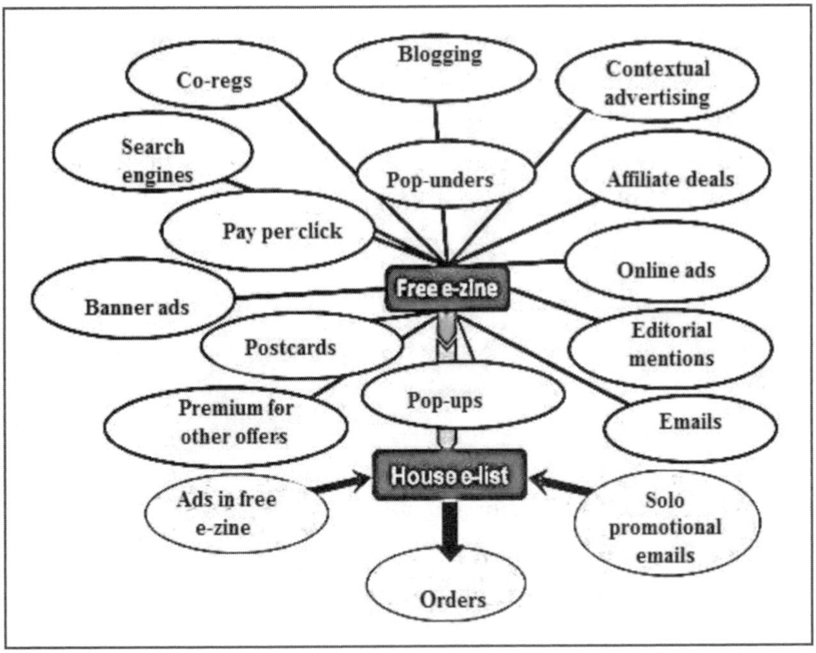

methods can also be used to drive traffic to the page; these include organic search traffic, online ads, blog posts, and email marketing. But I'll concentrate here on integrating direct mail into our sales funnel.

THE LANDING PAGE

When the prospect visits the URL in the direct-mail piece or other traffic driver, they arrive at a landing page, which is the next step down in the sales-funnel process.

In Chapter 14, we showed you how to build a landing page that is optimized to work in the sales funnel, particularly in ones where you first generate a lead and then convert it into a sale.

To recap, the prospect arrives on your lead-qualifying landing page (Figure 14.1 on page 233). There are three boxes they can select to determine their level of interest: 1) send me the lead magnet, 2) send me information about the product or service, and 3) have a salesperson call me. The prospect can click one, two, or all three options. Prospects who choose number three are the most qualified leads. Those who choose only number one are the coldest leads and may just be "freebie seekers"—people who like free content—rather than real sales leads.

But whichever options the prospect chooses, they must at least submit their name and email address. That way, you can follow up the lead via inexpensive email—multiple times if you like.

FULFILLMENT: DELIVER WHAT YOU PROMISED

Fulfillment means you send the prospect the lead magnet, premium, product information, white paper, or whatever it is they requested from your landing page.

The fulfillment materials can be sent as digital or hard copy. These days digital fulfillment is more common: PDF for documents, MP3 for audio, streaming MP4 for video. We know from experience that rapid inquiry fulfillment increases conversion to sale.

But some marketers believe a physical package has more impact, so they prefer to fulfill with hard copies: printed brochures, audio CDs, DVDs, and even physical objects with their company logos on them, such as pens, tiny flashlights, keychains, and other small gifts. If multiple items are sent in a big envelope or box, we call this a *shock and awe* fulfillment package because the prospect is being deliberately overwhelmed by the sheer volume of materials, which gets attention in a way a PDF white paper can't.

Other marketers fulfill inquiries immediately with digital materials and then send hard copies that arrive on the prospect's desk a few days later. We call physical fulfillment following electronic fulfillment the *thud factor* because the envelope lands on the prospect's desk with a thud.

The fulfillment can be automated or manual. You can easily automate digital fulfillment by triggering an autoresponder email as soon as the prospect submits the online form. The email thanks them for their interest and provides links to the digital fulfillment materials so they can download them.

The problem with automated fulfillment, though, is that your competitors can grab your materials without your knowledge, as can totally unqualified prospects. To avoid this, you can set the response form to notify you when a request is submitted. If it is legitimate, you fulfill it. If it's clearly not a genuine lead, you disregard it. To avoid having to fulfill all inquiries, you can say, "Submit the form below to see if you qualify for this special free offer." If a nonprospect complains that he didn't get your free material, you can politely explain that he did not qualify. I will generally send a nonqualified person my lead magnet but not my sales literature or pricing.

AUTORESPONDER EMAIL FOLLOW-UP

To increase results from a multichannel marketing campaign using the funnel we are working through now, the people who submit their names and email addresses should get a series of follow-up emails sent via automated autoresponder software such as AWeber. The follow-up emails stress different sales points and may contain some engaging content. But they always encourage the recipient to click on a link to the sales page or shopping cart (see below).

Typically the autoresponder email series has between three and seven emails spaced a day or two apart. These emails can increase the conversion rate to purchase by anywhere from 10 to 30 percent.

ORDER PAGE

An order page is, as the name implies, a page on which you can order the product. The order page is quite similar to order forms in direct-mail packages, the key elements of which are discussed in Chapter 11. The idea is to give a quick, concise summary of the offer and all the reasons to accept it, then provide a button customers can click on if they want to order. The button links to the shopping cart where they can make the purchase.

SHOPPING CART

The shopping cart is software that enables the customer to order and pay for their purchase online. Two of the most popular shopping carts are 1ShoppingCart and Infusionsoft.

An interesting and potentially profitable A/B split test is to send half your prospects to the order page and the other half directly to the shopping cart. Sometimes you actually get a better conversion rate going straight to the shopping cart without ever using an order page.

SELLING OUTSIDE THE FUNNEL

The idea of the funnel is to "nurture" the prospect along the sales cycle: get a lead, capture the name and email address, and progressively sell them until they are ready to buy.

Although funnels usually work, sometimes you can successfully bypass them. For instance, with a strong direct-mail package that does a complete selling job, test sending the respondent directly to the shopping cart or order page instead of the landing page. See which option—landing page, order page, or shopping cart—works best for each campaign.

The test will only show which approach works best for that specific promotion. It will not establish a universal rule that says you should always send direct-mail responders to a landing page/order page/shopping cart. Having said that, I find that sending the direct-mail recipient to the full landing page first usually gets the best results.

FINAL THOUGHTS

People consistently predict that new technology will make current technology obsolete. These predictions often come true, but sometimes they don't. For instance, people thought TV would be the end of radio and movie theaters, and photography would be the death knell of drawing and painting. Neither has yet come to pass.

Similarly, when the web and email came along, some marketing pundits said it would be the end of old-school direct mail. Instead, direct mail is more robust today than it was a decade ago, both as a stand-alone marketing tactic and as an element in an integrated multichannel campaign.

On the other hand, one thing the internet did make obsolete was physical video. Streaming video in general, and Netflix in particular, put Blockbuster and most other video rental stores, both chain and independent, out of business. As for music, the iPod has certainly hurt CD sales, but CDs still sell briskly, and even vinyl is making a small comeback.

But because of some pros' enthusiasm for digital marketing, the ability to plan, write, design, and execute moneymaking direct-mail campaigns has largely become a lost art. As a result, a great number of marketers today don't know how to make direct mail work and make it profitable.

But after reading this book, you do know how it works, which means you are on your way to becoming a direct-mail pro. And mastering direct mail can help you strengthen your business, make more money, get more customers, generate more leads, increase your sales, and make you a hero to your clients or boss. Given all that, there is plenty to like about direct mail—at least it seems that way to me. Best of luck on your journey to becoming a successful direct-mail marketer—or, if you already are one, to boosting your response rates and results to record levels!

DIRECT-MAIL VENDORS

Direct-Mail Consultants

McCarthy & King
http://www.mccarthyandking.com/

Simpson Direct
http://www.simpson-direct.com/

Envelope Manufacturers

Tension Envelope
https://tensionenvelope.com/

XpressEnvelopes.com
https://xpressenvelopes.com/

Fulfillment Services

RedStag Fulfillment
https://redstagfulfillment.com

Speaker Fulfillment Services
http://speakerfulfillmentservices.com/

Graphic Designers

Wm. Fridrich Design
http://www.fridrichdesign.com/

Lori Haller, Designing Response
http://lorihaller.com/

Printers

Seda's Printing
https://www.sedasprinting.com/

Shawmut Communications Group
http://www.shawmutdelivers.com/

Letter Shops

Ballantine
https://www.ballantine.com/

Talon Mailing & Marketing
http://talon-mailing.com/

Mailing List Brokers/Data Services

Dunhill International List Co. Inc.
https://www.dunhills.com/

Macromark Inc.
http://www.macromark.com/

MeritDirect
https://www.meritdirect.com/

Reach Marketing
https://www.reachmarketing.com/

Worldata

http://www.worldata.com/

Mail Monitoring Services

Quad Graphics

https://www.qg.com/

US Monitor

https://www.usmonitor.com/

Find More Vendors at:

http://www.bly.com/newsite/Pages/vendors.php

BIBLIOGRAPHY

Benson, Richard. *Secrets of Successful Direct Mail.* Stamford, CT: Bottom Line Books, 2005.

Bird, Drayton. *How to Write Sales Letters That Sell.* London: Kogan, 1994.

Collier, Robert. *The Robert Collier Letter Book.* East Setauket, NY: Robert Collier Publications, 1937.

Hatch, Denny, and Don Jackson. *2,239 Tested Secrets for Direct Marketing Success.* Lincolnwood, IL: NTC, 1998.

Kennedy, Dan S. *No B.S. Direct Marketing,* 2nd ed. Irvine, CA: Entrepreneur Press, 2013.

—. *The Ultimate Sales Letter,* 4th ed. Avon, MA: Adams Media, 2011.

Rapp, Stan, and Tom Collins. *Maxi-Marketing.* New York: McGraw-Hill, 1987.

Simpson, Craig, with Dan S. Kennedy. *The Direct Mail Solution.* Irvine, CA:

Entrepreneur Press, 2014.

Stone, Bob, and Ron Jacobs. *Successful Direct Marketing Methods,* 7th ed. New York: McGraw-Hill, 2001.

ABOUT THE AUTHOR

Robert W. Bly is a freelance copywriter with four decades of experience in business-to-business and direct-response marketing. Dubbed "America's top copywriter" by McGraw-Hill, Bly has written copy for more than 100 clients, including IBM, AT&T, Intuit, ExecuNet, Medical Economics, and Indeed.com.

He has given presentations to numerous organizations, including the National Speakers Association, the U.S. Army, Discover Card, The Learning Annex, Social Media Marketing World, and New York University.

Bly is the author of more than 95 books, including *The Copywriter's Handbook* (Henry Holt) and *The Digital Marketing Handbook* (Entrepreneur Press). His articles have appeared in *DM News, Cosmopolitan, New Jersey Monthly, Baltimore City Paper, The Writer,* and many other publications. Bob writes a monthly column for *Target Marketing* magazine. *The Direct Response Letter,* his monthly enewsletter, has 65,000 subscribers.

Awards include a Gold Echo from the Direct Marketing Association, an IMMY from the Information Industry Association, and Copywriter of the Year from American Writers & Artists. Prior to becoming a freelance copywriter, Bly was a staff writer at Westinghouse and advertising manager for Koch Engineering.

He can be reached at:

Bob Bly
Copywriter/consultant
31 Cheyenne Drive
Montville, NJ 07045
Phone: 973-273-0562
Fax: 973-263-0613
Email: rwbly@bly.com
Website: https://www.bly.com/

INDEX